D1074768

THE CONCERT OF EUROPE

THE CONCERT OF EUROPE:
A Study in German and British International Theory
1815-1914

Carsten Holbraad

New York
Barnes & Noble, Inc.

© Longman Group Limited 1970

First published in the United States, 1971
by Barnes & Noble, Inc.

ISBN 389 04110 6

Printed in Great Britain by
The Camelot Press Ltd., London and Southampton

CONTENTS

ACKNOWLEDGEMENTS

We are grateful to the following for permission to reproduce copyright material:

The Controller of Her Majesty's Stationery Office for extracts from vols v, iv, viii, x, ix 2nd series; vols vi, i, cxxxii, clxxvi, ii, cxxx, clv, lvi, cxxxv, cxlii, cxxxix, cxxix, cxii, cxxxviii, ccxxxiv, ccxlii, ccxxxii, cclxv, clvi 3rd series; vols xlviii, xlvii, xlvi, xcii 4th series, and vols lv, lvi 5th series from *Hansard*; R. Oldenbourg Verlag for extracts from *Politische Schriften* by J. G. Droysen.

PREFACE

In 1950 Sir Charles Webster told the members of the International Congress of Historians at Paris that they would look in vain for an adequate book about the principles and practice of the European Concert of the nineteenth century. Since then some serious work has been done on the subject. Historians, notably F. H. Hinsley, and political scientists, particularly Stanley Hoffman, George Liska and R. N. Rosecrance, have described and analysed the system of the Concert; and a diplomatic historian, René Albrecht-Carrié, has presented the hundred documents that in his view best illustrate the nature, meaning and operation of the Concert of Europe. But nobody has dealt thoroughly with its theory. To help fill that gap is the aim of this study. Rather than examine the Concert of Europe from inside, I have looked at it through the eyes of the men who lived with it and thought about it. From the writings of statesmen, diplomatists, publicists, historians, international lawyers and political philosophers I have extracted the various views and ideas of the European Concert that Germans and Englishmen put forward in the nineteenth century. The result is an analytic account of the German and the British contribution to speculation about the Concert of Europe.

It was Professor Martin Wight, now at the University of Sussex, who originally inspired my interest in the theory of international politics, and later directed it towards the Concert of Europe. To him I am indebted also for advice in my research and stimulating criticism of the draft of this book. My colleague here at the Australian National University, Professor Hedley Bull; my former colleagues at Carleton University in Ottawa, Professors Charles Dalfen and Michael Fry; Mr F. H. Hinsley at St John's College, Cambridge; Professor Richard Hiscocks at the University of Sussex; Mr Colin Jacobson; Professor F. S. Northedge at the London School of Economics and my father-in-law the late Mr

Andreas Vlachoutsicos read some or all of the chapters. I am grateful to them for the interest they showed and the many helpful suggestions they made. Mrs Ilse M. Mullins assisted me by drafting most of the translations of passages quoted from German sources. Finally, I record my gratitude to my wife, who encouraged and helped me at all stages of the work.

Canberra, November 1969.   C. H.

INTRODUCTION

The Concert of Europe, like the League of Nations and the United Nations, originated in war. The Revolutionary and Napoleonic Wars in one way united and in another divided the states of Europe. While revolution and invasion, by endangering the tranquillity and security of all, forced the powers to make common cause, the long struggle with France, by testing the strength of each, separated the stronger from the weaker ones. The product of the two influences was the coalition of Austria, Prussia, Russia and Britain. When the war was over the victorious allies retained the special position they had acquired in Europe. They took charge of the negotiations at Vienna, redrew the boundaries of states, prepared the peace treaties and, finally, renewed their wartime alliance. The treaty of the Quadruple Alliance was signed at Paris on 20 November 1815. Though primarily designed to provide against the dangers of a return of Napoleonic régime in France, it also contained a plan for the conduct of European politics in general. The sixth of its seven articles ran as follows:

> To facilitate and to secure the execution of the present treaty, and to consolidate the connections which at the present moment so closely unite the four Sovereigns for the happiness of the world, the High Contracting Parties have agreed to renew their meetings at fixed periods, either under the immediate auspices of the Sovereigns themselves or by their respective Ministers, for the purpose of consulting upon their common interests, and for the consideration of the measures which at each of these periods shall be considered the most salutary for the repose and prosperity of nations and for the maintenance of the peace of Europe.

On the basis of this article the great powers managed the affairs of Europe in the postwar years.

Already at the Congress of Aix-la-Chapelle in 1818 Britain

found herself in fundamental disagreement with the Continental powers about the political aims of the new system. The gulf that developed between the allies in the following years led to a breakdown of the congress system in 1822. But the practice of consulting and cooperating survived. Though they never made a habit of it, the great powers resorted to it so often throughout the century that together they sometimes assumed the character of an institution of European politics. This system of diplomacy became known as the Concert of Europe.

Unlike the League of Nations, its successor, the Concert of Europe was not an orderly organization with a permanent structure. At best, it was an informal institution which enjoyed no more than intermittent existence. Till the middle of the century the four founders of the congress system and France, who had been admitted at the Congress at Aix-la-Chapelle, were the only members. At the Paris Congress in 1856 the Ottoman Empire was formally accepted as a partner in the Concert, though in reality only admitted as a member of the international society of Europe. At the London Conference on Luxembourg in 1867 united Italy joined. And in 1871 the German *Reich* took the place of Prussia. In the last decades of the century some non-European great powers, particularly the United States, associated themselves for some purposes with the members of the European Concert. Most of its work was done in congresses of heads of governments or foreign ministers, or in conferences of ambassadors presided over by the local foreign minister. Sir Charles Webster counted eight of the former and eighteen of the latter.[1] The meetings were distributed irregularly throughout the century, far more falling before 1871 than after. Except for the early congresses, which were based on Article VI, the meetings were *ad hoc*. Often their subject was some aspect or other of the Eastern question; but the representatives of the great powers dealt also with a considerable number of other issues, ranging from the Belgian question in the early eighteen-thirties to African affairs in the middle eighties. The last meeting was the London Conference of 1912–13 on the Eastern question. The Concert of Europe dissolved finally in the First World War.

The development and the activities of the Concert of Europe may be studied in the protocols of the congresses and conferences

1. Webster: *The Art and Practice of Diplomacy,* p. 59; the meetings are listed on p. 69.

and in the despatches and letters of the men who conducted the work. These documents might reveal both the separate interests and the common concerns of the great powers, the tensions within the Concert as well as the relations with the other members of the states system. Research among such sources would provide material for a chronological account of the practice of the institution; and analysis of this practice could lead to a set of generalizations about the nature and functions of the Concert of Europe.

However, the Concert of Europe was more than a practice which developed into an institution. It was also an idea. The notion of an informal association of great powers survived the collapse of the congress system in the eighteen-twenties and retained a place in the political thought about international relations till the end of the century. Eventually it became commonly known as the Concert of Europe. But this did not happen till a late stage. In the language of diplomacy 'concert' originally meant either an *ad hoc* diplomatic arrangement involving some measure of cooperation between two or more powers or a temporary political situation implying some degree of agreement between the parties. In such senses it came into use early in the seventeen-nineties. [2] When Gentz, some years after the end of the congress system, reported that 'la France marchera en tout et partout de plein concert avec l'Autriche' [3] or referred to 'le manque d'union et de concert dans les vues et la marche des Puissances' [4] he was following this usage. Gradually the word acquired also another meaning. To the extent that Castlereagh and Metternich regarded the new political system as lasting, they used 'the concert' to refer to an established diplomatic arrangement. [5] 'The

2. Kaunitz used the term in its simplest sense as early as 21 December 1791: see Sorel: *L'Europe et la Révolution Française*, ii, 345. Grenville used it in December 1792, when he suggested 'a concert between other Gov[ernmen]ts to provide for their own security': see Temperley and Penson, eds, *Foundations of British Foreign Policy from Pitt (1792) to Salisbury (1902) or Documents, Old and New*, p. 9. There is a British pamphlet of 1793: *Letters on the Subject of the Concert of Princes and the dismemberment of Poland and France*, by a Calm Observer (viz. Benjamin Vaughan). See also Grenville and Malmesbury in 1794: *Diaries and Correspondence of James Harris, First Earl of Malmesbury*, 2nd edn, 1845, iii, 83–4 and 119.

3. *Dépêches inédites du Chevalier de Gentz aux Hospodars de Valachie, pour servir à l'histoire de la politique européenne (1813 à 1828)*, ii, 463. Gentz was referring to the situation at St Petersburg in 1825.

4. *Dépêches*, iii, 249 (letter of 3 April 1827).

5. Examples, with detailed references, of the various usages of the terms discussed on this and the following pages will be given in later chapters.

European Concert' or 'The Concert of Europe'—of which the
French equivalent, 'le concert européen', appeared in the treaty of
Paris of 1856—became common in the English language in the
second half of the century. Queen Victoria used it at the time of
the Crimean War in a sense much closer to the later meaning of
the term than to the traditional idea of 'concert'.[6] But it was
during the great crisis in the Eastern question in the late seventies
that 'the Concert of Europe' gained wide currency in its quasi-
institutional sense.[7] Since then the term has stood for the idea of a
loose association of great European powers consulting and acting
together occasionally.

In the earlier part of the century this notion appeared under
various synonyms. In the decade after 1815 as well as later
Englishmen often called it simply 'the European system'. Castlereagh used a variety of names, the more common ones being 'the
confederacy', 'the great alliance' and 'the union'.[8] The first of
these, which was used also by some of the Whig opponents of the
Continental union of sovereigns, was replaced by 'confederation'
almost a hundred years later in W. Alison Phillips's study of the
congress system.[9] Other advocates of the idea used different
names. While Gladstone sometimes called it 'the great European
combination of Powers' or 'the great Council of Europe', Salisbury on one or two occasions in the late nineties referred to it as
'the inchoate federation of Europe'. A number of the early
assailants of the idea of the Concert of Europe, who were inclined
to see the Holy Alliance as the ideological cloak of the new system,
refused to distinguish between the two arrangements and
described them collectively as 'the Holy Alliance'. Others, with a
liking for drawing parallels with classical times, sometimes

6. On 11 January 1855 Victoria reminded Frederick William IV that she had warned
him repeatedly of the dangers of 'separating from the Concert of Europe': see
Queen Victoria, *Further Letters ... from the Archives of the House of Brandenburg-
Prussia,* p. 53. In a letter to the King of 26 January 1856 she again referred to 'the
Concert Européen', see ibid., p. 62.
7. It is significant that *Hansard,* which earlier in the century had given the word as
'concert', after Gladstone's second ministry spelled it with a capital C. By 1900
'Concert of Europe' figured in the Index: see 4th ser., lxxxvii (under 'China').
8. All these terms appeared frequently in Castlereagh's correspondence and speeches.
In 1814 and 1815 they meant the coalition against France, in the following years the
peacetime alliance of the four victorious powers and after 1818 often the quintuple
arrangement introduced at the Congress of Aix-la-Chapelle.
9. *The Confederation of Europe, a Study of the European Alliance, 1813–1823 as an Experiment in the International Organization of Peace,* 1914.

resorted to such words as 'the Amphictyonic council of Sovereigns' or, more often, 'the Areopagus of Europe'.[10]

In the Austrian Council of Ministers in 1864 Francis Joseph made a reference to 'das europäische Concert'.[11] And in a speech in the *Reichstag* in 1898 Bülow touched upon Germany's role among the powers in connection with the Cretan question and, punning elaborately, used the term 'das europäische Konzert'.[12] But this expression appeared only rarely in German writings of the nineteenth century. The commonest synonym was 'die europäische Pentarchie', which was used by supporters and opponents of the idea alike.[13] As in England, some enemies of the system identified it with the Holy Alliance, while others called it 'der Areopag von Europa'. The most outspoken scoffers introduced new names. Constantin Frantz censured 'die Grossmachts-Corporation', and Bismarck referred ironically to 'der europäische Seniorenconvent'.

The ideas behind all these terms form the subject of the present study. The Concert of Europe is seen through the eyes of the men who lived with the institution and speculated about it, rather than through the records of its diplomatic activities. My aim is to present the body of ideas produced by contemporary speculation about the institution, not to analyse its practice. The sources are the speeches and writings, especially the more contemplative pieces, of the statesmen and the principal diplomatists, the works of the international lawyers and the relevant writings of the

10. The use of the latter, which in England may be traced back at least to the early eighteen-twenties, when first Castlereagh and then Canning were trying to curb the 'areopagitical spirit' of the Continental great powers, was censured by the historian E. A. Freeman. In a lecture delivered at Oxford in 1887 he referred to that body 'which those to whom the history of old Hellas is a blank think it fine to call the "European Areopagus"'. 'This very common phrase,' he explained in a footnote, 'is one of the queerest of popular confusions. It is hard indeed to see the analogy between a meeting of envoys from several states and the highest criminal court in a particular state. Would anybody say that the Berlin Treaty was made by the "King's Bench of Europe"? There seems to be a twofold blunder at work. First, the Athenian Areiopagos is confounded with the Amphiktyonic Council; secondly, the nature of the Amphiktyonic Council is altogether misconceived.' *Four Oxford Lectures, 1887: Fifty Years of European History and Teutonic Conquest in Gaul and Britain*, p. 56.
11. Clark: *Franz Joseph and Bismarck. The Diplomacy of Austria before the War of 1866*, p. 533.
12. *Fürst Bülows Reden, nebst urkundlichen Beiträgen zu seiner Politik*, i, 24–6.
13. Though much rarer than the German equivalent, 'pentarchy' appeared also in British writings. For example, both the international lawyer John Westlake and the historian A. W. Ward used it occasionally.

historians and the political philosophers of the period between the end of the Napoleonic Wars and the outbreak of the First World War.

To obtain a complete picture of the theory of the Concert of Europe it would be necessary to include not only the ideas developed in each of the great powers, Austria, Prussia, Russia, Britain, France, Italy and Germany, as well as in the outside great powers, especially the United States and Japan, but also the notions advanced in the lesser states, particularly in those which at one time or another were directly affected by the decisions of the great powers. The present study is limited to the views expressed in Germany—Austria, Prussia, the German Confederation and the *Reich*—and Britain.[14] Between them these countries account for a large part of the theory of the Concert of Europe. While most of the ideas that guided the system in the earlier years were developed by Austrian and British statesmen, many of the critical observations came from representatives of the lesser German states. The chief advocates of the later Concert were to be found in England, and some of its most determined opponents in Prussia and the German *Reich*.

The first stage of the enquiry has been to collect, analyse and arrange the German and British contributions to the theory. This cannot be done satisfactorily without establishing standards for assessing their importance. To decide whether particular references to the Concert of Europe are fortuitous or significant it is necessary to examine them in their context. It is not enough to analyse them in their immediate verbal setting, and in the background of the political situation in which they arose. They must also be seen in relation both to the political thought of the individual writer, and to other contributions to the theory of the Concert of Europe. Of these, the latter relationship is the more important. Since the aim of the study is to present the theory of the institution rather than to cast light on the thought of individuals, each contribution must be evaluated from the point of view of the general stock of ideas rather than from that of its source. This does not mean that a reference to the European Concert will be plucked out of its particular setting, but that the weight attached to it will depend more on the place it gained in the general theory than on the part it played in an individual system of thought. For

14. I am planning a complementary study of French ideas of the European Concert.

example, in 1897, during the crisis over Armenia and Crete, Lord Salisbury twice spoke at length about the Concert of Europe. Comparing it in a striking simile to a steam roller, he called it 'the inchoate federation of Europe' and suggested that it could be the beginning of international organization.[15] The apparently progressive character of this idea and the optimistic spirit in which it was advanced were out of line with the philosophy and temperament of Salisbury. In a study of his international thought probably little importance would be attached to these remarks. They might even be dismissed as erratic and wistful, provoked by the immediate political situation and expanded for rhetorical reasons. But they amounted to perhaps the most explicit formulation of a certain type of thought about the Concert of Europe which was prevalent in England in the last decades before the First World War. Spoken by the Prime Minister in the House of Lords and at a Guildhall banquet, they gained notoriety and were much quoted. In the following years men who had little in common with Salisbury defended his idea of the European Concert with conviction and others attacked it with passion. Its place in the history of ideas about the Concert of Europe was out of proportion to its place in Salisbury's thought, but it is the former that concerns us here. This example may show that the processes of collecting, analysing and arranging the various contributions are mutually dependent and cannot be carried out separately. The tasks of selection and weighting, which form part of the process of collecting, involve analysis; and analysis of any particular contribution cannot be done satisfactorily without regard to the whole pattern of thought about the Concert of Europe.

The method of arrangement, too, requires some explanation. Nearly all contributions to the theory presented the diplomatic system of the Concert of Europe as an instrument which served or could be made to serve some political end. Normally they contained both an observation on the nature of the Concert and a notion of its function. Either element could serve as criterion of classification. But because in most contributions the emphasis was not so much on the nature as on the function of the system, the latter has been found the more convenient. So the arrangement has been carried out according to what the institution was thought

15. This part of Salisbury's contribution to the theory of the Concert of Europe is discussed in more detail on pp. 176–82 below.

to do rather than what it was seen to be, according to ends rather than origins. On this basis the material has fallen naturally into three broad groups. The first is represented by those who envisaged the Concert of Europe as an instrument for preserving the dynasties or the boundaries of the Vienna settlement of 1815; the second by those who saw it as a system of maintaining the balance of power in Europe; and the third, by those who held it up as a means for humanitarian reform or as the germ of international organization. These groups have been labelled, respectively, the conservative, the balance of power and the progressive. These terms, it must be borne in mind, simply reflect a certain classification of thoughts about the Concert of Europe. They do not imply that the individuals within each group necessarily had anything else in common than that they subscribed to broadly similar ideas of the function of the European system. In fact, not all those thinkers who here have been described either as conservative or as progressive were so in other matters, whether of domestic or of European politics. On the other hand, men who according to conventional terminology would be called either conservatives or progressives did not all hold conservative or progressive views of the Concert. Also, there were thinkers who believed in the system of the balance of power but did not subscribe to any balance of power idea of the Concert. Nevertheless, as will become clear in the following chapters, there was marked correlation between speculation about the Concert of Europe and political thought in general in the cases of both conservatism and progressivism. This correlation, which prevents the terminology adopted here from becoming wholly misleading when related to conventional usage of the terms, causes a danger of confusion. To guard against this it must be said that in the following pages 'conservative' and 'progressive', whether appearing as adjectives or as nouns, 'conservatism' and 'progressivism' as well as 'balance of power thought' and 'balance of power thinkers' are, unless otherwise indicated, employed to refer simply to the particular types of views of the Concert of Europe already outlined.

The German and the English material have been arranged separately. In the case of each country, opposite the three groups of positive contributions have been classed the ideas that contained a criticism of them or implied their rejection. Finally, for reasons which will be made clear in the individual chapters, several of the twelve groups that resulted from this classification have been subdivided.

The second stage of the treatment is to analyse the various groups of ideas. This will be done both logically and historically. The essence of the former exercise is to determine how much common ground there was between the contributions within a group, whether, that is, the broad agreement about the function of the Concert of Europe, given by the system of classification, extended, in the first place, to the nature of this institution and, more widely, even to assumptions, values and concerns relating to European politics and international society in general. The object may be said to be to decide whether, and to what extent, each group of thoughts added up to a distinct theory of the European Concert in international politics. Any reasonably coherent theory arrived at through this process will be compared and contrasted with theories distilled from other groups.

But the material must be examined also historically. Arranged in a rough chronological order,[16] each set of ideas composes a stream of thought which may be followed from source to end. If it is of some richness as well as of considerable length, such a stream amounts to what here will be called a tradition of thought about the Concert of Europe. In both German and British speculation several such traditions can be discerned. The following chapters will trace the internal development of each of them by following the shifts of emphasis and the changes in trend which formed the character and shaped the course of the tradition. They will also outline the historical relationships between the various traditions of thought. These, it will be shown, took three forms, namely, a clash between a tradition supporting the Concert of Europe and another opposing it; a rivalry between two or more traditions coexisting within the same country but advancing different ideas in support of the Concert; and conflict between the tradition that prevailed in Germany and the one that became dominant in Britain. This three-level drama is the major theme of the present study. When the rise and fall of the various traditions of thought have been traced and the tensions and rivalries

16. Considerable overlapping in the chronological arrangement of contributions is unavoidable when the various thinkers within a group are dealt with in turn. Normally the thoughts of the individual about the Concert of Europe were developed over a period and advanced in stages.

between the principal ones outlined, patterns in the German and the English speculation about the Concert of Europe may be discerned.

Though this is primarily a study of the theory of the Concert, some account must be taken of the historical situations in which the ideas evolved. Political thought is not only a creation of the intellects of individuals, but also a product of the social forces that impinge upon them. The various sets of ideas about the Concert of Europe, whether considered as groups of notions, as composite theories or as traditions of thought, bear close relation to the conditions of the times and places in which they originated and developed. In the following chapters the chief features of each of them will be related not only to the common elements in the personal background of the men who formulated the ideas but also to the special characteristics of the political situation of the state in which they were conditioned. In particular, the thoughts that gained currency in Germany will be seen in relation to the positions of the various states within the German Confederation and to the situation of Prussia and the *Reich* in Europe, and the views that secured dominance in England in relation to Britain's role in Europe and place in the world.

However, political ideas, from one point of view products of history, are, from another point, factors in politics. The ideas of the Concert of Europe were not merely generalizations about experience, reflecting the interests and the problems of the societies in which they were produced, but also sources of inspiration and guides to action. In the concluding sections an attempt will be made to indicate briefly how the German and the British contributions to the theory of the Concert of Europe affected the course of events in Europe and the world in the nineteenth and twentieth centuries. Thus the study leads, in one direction, towards the triumph of German nationalism, and, in the other, towards the establishment of the League of Nations, after the First World War.

Part One
GERMAN IDEAS OF THE CONCERT OF EUROPE

INTRODUCTION

In Germany the pattern of speculation about the Concert of Europe clearly reflected the course of history. The conflicts and rivalries between the different traditions of thought paralleled the tensions and struggles between the various sides in politics. In the first half of the century after 1815 the conservative ideas, which presented the Concert of Europe as a means of preserving the territorial and dynastic arrangements of the Congress of Vienna, dominated the scene. But they were opposed by others, which exposed the Concert as, variously, a system of great power dictatorship, an instrument for political repression, an obstacle to territorial revision, and a tool of social reaction. In the same period the governments of Austria and Prussia encountered the criticism of statesmen in the secondary states of the German Confederation, the opposition of liberals in south Germany, the antagonism of national liberals in Prussia, and the hostility of revolutionaries everywhere.

In the beginning of the second half of the century the progressive ideas, which projected the Concert of Europe as an organ of a developing international society, still had a few advocates. But soon they lost all support, while a set of ideas which ignored the European Concert and international society and revered the Prussian state and national power rapidly won acceptance. This was the time when the German liberal movement faded into insignificance, and Bismarck went on to unify Germany and consolidate the *Reich*.

Within a few decades of the restoration after the Napoleonic Wars, the balance of power ideas, which identified the Concert of Europe with the balance of power, made their appearance. By the second half of the century they had outrivalled the conservative ideas and were establishing themselves as the principal German theory of the European Concert. About the same time Prussia challenged and defeated Austria and became the leading German state. In the following decades the balance of power theory underwent a development corresponding to the change in the foreign policy of Prussia and Germany. It transformed itself in step with the ascending scale marked by Bismarck's struggle to enhance the influence of Prussia in Europe, his efforts to maintain the position of the *Reich* after 1871, and his successors' bid for a German role in world politics. These analogies point to the inter-action between political ideas and historical circumstances.

Chapter One

THE CONSERVATIVE THEORY

1. Development

The conservative group of thoughts about the Concert of Europe comprised two distinct ideas about the function of the system. One was the doctrine of preserving the territorial settlement of 1815 and the other that of maintaining the dynastic order sanctioned by the Congress of Vienna. In Germany, but not in Britain, the two were generally tied up with each other. Their chief advocates were the statesmen of Austria and Prussia. To them the major evils of European politics were aggression, especially by France, and revolution, whether in Germany, in Italy, or in other countries. From the history of Revolutionary and Napoleonic France they had learnt that these evils were closely connected. While domestic revolution might lead to foreign aggression, invasion could prepare the way for revolution. In the Concert of Europe they saw a protection against both dangers.

But the two elements of conservative thought did not always carry equal weight. In the first years of the congress system, when it seemed certain that the greatest danger to the tranquillity of Europe was that of a new revolution in France followed by a fresh invasion of her neighbours, the emphasis was on protecting the restoration in Paris in order to preserve the boundaries of the peace settlement. But after 1818, when it became clear that the real danger to the new order was the revolutionary movements in the various countries that had been occupied by Napoleon, the stress was on defending the European thrones against the internal enemies. For the next four decades both Austrian and Prussian conservative thought was in general dynastic more than territorial.

Austrian contributions

The conservative ideas of the Concert of Europe belonged to Austria in particular. They corresponded with the interests of the

Habsburg Empire more than with those of any other great power. Placed at the centre of the Continent between France and Russia, the two potential aggressors, this Empire had a strong motive for maintaining the balance of power that had been arranged at Vienna and preserving the boundaries that had been laid down in the peace treaties. Since she had taken the leading part in the German Confederation, while Prussia had been relegated to the secondary role and the lesser states reduced to near impotence, Austria had good reason to be satisfied with the particularist solution that had been imposed on Germany as part of the European restoration. Above all, as a multinational power administered according to autocratic principles, she had every need to keep down the movements that, in the name of the new ideas of nationality and popular sovereignty, threatened to overthrow the Monarchy and break up the Empire. The future of the Habsburgs depended on territorial stability and dynastic conservation.

It was among the servants of the Habsburg Monarchy that the conservative ideas of the Concert found their two leading advocates. The one was Gentz, a prolific publicist with a European reputation, and the other Metternich, Austrian Chancellor for nearly forty years. Friedrich Gentz had left his native Prussia in 1802, when he was thirty-eight years old, and had settled in Austria. There he had been charged with the task of supervising the Austrian press and keeping an eye on newspapers published abroad. But he also helped Metternich to revise, and at times to formulate, state papers. And after the war he gained prominence as secretary to the congresses of sovereigns and ministers. In all capacities he was an inspiring influence.

Contrary to Metternich, his protector, Gentz was not conspicuous for constancy in his political philosophy. As a young man he had been excited by the ideas of the French Revolution. Later he had been strongly influenced by the writings of Burke, some of which he had translated. But with the restoration, which allowed him to interrupt his career as a journalist and pamphleteer and take up the life of a diplomatist and courtier, he embraced the legitimist doctrines of his absolutist masters. His European thought underwent a comparable transformation. The dominant influence on his earlier speculation about the states system had been the Napoleonic bid for universal dominion. In 1801 he had written a long pamphlet in answer to a French writer who, in defence of French hegemony, had attacked the old order of Europe.[1] Five years later he had published his *Fragments upon the Balance of Power in Europe* with a passionately anti-Napoleonic Introduction. In the latter work he had analysed the political structure of pre-revolutionary Europe, presenting the balance of power as an informal system of collective security, and called upon the princes of Europe to return to the traditional maxims of European politics. But after the fall of Napoleon he repudiated the old balance of power in favour of the new system of politics. In a report of March 1818, prepared for Prince Ianko Karadja, the Hospodar of Wallachia, whom he kept informed about current developments in European affairs, he described the congress system and contrasted it with the separate alliances and power balances of prewar Europe:

Le système politique qui s'est établi en Europe depuis 1814 et 1815 est un phénomène inouï dans l'histoire du monde. Au principe de l'équilibre ou, pour mieux dire, des contre-poids formés par des alliances particulières, principe qui a gouverné, et trop souvent aussi troublé et ensanglanté l'Europe pendant trois siècles, a succédé un principe d'union générale, réunissant la totalité des États par un lien fédératif, sous la direction des cinq principales Puissances, dont quatre ont une part égale à cette direction, tandis que la cinquième se trouve encore, jusqu'à ce moment, placée sous une espéce de tutelle, dont elle sortira bientôt pour se mettre sur la même ligne avec ses tuteurs. Les États de second, de troisième, de quatrième ordre se soumettent tacitement, et sans que rien n'ait jamais été stipulé à cet égard, aux décisions prises en commun par les Puissances prépondérantes; et l'Europe ne semble former enfin qu'une grande famille politique, réunie sous les auspices d'un aréopage de sa propre création, dont les membres se garantissent à eux-mêmes, et garantissent à chacune des parties intéressées, la jouissance tranquille de leurs droits respectifs. Cet ordre de choses a ses inconvénients. Mais il est certain que, si l'on pouvait le rendre durable, il serait, aprés tout, la meilleure des

1. Gentz: *Von dem Politischen Zustande von Europa vor und nach der Französischen Revoluzion* . . . see also Gentz: *Ueber den Ursprung und Charakter des Krieges gegen die Französische Revoluzion.*

combinaisons possibles pour assurer la prospérité des peuples et le maintien de la paix qui en est une des premières conditions.[2]

When Gentz called the postwar states system 'the federation of Europe', he was only following the terminology of his generation. 'Federation' was then used in a loose sense, close to that of 'confederation' today, and had not yet acquired its distinct modern meaning. Alternative terms used by him were 'the general union' and 'the European league'. The group of principal powers, which formed the nucleus of the system, he referred to as 'the great alliance', 'the union of great powers' or 'the union of sovereigns'. The relationship between that body and the other states was a recurrent theme of his writings.

At the outset of the Congress of Vienna Gentz had agreed that the four powers who had defeated Napoleon and proved their greatness had an incontestable right to take the initiative in the peace negotiations.[3] But towards the end of the negotiations he had observed that the dictatorship exercised by Austria, Russia, Britain and Prussia throughout the duration of the Congress, though 'non-seulement un mal nécessaire, mais même un bien réel' in the confusion and disturbances of that period, had become on several occasions a source of abuse, injustice and vexation for the states of lesser rank.[4] Then he had thought that the existence of disagreements and disputes between the great powers was a valuable safeguard for the independence and interests of the smaller states.[5] Less than three years later, according to his report to the Hospodar, he was admiring the way in which the smaller states tacitly submitted to the joint decisions of the great and willingly accepted the new system as the best guarantee of their

2. Gentz: *Dépêches,* i, 354–5. See also *Schriften von Friedrich von Gentz. Ein Denkmal,* iii, 'Ueber de Pradt's Gemälde von Europa nach dem Kongress von Aachen', pp. 121–2 and 'Gegen die Beurtheilung des Kongresses von Aachen in der französischen Minerva', pp. 85–6.
3. *Dépêches,* i, 97–8. 'Le congrès n'aurait jamais pu marcher,' he had argued, 'si l'on avait voulu réunir dès le commencement tous les plénipotentiaires grands et petits' (p. 97).
4. Ibid., i, 157.
5. Ibid. The four great powers, he had pointed out, 'n'étaient au fond d'accord que lorsqu'il s'agissait de donner la loi aux autres. Mais leurs propres intérêts ne les jetaient que trop souvent dans des discussions intestines, quelquefois très alarmantes pour le repos général. Ces discussions offraient, il est vrai, une chance de salut aux États faibles, dont l'indépendance et les intérêts auraient été encore plus menacés par l'union constante des dictateurs. . . .'

rights. By 1818 he had become an enthusiastic supporter of the idea of political direction by the principal powers.

With the Congress of Aix-la-Chapelle his attitude to the new system underwent further development. That meeting marked fresh changes in the role and relations of the union of great powers, he insisted in a public answer to a French critic:

> Henceforth these principal powers are nothing more than the most important and most natural protectors of the general order, repeatedly confirmed by treaties, and of the peace, affirmed by all Christendom and more than ever before established upon political, economic, moral and religious foundations. Moreover, the smallest sovereign state is as independent as France, England or Russia within its own territory and in the domain of its laws; and everywhere the mutual relations of states are dealt with according to traditional principles of international law and in purely diplomatic forms.[6]

Four years after the war he was apparently firmly persuaded that the problem of ensuring justice in the relations between strong and weak states, which had disturbed him from the time of the partition of Poland till the years of the Congress of Vienna, had been solved satisfactorily within the new system of European politics. But Gentz was no longer an independent observer. While the political comments he made in private letters now were the reflections of a deeply committed insider, the articles he published were the work of a man who had undertaken to handle the public relations of the union of sovereigns.

Gentz became a loyal supporter of the diplomatic concert of the sovereigns. But their Holy Alliance he could not defend. This pact he described as a political nullity, an invention without a real aim or an important result, 'une décoration de théâtre imaginée peut-être dans un esprit de dévotion mal entendue, et surtout bien mal exprimée, peut-être aussi dans un simple mouvement de vanité, conçue par un des principaux acteurs sur la scène du monde et secondée par la complaisance ou la bonhomie de ses associés'. It would soon be forgotten, he prophesied, and would one day figure in the diplomatic code of the nineteenth century only as a monument to the whimsicality of men and monarchs.[7] The close

6. *Schriften,* iii, 96–7.   7. *Dépêches,* i, 223–4.

union of the principal sovereigns and their first ministers, which was derived from a practical concern for the safety of Europe and based on political principles, and the loose pact of nearly all the Christian monarchs of Europe, which was inspired by mystical insights and founded on religious ideas, were kept quite separate in his mind. The former was a system of diplomacy, the latter, in the words of a wit whom he quoted, 'l'apocalypse de la diplomatie'.[8]

In the first three or four years after the war Gentz's conservatism was territorial. Like most men who had lived through the long struggle with France, he feared another European war after the fall of Napoleon and welcomed the renewal of the Quadruple Alliance as a safeguard against aggression and a protection for the peace settlement.[9] In a draft which he prepared for the Declaration of the Congress of Aix-la-Chapelle he wrote that the only aim of the union of sovereigns was to maintain the peace and guarantee the transactions on which it rested.[10] It was after this Congress that he acclaimed the union of the five great powers as simply the protector of the federation of European states. By preserving the legal order and territorial structure of the states system, it maintained peace and security throughout Europe.

As in some quarters after 1919, there was a feeling in Vienna after 1818 that the problems of peace and security had been solved. International tension had abated and France had joined the congress system. 'The *external* relations of the states', Gentz could write in 1819, 'are ordered and settled for a long time to come; the *political* peace in *Europe* is secured better than it has been for centuries....'[11] But it was only the political situation of Europe, the external relations of states, that caused satisfaction. The social condition offered no ground for optimism. 'L'intérieur de tous les pays européens, sans en excepter aucun,' he wrote after the Congress of Aix-la-Chapelle, 'est travaillé par une fièvre ardente, compagne ou avant-coureur des convulsions les plus violentes que le monde civilisé ait éprouvées depuis la chute de l'empire romain. C'est la lutte, c'est la guerre à mort entre les anciens et les nouveaux principes, entre l'ancien et un nouvel ordre social.'[12] Fear of revolution determined his thought about the Concert of Europe after 1818.

8. *Schriften,* iii, 150–1.　　9. *Dépêches,* i, 200.　　10. *Schriften,* iii, 72.
11. Ibid., iii, 149.
12. *Mémoires, Documents et Écrits divers laissés par le prince de Metternich,* iii, 174.

Since the fall of Napoleon and the restoration of the Bourbons Gentz, in common with most men who had experienced invasion by France, had dreaded a revolutionary outbreak in Paris. Remembering that a French revolution was apt to lead to foreign aggression and European war, he had subscribed to the view that the primary function of the new system of politics was to protect the Bourbon monarchy.[13] After 1818, when revolutionary outbreaks occurred in countries other than France, this attitude changed. Now revolution abroad alarmed him not because of its political and international repercussions but because of its tendency to spread from country to country. A revolution anywhere in Europe threatened the social order everywhere. The European federation of states was like a body, he thought, and revolution like a disease which, once it had established itself in any part, might spread to the rest of the organism.[14] To protect Europe against all such attacks now became in his view the most important function of the union of great powers. The principal sovereigns were protectors and keepers of the existing public order, he explained after the Congress of Aix-la-Chapelle.

> ... leur union intime, 'calme et constante dans son action', est le contre-poids du mouvement désordonné que tant d'ésprits turbulents, sortis de leur sphère, voudraient imprimer aux affaires humaines; le noyau des forces organisées que présente cette union est la digue que la Providence paraît avoir élevée elle-même pour conserver l'ancien ordre de la société, ou pour en ralentir et en adoucir au moins les changements devenus indispensables.[15]

Behind the mystical language, almost reminiscent of the Act of the Holy Alliance, to which Gentz resorted in this passage was the idea of the balance of power. But it was a balance fundamentally different from that which he had discerned in the prerevolutionary states system. While the old balance among the powers of

13. Gentz: *Briefe an Pilat*, i, 190–1.
14. *Schriften*, iii, 265–6: 'And who could still call it into question,' he asked rhetorically in an article of 1824 about the right of states to grant political asylum to foreign revolutionaries, 'since Europe, through innumerable ties and daily closer intercourse between sovereigns and peoples, has formed itself into a true federative body, in which no member can be mutilated, wounded or poisoned without the harm penetrating more or less deeply into all the others?'
15. Metternich: *Mémoires,* iii, 175. See also Gentz: *Schriften* iii, 68–9.

Europe had been political and complex, the new one between the powers of the 'sacred union' of sovereigns and the forces of the revolutionary movements was social and simple. Under the impact of the social forces of the postwar world, which caused so much tension in the restored Europe, Gentz had turned his attention from the external relations of states to their internal condition. Focusing on the horizontal cleavage between rulers and revolutionaries, which seemed to cut right across the society of Europe, he had set aside his traditional ideas of international politics and adopted a cosmopolitan view of European society. In emphasizing the solidarity of the monarchs on the one side and the universal character of the revolutionary pressure on the other he was inclined to ignore, at least in his public utterances,[16] the vertical divisions between the members of the states system, which previously had appeared to him to be the outstanding feature of the European federation of sovereign states.

The function of the union of sovereigns was to preserve the social structure of Europe by maintaining the internal relations of the states. The method was armed intervention to suppress revolutionary outbreaks. Gentz maintained that the principal sovereigns of Europe had a right to send armies into a state which was in the throes of revolution. Since a local revolution constituted a European emergency, intervention was not only a deed of loyalty towards a fellow sovereign but also an act of self-defence. Hence it was justified even when the threatened government had not made a request for intervention. On the occasion of the Greco-Turkish war in 1823 he wrote to the Hospodar:

> Les Puissances alliées ne se sont jamais arrogé un droit d'intervention dans les affaires internes d'un État indépendant, elles n'ont jamais prétendu influer ni sur les institutions, ni sur la législation, ni sur l'administration d'aucun pays; elles ne se croiraient pas même autorisées à une intervention pareille, uniquement parce qu'un pays serait déchiré par des désordres et des troubles dans son intérieur. Les souverains ne sont en guerre permanente qu'avec *le principe révolutionnaire* tel qu'il

16. Of course, being close to so many of the leading statesmen of the age, Gentz could not be unaware of the tensions that divided the great powers in the postwar years. In private conversations he felt free to discuss them. Ranke, who stayed a year in Vienna on his way to Italy in 1827, reported that it made a great impression on him to hear Gentz talk about the secret history of that period and reveal the various issues and conflicts that had divided the members of the congress system.

s'est élevé, et qu'il a désolé l'Europe depuis trente ans. Ce principe, ils le regardent comme un ennemi commun de tous les Gouvernements établis, comme un incendie, que (dans l'ordre civil même) on se croit autorisé et appelé à éteindre chez son voisin, pour ne pas en être atteint soi-même, sans que pour cela on prétende se mêler de ce qui se passe dans la maison ou dans la famille de ce voisin.[17]

It was necessity which in his view justified intervention.

However, Gentz's conversion to the cosmopolitan doctrines of the legitimists was never complete. Even when the union of sovereigns was at its strongest he was conscious that the new system could not last indefinitely. Created in the unique circumstances of the restoration period, it lacked a basis of distinct and permanent common interests, he explained in his confidential report of March 1818. Eventually the divergent interests and opposed tendencies of the great powers would override the bonds that now tied the sovereigns together. Then Europe would revert to 'cet état d'opposition et de lutte, auquel la diversité de position, d'intérêts et d'opinion entraînera toujours une masse de Puissances indépendantes, dont chacune a nécessairement son caractère et son système particulier'.[18] The present system would probably last another ten, perhaps even twenty, years, he then thought. But already in the early twenties he witnessed the gradual deterioration of European unity. When the congress system finally broke down, and his career in diplomacy came to an end, he reached the second major turning-point in his intellectual development. In the last half-dozen years of his life he took a more moderate line in the social issue and almost returned to the political ideas that had guided him in his youth.

Metternich, who was born at Coblentz on the Rhine and came from a family with a long tradition of service in high positions, lived most of his life in Vienna and spent more than fifty years in the service of the Habsburgs. In 1809, when he was still in his middle thirties, he became the Foreign Minister of Austria. For thirty-nine years he remained the first minister of the Habsburg Monarchy and one of the leading statesmen in Europe. The greatest moment of his career was when he confronted Napoleon towards the end of the war. Recalling their famous meeting at

17. *Dépêches*, ii, 195–6.   18. Ibid., i, 355–6.

Dresden in 1813, he later related how the dictator had abused him and threatened Austria and how he in turn had urged the aspirations of Europe and stressed the need for peace. '. . . à ce moment décisif', he wrote, 'je me regardai comme le représentant de la société européenne tout entière.'[19] This feeling of standing for the society of Europe, of carrying the world on his shoulders,[20] stayed with him till his fall in 1848. Only, the identity of his opponent changed. In the earlier years it was Napoleon, in the later the revolutionary movement. In his efforts to prevent aggression as well as in his struggle to stave off revolution he called into play the political system that had been introduced at the Congress of Vienna and developed at the Congress of Aix-la-Chapelle.

In the postwar decade the problems connected with the composition, the organization and the role of the union of principal powers occupied Metternich a great deal. Within a few years of the restoration the position of the defeated power came up for revision. France, he agreed at the outset of the Congress of Aix-la-Chapelle, could not be left isolated but should be linked to the other great powers in some way. It ought not to be done, however, by extending the Quadruple Alliance to include the ex-enemy in a general alliance of the five powers. It was important, he thought, to maintain the permanent stipulations of the treaties of the Quadruple Alliance and the provisions for a *casus foederis* against France; it was not in the interest of the peace of Europe to create a quintuple alliance which would lack a *casus foederis*. The measure he favoured was a diplomatic association based on Article VI of the Treaty of 20 November 1815, 'un concert diplomatique (autre qu'un traité) entre les cinq Cours, ayant pour but unique et explicite le maintien de la paix générale'.[21] In this proposal he revealed his stubborn distrust of the ex-enemy. Even many years later he asserted that he would have preferred a diplomatic measure which made a clearer division between the revolutionary power and the old allies to the political arrangement by which France in 1818 was admitted to the union of great powers and allowed to take part in the congresses.[22] In his retirement, how-

19. *Mémoires*, i, 148.
20. Ibid., iii, 365: 'Je sens que je porte le monde sur mes épaules'.
21. Ibid., iii, 168.
22. Ibid., vi, 559 (letter of 26 September 1841).

ever, he took a more detached and generous view of the formation of the five-power Concert. It had evolved as the natural successor to the Quadruple Alliance, he explained in a chapter of his autobiography, which had safeguarded the peace of Europe between the Congresses of Vienna and Aix-la-Chapelle.

A la place de la Quadruple Alliance, qui n'avait plus de raison d'être une fois qu'on eut atteint le but politique poursuivi en commun, se forma une pentarchie morale, dont le Congrès d'Aix-la-Chapelle détermina plus tard les attributions, en même temps qu'il délimitait en principe ses pouvoirs et réglait sa manière de procéder. Ainsi l'Europe était assurée, autant qu'il était possible, d'une paix solide et durable.[23]

For Metternich, whose partiality for the oligarchic system of European politics was tempered with respect for the sovereign rights of independent states, the relationship between the Concert of the five powers and the other states in Europe presented some difficulties. Complaints about domination by the principal powers over politics and diplomacy had already been made in the early days of the Congress of Vienna. They were brought up again in connection with the first peacetime meeting of sovereigns. During the period of preparation for the Congress of Aix-la-Chapelle Count Capo d'Istria had an interview with Metternich, in which he criticized the form of the proposed meeting and pointed to the danger of jealousy arising among the powers that were to be excluded. In his report of the conversation Metternich pointed out that by the Treaty of 20 November 1815, which had been ratified and recognized by all the courts of Europe, the five powers that were preparing to assemble were not only called on, but even obliged, to take part in the meeting. That they did so was no ground for jealousy for those who had neither the right nor the duty to participate. No government, he thought, was afraid of leaving it to the five powers to deal with the problem that the Congress had been convened to solve. What all the other governments feared was that the representatives of the leading powers intended to busy themselves with other affairs as well. To allay that fear he thought it necessary for the sovereigns and ministers of the Quadruple Alliance not only to restrict their negotiations with France exclusively to the matter in question, but also to

23. Ibid., i, 215.

acknowledge well in advance of the conferences an obligation to keep to their proper business. [24] On the eve of the Congress, when he was preparing his plan for the establishment and organization of a diplomatic Concert of the five powers, Metternich again gave some thought to the attitudes and reactions of the lesser states. Having outlined his project, he suggested a number of means by which he thought it possible to introduce the new arrangement without arousing suspicion and alarm in the other governments. [25] The various statements of principles and intentions which he then proposed found formal expression in the Declaration of Aix-la-Chapelle.

Four years later a bitter attack by the sovereign of a small state on the diplomatic practice of the new system provoked Metternich to take up again the subject of the principles governing the relationship between the powers of the Concert and the rest of Europe. Shortly after the Congress of Verona the King of Württemberg issued a circular note with a strong complaint about high-handed treatment of states which were not represented at the meeting. Making a distinction between powers which had inherited the former influence of Napoleon and 'des États mineurs', which had been brought to a state of tutelage, he went so far as to cast doubt on the future safety of the lesser states. Offering the opinion that the means employed by the leading powers in their supervision of Europe involved the introduction of legal principles of a rather alarming character, he suggested that the various diplomatic innovations associated with the new system of politics justified at least an express reservation about the inalienable rights of all independent states. The more particular reason for the King's dissatisfaction and complaint was the novel practice of excluding states of the second order from negotiations conducted in the interest of all members of the family of Europe and of granting them no opportunity to express and explain their individual views and concerns. [26] Metternich made angry comments in the margin of the document.

No action, he wrote, and no utterance of the monarchs of Austria, Prussia and Russia had given the cabinet of Württemberg

24. *Mémoires*, iii, 145.
25. Ibid., iii, 168–9.
26. Ibid., iv, 28–9. For a more detailed discussion of the King's protest, see below pp. 45–6.

any right to ascribe to them the intention of treating independent states as minors: 'Loin de prétendre exercer une *tutelle* quelconque, ces Monarques, dans les occasions mêmes où leurs secours étaient hautement réclamés, ont toujours respecté jusqu'au scrupule l'autorité, l'indépendance et les droits des souverains légitimes auxquels ils accordaient ces secours.' From the incontestable right of these sovereigns to supervise their own states and invite the other governments to follow their example it was a long way to the so-called right to general supervision, that 'chimère gratuitement imaginée par les hommes qui font le métier de calomnier les Monarques'. Nor had the three monarchs introduced disquietening principles into the public law of Europe: 'Ils n'ont rien introduit, rien *innové*; le but unique de leurs efforts est de maintenir le droit public et tous les droits individuels, *tels qu'ils existent.*'[27]

The complaint about exclusion of smaller states, too, was without foundation, he insisted. In the years of the Congresses of Vienna and Aix-la-Chapelle it had undoubtedly happened that treaties had been concluded, accepted and signed, sometimes directly and sometimes by way of assent, by all the states of Europe. But during that period 'les Souverains, fondateurs de la grande Alliance, étaient considérés, de l'aveu unanime des Gouvernements, comme les interprètes de leurs intérêts communs, et par conséquent pleinement autorisés à délibérer et à traiter au nom de ces Gouvernements...'. At the Congresses of Laybach and Verona, on the other hand, conventions had been arranged without general participation by states of the second order. But the powers represented there had been conducting transactions which were strictly limited to matters 'auxquels les trois Monarques ont cru devoir attacher un intérêt majeur'. They had been under no obligation to consult the German courts or the cabinets of other states not directly involved. The exclusive form of congress was both proper and preferable, he argued. From the legal point of view, it was clear that the sovereigns of the principal powers needed neither the consent nor the concurrence of states of the second rank for such meetings. To an experienced statesman, it was obvious that a general assembly of diplomatic representatives of all the courts in Europe would be an unsuitable instrument for dealing with complicated affairs and delicate questions and a poor

27. Ibid., iv, 30.

substitute for the close union of the prudent cabinets of the leading powers. With the point that the revolutionary partisans of Europe, too, opposed these meetings, rightly regarding them as the principal obstacle to the accomplishment of their plans, he clinched his argument in defence of the congress system.[28]

Metternich did not acknowledge the existence of a conflict between the political system of congress diplomacy and the legal principle of state equality. Through legalistic argumentation he managed to reconcile the two to his own satisfaction. Yet, though he paid tribute to both, it is clear that he put the authority of the oligarchs before the rights of the other states. The idea of an exclusive union of principal powers directing the diplomacy and controlling the political life of Europe appealed to his aristocratic temperament. But there were more compelling reasons why he should accept it. He believed that only the concerted efforts of the great powers could prevent European war and stave off social anarchy.

Till the year of his resignation the European policy of Metternich was to maintain peace and security by preserving the settlement of Vienna. In the treaties and boundaries of 1815, the work of statesmen who had been inspired by the idea of a durable peace and guided by the principles of the balance of power,[29] he saw a solid foundation for European peace and political order. In the Concert of the powers, which had developed from a system introduced to secure the good relations of the allies and facilitate the execution of the peace treaties, he found a suitable instrument for protecting the legal basis and territorial structure of the states system. Maintenance of peace, he implied in the course of an examination of the postwar efforts of the principal governments, depended on preservation of 'circonscriptions territoriales, et le respect dû aux traités'.[30] The powers responsible for guarding the peace of Europe, he insisted many years after the war, 'dans leur intérêt individuel comme dans l'intérêt général, doivent ainsi reconnaitre comme règle immuable de leur conduite politique *le respect des traités* existants, dont la délimitation des États forme

28. *Mémoires*, iv, 30–1.
29. In his autobiographical notes, Metternich described the peace aims that had guided him in 1811 and 1812: 'Le seul moyen, c'est de faire rentrer la France dans des limites qui permettent d'espérer une paix durable et de rétablir l'équilibre politique entre les grandes puissances' (*Mémoires*, i, 127).
30. Ibid., iv, 232.

la base essentielle et principale'.[31] In the politics of Europe the role of the Concert was to safeguard the legal and territorial *status quo*.

But the activities of the Concert could not be limited to the political relations of states. Often political problems were inseparable from social issues. In some situations, the attitude of a foreign power or the efforts of a revolutionary movement could add a social side to a political matter.[32] In other circumstances, the tendency of anarchy to lead to civil war or foreign aggression could give political importance to a local revolution.[33] Hence, nearly all the problems that faced the powers had two aspects: 'Elles ont un côté *politique,* et elles en ont un second que je ne crois pas pouvoir désigner autrement qu'en le qualifiant de *révolutionnaire.'*[34] Even in its defence of international law and the political order, the Concert of Europe had to take account of moral and social factors.

However, it was not mainly for reasons of European politics that Metternich was anxious to extend the sphere of the Concert to the field of social relations. The revolutionary movements not only presented an indirect threat to the security of states and the peace of Europe; by undermining the social order, they also endangered the future of civilization. Metternich, who in common with Gentz likened the society of Europe to an organism and revolution to a disease, saw himself in the role of the doctor who would prevent 'le germe révolutionnaire' from destroying the organs of civilization.[35] It was his conviction, his 'arch lie' Gentz said,[36] that all revolutionary outbreaks could be traced to secret societies and be dealt with by force. He did not see a number of independent revolutionary movements, each taking advantage of local conditions, but one vast international conspiracy against all the governments of Europe. The network of secret societies was directed from Paris. It was there that the canker had struck first

31. Ibid., v, 326.
32. Thus the Ottoman question, Metternich pointed out in 1841, which had started in 1840 as a political question, had become, as a result of the attitude taken by France, also a social question (ibid., vi, 580). He made a conceptual distinction between 'questions strictement politiques' and 'questions sociales'.
33. This was so especially in the case of a large state: 'L'anarchie consommée dans un grand État le conduit toujours à la guerre intestine ou à la guerre extérieure, et souvent aux deux fléaux à la fois.' (Ibid., v, 57).
34. Ibid., v, 373.
35. See, e.g., ibid., iii, 434–6.
36. Mann: *Secretary of Europe: the Life of Friedrich Gentz, Enemy of Napoleon,* p. 304.

and from there that it was spreading to the rest of Europe.[37]

The remedy Metternich proposed was a general union of European governments.[38] Such an alliance, he argued, would be supported by the large majority of the people of Europe, who was always inclined to be law-abiding and conservative.[39] It should be led by the principal powers. Though he was often reduced to falling back on a narrow entente with the autocratic governments of Russia and Prussia, Metternich generally wanted to bring the governments of all five powers together in a conservative union. Even when the British had dissociated themselves from the repressive policies of the continental powers and the French had become revolutionary, he did not discard the idea of opposing the revolutionary movement with the full strength of the Concert of Europe: 'La réunion des *cinq* puissances est écrite dans l'avenir,' he wrote to Paris in 1836, 'car en elle se trouvera le rétablissement de la paix morale du corps social . . . .'[40] In his opinion, the social conflict in Europe transcended the political issues between states.

Metternich believed that a new balance of power had arisen in Europe. Rather as the prewar equilibrium of the states system had been disturbed by French aggression and replaced by conflict between France and the Coalition, so the stability and repose of the social structure had been upset by revolutionary pressure and succeeded by struggle between the forces of destruction and preservation.[41] But, while France had been defeated, revolution had been only staved off. While the political conflict had been transformed into a solid balance of power, the social struggle had been consolidated in a precarious balance of forces. The essence of Metternich's theory of the balance of power was the distinction between a balance of rest and stability and a balance of strain and instability. In relations between states, the former was a situation

37. *Mémoires,* v, 44.
38. In his 'Profession de foi politique', Metternich recommended the idea of a 'ligue entre tous les Gouvernements contre les factions dans tous les États' and suggested that 'L'union entre les Monarques est la base fondamentale de la politique à suivre pour sauver aujourd'hui la société de sa ruine totale' (*Mémoires,* iii, 441).
39. Ibid., iii, 443–4; v, 45 and 53.
40. Ibid., vi, 137.
41. 'Deux éléments sont et seront toujours en lutte dans la société humaine: l'élément positif et l'élément négatif, l'élément conservateur et l'élément destructeur,' he wrote after his retirement (ibid., vii, 639). In the years after the fall of Napoleon the faction that carried the latter element had become strong enough to upset the natural balance of society; the need for a counterweight had been met by the governments.

of solidarity, peace and security; in the affairs of society, one of unity, tranquillity and prosperity. The latter was always a state of emergency.[42] In Metternich's Europe the uneasy balance between the social forces of stability and movement[43] served to prop up the existing order and keep off revolutionary anarchy. Both Gentz and Metternich saw the social balance of power as a simple mechanism. Gentz, at least in his more reflective moments, thought of it as a device for regulating an inevitable transition from the old to a new order of society. But Metternich invariably regarded it as a contrivance for postponing a final collapse into chaos. Neither of them liked to see the scales of the balance turn and move against them. But, while Gentz wanted to slow down and control the movement, Metternich wished to stop and delay it.

The instrument of his policy was the Concert of Europe. Metternich persistently maintained that the principal function of the Concert was to support the existing social order by upholding the principles of stability, government and law against the ideas of movement, revolution and anarchy. '. . . le résultat le plus heureux de l'entrevue,' he informed his Emperor shortly before the meeting at Aix-la-Chapelle, 'sera donc celui-ci: *Qu'il n'y aura rien de changé dans l'ordre de choses existant*; ce résultat *vaudra le plus beau triomphe* à Votre Majesté et aux Cabinets qui, depuis 1815, n'ont cessé de suivre une marche positive, qui n'ont jamais fait appel à l'esprit d'innovation et qui ont toujours soutenu le droit seul, le droit pur et simple.'[44] 'Le premier des principes à suivre par les Monarques, unis de volonté comme ils le sont par l'uniformité de leurs voeux et de leurs jugements,' he advised the Tsar two years later at Troppau, 'doit être celui d'opposer la stabilité des institutions politiques au mouvement désordonné qui s'est emparé des esprits; la fixité des principes à la manie de leur *interprétation*; le *respect pour les lois en vigueur* à leur *renversement*.'[45] 'Le principe que les Monarques doivent opposer à ce plan de destruction universelle,' he reminded him at Laybach, 'c'est celui de la *conservation*

42. 'Ce n'est pas, en un mot, l'état de controverse et la lutte entre les Gouvernements et les peuples que nous envisageons comme l'ordre régulier du corps social, mais bien positivement comme un malheur propre aux temps de trouble et d'anarchie.' (ibid., v, 374).
43. Significantly, he grouped all his enemies together under the title of 'le mouvement': 'L'Italie *du mouvement* (les denominations de libérale, radicale, progressiste, ne comptent pas pour nous) . . .' (ibid., vii, 227).
44. Ibid., iii, 145–6.
45. Ibid., iii, 443.

de toute chose legalement existante. Le seul moyen de parvenir à ce but pourra être celui *de ne pas innover.*' [46] And the Circular Note that the representatives of Austria, Russia and Prussia prepared at the Congress of Verona and which Metternich arranged to have published referred to 'les principes conservateurs' as 'les principes sur lesquels repose le concert européen'. [47]

The counterrevolutionary measures that Metternich advocated were intervention and repression. In common with Gentz, he believed that sovereigns had both a right and a need to interfere in the affairs of a state afflicted with revolution. The right, he suggested, was nothing but 'le simple exercice d'une faculté dont l'emploi est la conséquence du libre mouvement de tout État indépendant'. [48] The so-called principle of non-intervention was merely a word devoid of meaning, a phrase without practical significance. [49] It had become popular in Britain and France but could never gain acceptance in Austria:

> Faux dans sa base, il peut être soutenu par un État insulaire. La nouvelle France n'a pas manqué de se l'approprier et de le proclamer hautement. Ce sont les brigands qui récusent la gendarmerie, et les incendiaires qui protestent contre les pompiers. Nous n'admettrons jamais une prétention aussi subversive de tout ordre social; nous nous reconnaîtrons, au contraire, toujours le droit de nous rendre à l'appel que nous adressera une autorité légale en faveur de sa defense, tout comme nous nous reconnaissons celui d'aller éteindre le feu dans la maison du voisin, pour empêcher qu'il ne gagne la nôtre. [50]

But it was not only the rules of law and the demands of necessity which guided the great sovereigns. [51] They were also conscious of

46. *Mémoires*, iii, 505.
47. Ibid., iii, 617.
48. Ibid., v, 541.
49. Ibid., v, 540–1.
50. Ibid., v, 46.
51. Metternich made that distinction himself: 'A côté de la question de droit, qui, je le répète, est pour nous claire comme le jour,' he wrote about the annexation of Cracow in 1846, 'l'affaire a encore bien d'autres côtés, dont nous nous croyons appelés à être les juges natures. Parmi ces questions, celle de la nécessité mérite la première place' (ibid., vii, 361).

This particular act of intervention, which Metternich described as 'une mesure de police' (ibid., vii, 361), is interesting because it represents the triumph of the principle of dynastic over that of territorial conservation. It was carried out in the name of counterrevolution and amounted to a modification of the Vienna settlement.

a duty to aid any legal authority which had been attacked by the common enemy.[52] Metternich always preferred any such act of succour to be carried out by the Concert of Europe rather than to be undertaken by an individual power.

Une considération qui à nos yeux a la plus haute valeur (he wrote a few months after the July Revolution of 1830), c'est celle de la différence immense qu'offrira toujours, dans son point de départ et dans ses conséquences, tout secours prêté à un État par une puissance voisine agissant d'après une impulsion particulière ou des calculs isolés, et celui qui serait l'effet d'une solidarité avouée par les puissances.[53]

Metternich's motto was 'la force dans le droit'.[54] But the basis of his system of politics was neither the principle of legitimacy nor the idea of the divine right of sovereigns.[55] It was with legal facts that he was concerned and as a 'conservateur'[56] that he described himself. He wanted to maintain all established governments and existing institutions because he believed that a defeat of authority in any state could lead to a collapse of order throughout the society of Europe. For Metternich, as for Gentz, the Concert of Europe was primarily an instrument for conserving the dynastic order of Europe.

Austrian conservative thought about the Concert of Europe hardly survived Metternich. As long as he was chancellor it was still possible to maintain that the interests of the Habsburgs in upholding the territorial and dynastic order of 1815 coincided with the needs of Europe. After 1848 this could no longer be done. In the fifties and sixties, which were dominated by national movements and marked by wars between great powers, there was no basis for a conservative Concert of Europe. So Metternich's successors gave only little thought to the Concert. Schwarzenberg,

52. Ibid., v, 44.
53. Ibid., v, 56. See also iv, 605–6: 'Si l'on veut que des mesures de ce genre [necessary to conserve 'la santé publique'] produisent leur effet, it faut qu'elles soient prises par plusieurs États agissant de concert; des alliances entre les Gouvernements en sont la condition indispensable' (October 1829); and vii, 473: '... y rétablir l'ordre au moyen d'un concert, serait plus avantageux à notre avenir que de le faire par une intervention isolée, quand même elle nous serait possible ...' (*re* Italy in August 1847).
54. See, e.g., ibid., i, 2, and vii, 637.
55. See e.g., ibid., vi, 189.
56. See, e.g., ibid., vii, 243.

who relied on the Austrian army to defend the interests of the Monarchy, was not a man of ideas. Francis Joseph, though he adhered to the legitimist doctrines of his predecessors and subscribed to the principles of territorial and dynastic conservatism, rarely applied them to the Concert of Europe. In the fifties, when another Napoleon became Emperor of France and war broke out between three of the great powers, he looked to a league with Prussia and the lesser German states as his instrument for a conservative policy. In the sixties, when Prussia defeated Austria and took over the leadership in central Europe, he turned his back upon Germany and concentrated on the Balkans. In the second half of the century Austria contributed little of importance to the theory of the Concert of Europe.

Prussian and other contributions

Among the statesmen of Prussia, who were as afraid as the Austrians of the national and revolutionary movements and tended to lean on Metternich for support and protection, there were many who held conservative views of the Concert of Europe. In the thought of these men, too, the emphasis was generally on the doctrine of dynastic conservation.

In 1817 Frederick William III believed that all other interests should be subordinated to that of maintaining the legal order and the general tranquillity of Europe. 'L'un et l'autre tiennent à la conservation de la paix et à la stabilité de la restauration.'[57] Three years later he recognized in the revolutionary movement his most dangerous enemy in postwar Europe. Only the close and lasting union of the allied sovereigns, he wrote to Tsar Alexander, could wreck the efforts of the revolutionaries. '... la réunion de nos efforts est devenue un des principaux moyens dont la Providence s'est servie pour assurer à l'Europe les bienfaits qu'il s'agit aujourd'hui de lui conserver.'[58]

If for some years, after France had been admitted to the Concert and revolution had broken out in various Mediterranean countries, fear of revolution had tended to become separated from distrust of France, after the revolution of 1830 in Paris they were again firmly linked in the minds of men. The European thought of Frederick

57. *Briefwechsel König Friedrich Wilhelm's III und der Königin Luise mit Kaiser Alexander I*, p. 291 (letter of 6 December).
58. Ibid., p. 310 (letter of 24 September 1820).

William IV, an ardent adherent of the conspiracy theory of revolution, was a product of this combination. 'The pestilence of radicalism'[59] was spreading from Paris and endangering all of Europe. We know, he wrote to his friend Bunsen at the outset of the empire of Napoleon III,

> that Louis Buonaparte has made a deal with the leaders of insurrectionary efforts throughout Europe. Mazzini and Kossuth and others were on hand, hiding in or near Paris. A sign from the incarnation of revolution, sent out from the Tuileries, will light the flame of revolt in Poland, Hungary, Italy, southern Germany and Belgium. Then Buonaparte will appear in the border countries as Empereur de la paix!!! and garant du droit de tous les peuples.[60]

To provide against the danger that France presented to the social and territorial order of Europe, the King wanted to reestablish the Great Alliance that had beaten her a generation earlier. Only the language of a physical and moral union of the great powers of Europe, he thought after the revolution in Paris in 1848, would impress 'raving France'.[61] 'Contre l'Europe en armes pour la plus sainte des causes, le contraire de la révolution', he insisted four years later, 'la révolution est sans armes!'[62] 'The one thing that is important, right and decisive for the future of Europe', he wrote when the 'newly crowned bird-of-prey'[63] started his reign, 'is that the four powers should keep together and that, as a result, Napoleon, through the pressure of this unprecedented union of power, should feel: *"We would guarantee the treaties and, therefore, also the territories and not allow them to be seized or even touched. . . ."*'[64] While the aims of the Concert policy of Frederick William IV were to preserve the old order of society and to maintain peace in Europe, the principle was legitimacy.

59. Ranke: *Sämmtliche Werke*, xlix–l, 'Aus dem Briefwechsel Friedrich Wilhelms IV mit Bunsen,' p. 439 (letter of 4 December 1847): the only side of the Swiss question that mattered to the great powers, he told Bunsen, was 'whether the pestilence of radicalism, that is of a sect which deliberately has cut itself off from Christianity, from God, from all existing law, from divine and human law, and is finished and done with them, whether or not this sect, through murder, blood and tears, shall gain control in Switzerland and *thus endanger all of Europe*'.
60. Ibid., p. 534 (letter of 1852).
61. Ibid., p. 458 (letter of 9 March 1848).
62. Ibid., p. 534.
63. Ibid., p. 537.
64. Ibid., p. 536 (letter of 20 November 1852).

The European thought of the Prussian sovereigns was reinforced with contributions from a number of conservative statesmen and scholars. Friedrich Ancillon, writer on the history and politics of Europe, tutor to the young Frederick William IV and, eventually, foreign minister of Prussia, had a great deal in common with his cousin Gentz. In his earlier years, when he made a study of the states system, he was inspired by the classical idea of the balance of power.[65] But later in life, when he gained influence and received office in the Prussian government, he embraced the reactionary ideas of the rulers. The balance system that he expounded, before the fall of Napoleon as well as after the Congress of Vienna, was one of counter forces rather than equilibrium, 'Gegengewicht' not 'Gleichgewicht'.[66] Its parallels were in the physical world.[67] It involved movement, activity and growth and had little to do with Metternichian repose.[68] The effects of the political system of the earlier age, he found, had been to check the ambitions of leading states and to prevent situations of extreme preponderance of power. Its merits had been to minimize abuse of force, to protect the security and independence of all states and to bring about reasonable measures of order, harmony and stability in Europe.[69] Ten years after the war he maintained that the system introduced at the Congress of Vienna and developed at the later meetings of the powers, though in appearance a deviation from the older system of counter forces, was in reality its perfection.

65. See Ancillon: *Tableau des Révolutions du système politique de l'Europe, depuis la fin du quinzième siècle* (Brussels, 1839), i, 27.

66. Ibid., ii, 488: 'Le nom de système des contreforces convient beaucoup mieux ici que celui de système de l'équilibre. Ce dernier terme réveille des idées vagues et fausses.' Because of the inequality of forces, perfect equilibrium is never achieved. See also Ancillon: *Ueber den Geist der Staatsverfassungen und dessen Einfluss auf die Gesetzgebung*, p. 322, where he argues that 'Gleichgewicht' is neither possible nor desirable.

67. Ancillon: *Ueber den Geist*, p. 321–2: 'Just as in the celestial system the worlds, fixed in their orbits, remain still and ever unchanged, obeying and following simultaneously the force of gravity and the centrifugal force—and without the latter would collide, be lost and fallen; so all the states in Europe have maintained themselves, autonomous and independent, equidistant from overlordship and submission, despotism and slavery, alternately attracting and repelling each other in direct relation to their mass and in inverse relation to their distance. The larger and the closer they were, the more they repelled each other out of justified fear, if not in hostility then in distrust; the farther away from each other and the smaller their mass, the more disposed they were towards friendship with one another.' Ranke used the same metaphor thirty years later.

68. Ibid., pp. 322 and 327.

69. Ibid., pp. 323 and 326–7; Ancillon: *Tableau*, i, 22 and 32.

The five great powers, closely united among themselves and with the others, form a system of solidarity, by which one stands for all and all for one; in which power appears only as protection for everybody's possessions and rights; in which the maintenance of the whole and the parts within legal bounds, for the sake of the peace of the world, has become the only aim of political activity; in which one deals openly, deliberates over everything collectively and acts jointly.[70]

A step had been taken towards reconciling politics with morality and replacing violence with law, which would evoke the admiration and gratitude of future generations. But before the new system could take root and become a lasting guarantee for the security as well as the independence of states it would need to be developed and organized. 'As yet, it unfortunately appears to rest only on the lives and the great personages of the present rulers of the world.' Should it dissolve and disappear with the men who had set it up a return to the principles of 'interaction of counterforces' could be expected.[71]

Although he emphasized the continuity between the prerevolutionary and the post-Napoleonic politics of Europe and insisted on an essential similarity between the traditional balance of power and the new system of politics, Ancillon's conception of the postwar situation was clearly based on the notion of struggle between the union of sovereigns and the revolutionary movements. The essence of his idea of the Concert of Europe was the principle of preservation.[72] In a memorandum, which presumably was handed to the Tsar in 1818, he had not only suggested that the five great powers should combine to guarantee the existing possessions of all states against forcible disturbance and agree to meet in congress from time to time to decree such changes in the *status quo* as would be necessary, but also demanded that they should pledge one another to maintain legitimate sovereignty

70. Ibid., p. 332.
71. Ibid., p.331–3.
72. Haake: *Johann Peter Friedrich Ancillon und Kronprinz Friedrich Wilhelm IV von Preussen,* pp. 156–7: in an undated letter, in Haake's opinion from the summer of 1825, he writes: 'The Greek insurrection has been plotted by the same secret societies which threaten the social order in France, Spain, Portugal, England, Italy and which set the principle of destruction of what exists and of mobility in all relations against the principle of conservation upheld by the great union of sovereigns.'

everywhere.[73] And the similarity between his and Gentz's comments on secret societies, revolution and intervention extended to the metaphors.[74]

Wilhelm Traugott Krug, a liberal Kantian and anti-Hegelian professor of philosophy at Leipzig and a busy pamphleteer, had a different opinion of the old balance of power. He could see in it nothing but an apparition haunting the cabinets of Europe, arousing suspicion and ambition everywhere;[75] an idea that never could be realized;[76] something so unstable and unreliable that its pursuit had more often led to war than safeguarded peace.[77] As means of achieving the eternal peace at which he aimed he rejected the balance system as well as the ideas of a universal monarchy and a world federation of states. Instead he pointed to a material and political and, especially, a moral and religious improvement in the conditions of the peoples as the only way.[78] So when the Holy Alliance became known to the public he welcomed it with enthusiasm. It stood for the application of Christianity to politics, for the replacement of the traditional principles of power, conquest and war with those of justice, love and peace. It seemed to him to contain promises of liberal constitutions and practice throughout Europe and of harmonious relations among the states whose sovereigns had signed the treaty.[79] Drawing support from Plato's argument that the solution to the great problems of

73 H. v. Treitschke: *History of Germany in the Nineteenth Century*, iii, 113–14.

74. When reacting to the revolutionary situation in Belgium in 1830 he resorted to the familiar similes of the contagious disease, the erupting volcano and the spreading fire (paraphrase in Haake, p. 161).

75. Krug: *Gesammelte Schriften*, iv, 300–1; from *Griechenlands Wiedergeburt. Oder drei Worte über die griechische Sache* (1821–22).

76. Ibid., iv, 301.

77. Ibid., vi, 538; from *Dikäopolitik oder neue Restaurazion der Staatwissenschaft mittels des Rechtsgesetzes* (1824). Great powers with strong governments, he argued, would always preponderate; the alliances of the weaker states, which invariably lacked unity, could not provide an adequate counterweight. Elsewhere he made the point that the maxim of preserving a balance of power easily could serve as a pretext for starting a war; the balance of power needed the addition of 'an inner, merely moral, motive (for example, the sanctification of the state of possession and the treaties)' (iv, 80; from *Kreuz-und Querzüge eines Deutschen auf den Steppen der Staats-Kunst und Wissenschaft* (1818)).

78. Ibid., iv, 80 and 89; from *Kreuz-und Querzüge etc.*

79. Ibid., iii, 257–8; from '*La sainte alliance. Oder Denkmal des von Oestreich Preussen und Russland geschlossenen heiligen Bundes* (February 1816). He did not think that the Holy Alliance would bring eternal peace. The Christian world had to fight the Turks and the North African robber states as well as Britain (pp. 258–9). For his liberal idea of the Holy Alliance, see also iv, 405–28.

politics can lie only in the wisdom of kings, he put his faith in the monarchs.[80]

But fifteen years after the publication of the treaty of the Holy Alliance he had come to realize that mankind was not yet sufficiently developed to accept a system of politics 'which wanted to guide worldly affairs according to divine ideas'. European politics, he now observed, had once more moved towards the system of political preponderance. But this preponderance had not become the property of one state exclusively but of five states jointly, which was something new. Relations between the great powers and the smaller states could not be said to be conducted strictly according to the law of justice, which gave all states, irrespective of size, equal rights and equal duties. But, if the claim of the five governments that they were concerned merely with preserving peace and order was accepted, the existing system could be justified by reference to the maxim *salus populi suprema lex*. So long as the states had no elected judicial body to settle their disputes, the law of prudence demanded that the weak ones yield to the powers and avoid the greater evil. By that he referred not only to the temporary and limited harm of war between a couple of states but also to the calamity of revolution.[81]

Contrary to some of his conservative contemporaries and successors, Krug distinguished between the Holy Alliance and the Concert of Europe. While, at least in his later years, he conceived of the former as a set of ideas, the ideal counterpart of the existing institution,[82] he regarded the latter rather as an expedient compromise, a reserve position. He had a great deal in common with the men who later in the century presented the Concert of Europe as a stage in a development towards an organized society of nations. But he shared the concern about the social conflict and the dread of revolution so characteristic of his times. To his mind, the primary function of the new institution was as a safeguard against the great ideological war, which he was convinced would be the ultimate result of new revolutionary outbreaks.[83] Ancillon subordinating his theory of the balance of power to the rulers' idea of the Concert of Europe, and Krug adjusting his liberal

80. Ibid., iv, 89; from *Kreuz-und Querzüge etc.*
81. Ibid., v, 220–3; from *Portrait von Europa* (1831).
82. See e.g., ibid., iii, 265; third postscript to *La sainte alliance*.
83. Ibid., v, 222–3; from *Porträt von Europa*.

principles to his antirevolutionary feelings, are illustrations of the impact of social tension on two different strands of European thought.

Three men close to the court of Frederick William IV—Joseph von Radowitz, Leopold von Gerlach and Friedrich Julius Stahl—joined the King in defending the social order with arguments derived from Christian theology and in investing the Concert of Europe with ideas borrowed from the Act of the Holy Alliance. Radowitz, though a non-Prussian of Polish stock and a catholic, believed in Prussia's mission in Germany, and gained the confidence of the King. The aim and the result of revolution, he found, were 'to replace the principle of law, the divine order of the world, by an order chosen by man himself'.[84] The primary reason why it had become a frequently recurring phenomenon in the postwar world he discovered in the idolization of peace and order, of which leading statesmen had been guilty since the Congress of Vienna.[85] They had taken measures to drive war out of European politics and had failed to understand that war is as natural a part of human existence as peace. When repressed in the external relations of states, it was bound to reappear in their internal affairs. So the result had been that war with a foreign enemy had been replaced by struggle with the domestic opponent. Thus arose the need for the great powers to intervene in the affairs of other states. A world-shaking war, he believed in 1852, was the only means by which a proper reorganization of Europe could be effected.[86] He would have preferred the 'Pentarchie'[87] to devote fewer efforts to avoiding war in Europe and to concentrate instead on preserving the old monarchical order on the Continent.[88]

84. Radowitz: *Gesammelte Schriften,* iv, 46–7 (under '1831').
85. Ibid., iv, 62 (under '1836'): 'I find that one of the most important characteristics of this age is the way in which peace ["Ruhe"] is being idolized. If it is stated in purely abstract terms that peace and order are absolutely the highest good, then there can be no talk of right and truth. There is, of course, a peace of life, which gives expression to the concept of the organism; but there is also the peace of death. . . . It is unbelievable what influence "appeasement" ("Mässigung"), which stems from moral weakness and love of pleasure, has exerted in the last years. I am convinced that a far greater part of all the troubles that have befallen Europe since the Peace of 1815 has been due to this influence than to the efforts of all the factions.'
86. Ibid., iv, 325–6.
87. The term 'die europäische Pentarchie' appears on p. 106 of Radowitz, ii.
88. After the July Revolution in Paris he censured the powers for being far too tolerant towards France; they should have gone to war in defence of 'the long-established European principle of monarchy', he thought (iv, 39 and 43).

General von Gerlach, who in his earlier years together with Radowitz was a close adviser of the Crown Prince and in 1850 became adjutant to the King, was a fanatic. 'My principle of politics is and will be the struggle against the revolutionary movement', he declared when once Bismarck tried to reason with him.[89] It was the maxims of the Holy Alliance which guided his approach to politics and determined his attitude to revolution and 'Bonapartismus'.[90] They filled his mind so completely that he ignored the distinction between that alliance and the Concert of Europe. The congresses of the postwar years he was inclined to regard in retrospect as meetings of the Holy Alliance.[91] And the history of Europe from 1815 till the middle of the century he described as the struggle of the revolutionary movement with the Holy Alliance,[92] between those who rejected and those who accepted the fundamental ideas 'that the authority comes from God and that the sovereigns therefore must rule as servants appointed by God'.[93]

Stahl, philosopher and politician, was also a reactionary. Born in Munich of an orthodox Jewish family and converted to Lutheranism in his youth, he became professor of law at Erlangen. In 1840 Frederick William IV called him to Berlin. Unlike Gerlach, Stahl distinguished between the Concert of Europe and the Holy Alliance. But he had faith only in the latter. In the Holy Alliance— by which he generally meant the conservative alliance of the three eastern powers rather than the pact of 1815 between all the Christian sovereigns of Europe except the Pope and the King of England—he recognized the true heiress of the Holy Roman Empire. It had taken over the role of the highest authority in the world and the function of maintaining, by the grace of God, law and order throughout the Christian countries.[94] It was a guarantee

---

89. Bismarck: *Gedanken und Erinnerugnen*, i, 169 (letter of 6 May 1857).
90. See, e.g., his letter to Manteuffel of 18 February 1856 in *Preussens auswärtige Politik 1850 bis 1858* . . . ed. Poschinger, iii, 218, and his letter to Bismarck of 1 May 1860 in *Briefe des Generals Leopold von Gerlach an Otto von Bismarck*, ed. Kohl, p. 230.
91. *Denkwürdigkeiten aus dem Leben Leopold von Gerlachs*, ii, 725.
92. Ibid., i, 769.
93. Gerlach: *Briefe*, p. 230 (letter of 1 May 1860). See also *Denkwürdigkeiten,* ii, 724, for references to the history and principles of the Holy Alliance.
94. Stahl: *Parlamentarische Reden*, p. 32 (speech on the Eastern Question, 25 April 1854); see also ibid., p. 50 (speech on the Eastern Question, 24 April 1855) and Stahl: *Siebzehn parlamentarische Reden und drei Vorträge*, p. 230 (speech on the Italian Question, 13 May 1859).

41

system for the thrones as well as the territories of the European monarchs, a defensive alliance against the ungodly movements of revolution and nationalism.[95] Because he believed it to be a European interest that the holy struggle for right, legitimacy and monarchy against revolution should not acquire the character of being merely a fight for the persons of the sovereigns against the persons of their subjects, he would have liked to see the governments of the five great powers stand above the contending parties as a European Areopagus.[96] But he knew that only the rulers of Prussia, Austria and Russia could be relied on to fight the enemies of the social and political order of Europe.

In 1859, at the time of the Italian war, Stahl insisted that a substantial violation of the treaties of 1815 was a matter of serious concern to all of Europe.[97] But generally conservative thinkers in Prussia were more concerned with maintaining monarchical power than with guaranteeing territorial sovereignty. This was primarily a result of the pressure of the revolutionary movements on the one hand and the long absence of European war on the other. But it had to do also with the German question. Few Prussians, even among those who were guided by the cosmopolitan ideology of the restoration rather than by national feeling, were satisfied with the particularist order which had been imposed on Germany at Vienna. This arrangement not only denied Germany national unity but also relegated Prussia to the second place in Germany and the fifth in Europe. So the idea of the great powers blocking a revision of the territorial order of Europe could be of only limited attraction to these statesmen.

It is among the Germans who sympathized with Austria more than with Prussia that one expects to find men who placed the emphasis on the antirevisionist functions of the Concert of Europe. Jean Baptist von Schweitzer, the early socialist leader, is an example, though a rather special one. Born in Frankfurt am Main and brought up in the catholic faith, in his youth he combined

---

95. For Stahl, the national movement was part of the revolutionary movement. 'None of the ideas of revolution stands by itself,' he said in his speech on the Italian Question in 1859, 'they are *jointly connected*; whether they start their cry with "freedom and equality" or with "the rights of nationality" comes to the same; one watchword always ignites the other, until finally the entire legal and historical order stands in flames' (*Siebzehn parl. Reden*, p. 228); see also ibid., p. 235.
96. Ibid., p.179 (speech of 15 February 1851 on Schleswig and Holstein).
97. Ibid., p. 226.

hatred of Prussia with a vague loyalty towards Austria. During the European crisis of 1859, when he was still in his middle twenties, he attacked Napoleon III for trying to tear Italy away from Austria. In two pamphlets, of which one was published anonymously under the title *Oesterreichs Sache ist Deutschlands Sache* and the other was presented as a refutation of a pro-French work by Carl Vogt, he accused Napoleon of attempting to upset the Vienna settlement. The territorial treaties of 1815, he asserted, were to the European states system as a written constitution was to a state.[98] They were drawn up according to the system of the balance of power, and constituted the legal frame of the system of politics by which the great powers up to now had kept each other in check and secured peace, order and civilization in Europe. 'This is the significance of the treaties of 1815. As their natural protectors stand the great powers of Europe.'[99] For Schweitzer the enemy in 1859 was the French Empire and not, as for Stahl, the national movement. Schweitzer, himself an ardent patriot with a passionate desire for national unification, wrote his tracts at a time when he was still hoping for Austrian leadership of a united Germany. The difference of emphasis between the predominantly antirevolutionary and the predominantly antirevisionist element in German conservative thought generally reflected the diversity in the attitudes to the German question.

The conservative theory was in more than one way the sovereigns' theory of the Concert of Europe. Developed mainly by monarchs and ministers, it sprang from the will to preserve the territories and maintain the power of the rulers. Also, it presented the Concert as a union of principal sovereigns, as distinct from a system of states or a society of nations. In its typical form, it was, in the terminology of the time, a social rather than a political theory in the sense that it dealt more with conflict between the strata of the society of Europe than with relations among the members of the states system. At its centre was the doctrine of counterrevolutionary intervention.

Contrary to the other German views of the Concert of Europe, the conservative ones were not marked off clearly from the ideas of the Holy Alliance. The notion that sovereigns were servants of

98. Schweitzer: *Widerlegung von Carl Vogt's Studien zur gegenwärtigen Lage Europa's*, p. 16.
99. Ibid., p. 17.

God who had been charged with maintaining law, government, peace and order in the Christian society of Europe appeared also in some of the contributions to the conservative theory. The overlapping of the two sets of ideas led to a blurring of the distinction between the Concert and the Holy Alliance. In the years of the postwar congresses, when the Concert was clearly in evidence and the Holy Alliance existed primarily as an expression of sentiments and ideas, there was an inclination to regard the institution of the Concert as inspired by the doctrines of the Act of the Holy Alliance. In later years, when the five-power Concert functioned only intermittently and the name of the Holy Alliance had been connected with the union of the autocratic rulers of the three eastern powers, there was a tendency to overlook the Concert of Europe and concentrate on the 'Holy Alliance'.

After the death of Frederick William IV and the rise of Bismarck Germans became more concerned with changing the political structure of Europe than with preserving its social order. While new ideas of the European Concert came to the fore, the conservative tradition went into decline and nearly died out.[100] In one way, this reflected a growing feeling that the danger of revolution had receded. In another way, it was a result of the vigorous criticism to which the conservative ideas had been exposed for decades.

2. CRITICISM

The attack on conservative thought came from four camps. The moderate constitutionalists in the secondary states of the Confederation, the radical liberals throughout the smaller states, the national liberals in Prussia, and the revolutionaries wherever they were all opposed the Metternichian system and criticized the

100. Relics of the dying tradition of thought survived till late in the century. Though expressed in terms of an alliance of the autocratic governments rather than of the Concert of Europe, the idea of ensuring social stability through monarchical solidarity was one of the strains in the European thought of Bismarck after 1871 (see below pp. 98–9) and the essence of the outlook of both William I and William II. Other remnants of conservatism may be seen in a book by an international lawyer on the right and duty to intervene, which was published the year after the Congress of Berlin. Both elements of the conservative theory found expression in this work. On the one hand, the author recommended collective intervention by the great powers as the best means of preserving the international legal order; on the other, he suggested that a social democratic or similar victory in any state should be included in the list of legitimate grounds for intervention (Strauch: *Zur Interventions-Lehre*, pp. 28–9 and 35).

conservative Concert. While most of the supporters of the anti-revolutionary Concert of Europe came from Austria and Prussia, the majority of its opponents lived in the south of Germany.

The moderate constitutionalists

Two types of views may be distinguished in south German criticism. The one saw the congress system as a dictatorship of the great powers over the weaker states, and insisted on the rights of the secondary members of the Confederation. The other viewed the Concert as an instrument for political repression, and upheld the rights of the peoples. The supporters of the first view concentrated their criticism on the system and the methods of the Concert and requested some form of representation and participation of the states in the south. The adherents of the second censured the aims and the actions of the institution and demanded its overthrow and replacement. Some thinkers contributed to both sets of ideas and are difficult to classify. But, generally, the men that held moderate views on the constitutional issue belonged to the first group and the radicals in domestic politics to the second. Kings and ministers were clearly in the first group.

Already as crown prince William of Württemberg had reacted to 'the quadruple despotism' which had succeeded Napoleon's domination over Europe.[101] After the Congress of Verona, in a circular note for his ministers abroad, he complained about high-handed treatment of second rank powers and discussed the dangers of great power tutelage. It was not to the ends pursued and the work accomplished by the members of the Congress that the King objected. Indeed, he complimented the sovereigns on the care they devoted to upholding the monarchical principle, repressing subversive ideas and keeping an eye on the state of Europe.[102]

> Mais les moyens par lesquels cette surveillance agit (he admitted) nous paraissent en partie introduire dans le droit public des principes plus ou moins importants. Des traités conclus, des congrés rassemblés dans les intérêts de la famille européenne, sans qu'il soit permis à ceux du second ordre de faire valoir

101. Stein: *Briefwechsel, Denkschriften und Aufzeichnungen,* v, 263 (letter to Stein of 31 August 1815).
102. He did, however, draw attention to the excellence of the institutions he had introduced in his own state.

leurs intérêts particuliers, ces formes mêmes sur lesquelles on les admet aux traités et on leur fait connaître les décisions des cours prépondérantes, et l'attente de celles-ci de ne point rencontrer une différence d'opinion chez aucun de leurs alliés; ces différentes innovations en diplomatie justifient au moins une réserve expresse des droits inaliénables de tout état indépendant.[103]

He regretted especially the exclusion of the German Confederation from the meetings of the great powers.

The man thought to have inspired the King's note was Karl August von Wangenheim, Württemberg's representative in the Federal Diet. He wanted the smaller German states to become less dependent on Austria and Prussia and championed the so-called 'Triaspolitik'. A confederation of the smaller states within the German Confederation would be of advantage not only to themselves, he argued, but also to the two leading powers as well as to Europe in general. It would give the lesser states a say in German and European affairs and would improve the balance of power in both Germany and Europe.[104]

A. F. H. Schaumann, the author of a history of the second Peace of Paris published in Göttingen in 1844, continued this line of thought. Referring favourably to the scheme for a union of the south German states that the Bavarian minister Count Rechberg had prepared in 1815, he suggested that the governments of the smaller states should unite for the purposes of foreign politics and set up a new great power to represent the purely German interests in European diplomacy. Austria and Prussia ought to welcome such an addition to the power of Germany, he thought, and should secure entry for the sixth great power to the congresses where the fate of Europe was decided.[105] In a history of the Congress of Verona, published in 1855, he concentrated on the work of the Concert of Europe. Describing the European

---

103. Lesur: *Annuaire historique universel pour 1823*, pp. 693–4. An extract of this document, which was signed by Wintzingerode, is given in Metternich's *Mémoires,* iv, 28–9, together with Metternich's marginal comments (see above pp. 26–7).

104. *Die Wahl des Freiherrn von Wangenheim,* pp. 196 and 213 (letter to Metternich of 16 September 1818) and p. 276 (Denkschrift). Also Wangenheim: *Österreich, Preussen und* das reine Deutschland *auf der Grundlage des deutschen Staatenbundes organisch zum deutschen Bundesstaate vereinigt,* p. 101.

105. Schaumann: *Geschichte des zweiten Pariser Friedens für Deutschland,* pp. 289–90 and 292–3.

Pentarchy as 'the five-star constellation guiding the erring navigation on the ever rocking sea of the destinies of countries and nations', he criticized the action against Spain in 1823.[106]

Also Friedrich Ludwig Lindner, a liberal editor and writer and a close friend of King William of Württemberg, was against both the structure of the congress system and the principles of Concert politics. His *Manuscript aus Süd-Deutschland*, which caused a stir after its appearance in London in 1820 and provoked the indignation of Gentz, is one of the foremost expositions of the 'rein-deutsche' idea. Complaining about the practice of discussing and settling matters directly related to the interests of Germany without hearing German views other than those of Austria and Prussia of which the negotiations of the Congress of Aix-la-Chapelle in his opinion afforded an outstanding, though not an isolated, example, he pointed out that Germany's two great powers, with their separate interests and aims, were ill suited to represent her smaller states.[107] Not only Germany but also Europe needed a new and independent power in the European Areopagus. To recover the balance of power that she had lost, Europe required a certain number of states of definite sizes. Too few powers in the states system made for danger and insecurity, while too many small and weak states spelled confusion and friction. States of average size in central positions, 'mittlere Staaten', were the most useful members of the states system because they guaranteed the security of the greater powers and guarded the balance of power. So the interests of the various powers as well as the general interest of Europe, he concluded, demanded a united Germany strong enough to take her place alongside the five great powers.[108]

In his criticism of the suspicious attitude and restraining policy of the Metternichian Concert of Europe Lindner went further than most supporters of the 'Triaspolitik'. He attacked the establishment of the Concert with the passion of a radical. 'Do we want to blindfold ourselves so as not to see what times we live in?' he asked. 'Is it possible to misunderstand the condition of the world so much as to imagine that the agreements of half a dozen

---

106. Schaumann: *Geschichte des Congresses von Verona*, p. 9. The author did not distinguish between the Concert of Europe and the Holy Alliance. He presented the postwar congresses as meetings of the Holy Alliance (p. 3) and described Britain as a member of the Holy Alliance (pp. 98–9).
107. Lindner: *Manuscript aus Süd-Deutschland*, pp. 168 and 180.
108. Ibid., p. 221–9.

titled diplomats, overloaded with ribbons, could check the moving force of the century, could hurl mankind back into the chaos of feudal times?'[109]

The radical liberals

While the conservatives sometimes associated the Concert of Europe with the Holy Alliance, the radicals generally regarded the one as part of the other. In their attack on the political system of Europe the radicals in the smaller states of the German Confederation treated the Concert rather as the executive of the Holy Alliance. They concentrated on the latter.

Karl von Rotteck, who was born in Baden and taught history and political science at the University of Freiburg, inspired the liberals in south Germany for more than a generation after 1815. Observing that all the postwar congresses had been conducted in the spirit of the Holy Alliance, he concluded that the reactionary policy of the powers was based on the Act of the Alliance.[110] Though he accepted that the Holy Alliance had sprung from ideas and feelings rather than common material interests, he insisted that the religious convictions and personal sentiments of individuals were unsuitable as a foundation of law for others.[111] The notion that the Christian sovereigns of Europe were brothers, and the nations they ruled merely branches of one great family, had led to the establishment of 'a collective right to rule' on the monarchs' side and 'a collective duty to obey' on the side of the peoples. All the safeguards for rights and freedom that had accompanied the traditional separation of peoples and states having disappeared, the mankind of Europe was subjected to the universal dominion of the united sovereigns and their ministers. Each people, in the pursuit of its natural right to a share in the government of the country, faced an opponent that disposed of the collective force of all the governments in Europe.[112] Through-

109. Lindner: *Manuscrirt aus Süd-Deutschland*, p. 187.
110. K. v. Rotteck: *Allgemeine Weltgeschichte für alle Stände, von den frühesten Zeiten bis zum Jahr 1840*, iv, 245: 'The advancing development and completion of the system of the Holy Alliance and its influence on all the external and internal relations of the nations, on all the interests and on the whole destiny of this part of the world, indeed of the entire civilized world, make up the far predominant character of the most recent history.'
111. *Staats-Lexikon, oder Encyklopädie der Staatswissenschaften,* ed. C. v. Rotteck and C. Welcker, i, Allianz, heilige (signed 'R.'), 462–4.
112. Ibid., i, 465–7.

out the Continent the reactionary forces of the absolutists and the aristocrats were undermining or overthrowing constitutional governments.[113] This was the Metternichian conspiracy theory in reverse.

The peoples of Europe reacted by uniting against their rulers.

As the sovereigns of the Holy Alliance met in a union, so a holy alliance of the peoples, i.e. a spiritual fraternity of the liberals of all countries, took form. No longer does the history of the world revolve round a few individual elevated personalities, in comparison with whom the peoples vanish as nonentities; instead the peoples themselves step on to the scene; they themselves are the knights and the heroes of the drama; they become conscious of their worth. . . . The struggle is no longer between one people and another but between one man and another.

Rotteck had no doubt that in the long run the moral power of the league of peoples would prove stronger than the physical force of the Holy Alliance.[114]

In the realm of ideas the issue after 1815 was between what he called 'Vernunftrecht', natural law, for which the liberals stood, and 'historisches Recht', positive law, on which the governments of the Holy Alliance relied.[115] His son Hermann von Rotteck used this antithesis in a study of the right to intervene in the affairs of other states, which he published in 1845. He found that the idea of intervention conflicted with natural law and had failed to gain the status of a definite principle of positivist theory, but that the practice of intervention had become accepted in positive law since 1820.[116] The governments represented at the Congresses of Troppau, Laybach and Verona had been able to impose it on Europe because most of the sovereigns of the lesser states had been unwilling to meet the social pressure with a measure of reform and, fearing revolution more than a partial loss of

---

113. Rotteck: *Allgemeine Weltgeschichte,* iv, 270: ' . . . according to circumstances, cunning or violent . . . at all points watchful, tireless, with the goal fixedly in eye, forgetting all private dissension in an enduring, steadfast alliance against the common enemy.' His description of the work of the reactionary conspiracy can be compared to Metternich's accounts of the activities of the revolutionary movement.
114. Ibid., v, 8 and 11.
115. C. von Rotteck: *Gesammelte und nachgelassene Schriften mit Biographie und Briefwechsel,* i, 'Das Jahr 1828', p. 159.
116. H. v. Rotteck: *Das Recht der Einmischung in die inneren Angelegenheiten eines fremden Staates.* The conclusion he draws is on p. 93.

sovereignty in external relations, had been prepared to accept the dictatorship of the great powers in order to gain internal security. This attitude had facilitated the transformation of the Holy Alliance from an apparently innocent piece of mysticism to an antiliberal association of governments.[117] But, sharing his father's belief in the power of public opinion and the victory of truth, he thought that the two constitutionalist members of the 'Council of Five' would find the strength to counter the existing domination of Russia and her fellow autocracies.[118]

The historian and publicist Georg Gottfried Gervinus, who was thirty years younger than Karl von Rotteck, was born in Hessen and spent most of his life at Heidelberg. He, too, saw European politics as a duel between the Holy Alliance and the liberal movement of the peoples. In his *History of the Nineteenth Century*, of which the first volume appeared in 1855, he examined the formation and development of the Holy Alliance and described its encounter with the dominant social and political forces of the century. Though originally it had been presented as the crowning of the peace treaties and a foundation of a European political system, the Act of the Holy Alliance had turned out to be a cloak for the pursuit of the rulers' interests instead of an instrument for the preservation of peace and order.[119] The man primarily responsible for this development was Metternich. From the mistaken assumption that lasting peace was possible only among states governed in accordance with the principles of pure monarchy, he had directed the attention of the principal members of the new political system to the internal relations of states instead of to their external politics.[120] With the intention of applying the same treatment to Europe as he had given Germany at Karlsbad, he had gained influence over the sovereigns by scaring them with the prospect of revolutions.[121] Gervinus charged the rulers who had believed the story of the revolutionary conspiracy with ignorance of history. From the observation that the postwar social situations of nearly all European and South American countries presented identical features they had jumped

117. H. v. Rottek: *Das Recht der Einmischung in die inneren Angelegenheiten eines fremden weschsel*, pp. 65–6.
118. Ibid., pp. 94–5. He described public opinion as the sixth European power.
119. Gervinus: *Geschichte des neunzehnten Jahrhunderts seit den Wiener Verträgen*, i, 250–2.
120. Ibid., iv, 873.
121. Ibid., vii, 5–6.

to the idea of an international plot of revolutionaries. They had failed to realize that the reason why so many governments faced similar problems was simply that the new political ideas were universal and that the social forces operating in each country were akin.[122]

Gervinus saw clearly that the powers defending the principle of legitimacy throughout Europe were bound to be defeated by the new forces eventually. Their enemy was 'the tough and unremitting staying-power of the peoples and the progressing spirit of history, which, without any need for alliances, brings the peoples together to work for one single goal and which has as its tool the powerful drives of mighty masses, who do not have to hurry, for whom the particular moment often was dangerous but of whom time always will be a sure ally'.[123]

One of the most outspoken critics of the political system instituted at the postwar congresses was Joseph von Görres. He was a catholic from the Rhineland, a publicist with a record of opposition to Napoleon and strong feelings against Prussia who became professor of history at Munich. The titles of three books which he published between 1819 and 1822 indicate his view of the European situation: *Deutschland und die Revolution, Europa und die Revolution* and *Die heilige Allianz und die Völker, auf dem Congresse von Verona*. Like the south German liberals, he thought of the European congresses as meetings of the powers of the Holy Alliance and made no separation in his mind between the Concert of Europe and the Holy Alliance. The Christian principles of the Alliance appeared to him as an ideological cloak for the policy of territorial and social preservation.

In the political system introduced at the Congress of Vienna, which he saw as a general alliance of all against anyone who might attempt to disturb the peace and upset the settlement, the great powers had assumed supreme authority. This substitute for an executive authority, he wrote in 1819, had subsequently been dissolved at the Congress of Aix-la-Chapelle; and all that had been left to serve as basis for the European alliance had been a pure negativity in the mutual relations of all states. Instead of making

122. Ibid., vii, 1–4.
123. Gervinus: *Einleitung in die Geschichte des neunzehnten Jahrhunderts*, pp. 164–5. In this work he outlined his plan for a dissolution of the great monarchies into federal states.

efforts to weigh opposed forces, as under the old system of the balance of power, the men of 1818 had laid down that all oppositions had been abandoned or at least become dormant. They had disregarded the possibility of change in the existing relations between states, had decided that no power should disturb another state with demands and interference, and had looked forward to a lasting peace based on mutual restraint. In the meantime the Holy Alliance had been arranged in response to the feeling that such an absolute self-denial ought to be based on a positive principle.[124]

In the course of the ensuing struggle with the revolutionary movement the Holy Alliance had acquired a new ideological role. As the sporadic reactions of the peoples to the repressive policies of the governments had developed into a general movement, and local issues had become European problems, the instinct of self-preservation had driven the rulers closer to each other. The sovereigns had concluded an '*eternal alliance* as protection against and in defiance of all revolutionary movements'. But, since revolution was an internal, spiritual fire which could not be dammed up with a purely physical counterforce, the antirevolutionary coalition had needed a set of ideas. Hence there had been a revival of Christian principles in politics. The rulers had had a presentiment that only religion could pacify such an immense, widespread and deeply rooted strife, and that only an idea could succeed in controlling and guiding the great movement. But ideas were not empty words, Görres insisted, and could not be misused with impunity. Through the acknowledgement of the religious idea as the leading principle of politics, statecraft had been transferred from the narrow cabinet, where rightly only the initiates deliberated, to humanity in general, where anyone who possessed human feelings and who had not banned God from his heart was called upon to have a say.[125] He believed that only through the establishment of a 'Völkerrat', a council of nations, could the peoples of Europe be liberated from the sway of their united sovereigns.[126]

Though the national idea always exercised some attraction, it was liberal principles which in the first place guided the radicals

---

124. Görres: *Gesammelte Schriften,* iv, 78, from *Deutschland und die Revolution* (1819). He saw the Holy Alliance as the successor of the Holy Roman Empire (p. 79).
125. Görres: *Die heilige Allianz und die Völker auf dem Congresse von Verona,* pp. 29–32.
126. Sepp: *Görres,* ch. xviii.

in the southern and western states in their approach to German and European affairs. When the choice was between constitutional systems within the separate states and national unity under the antiliberal government of Austria or Prussia, they preferred the former. When the great powers resisted the democratic pressure and opposed the national movement throughout Europe, they resented the former interference more than the latter. Like the conservatives in Austria and Prussia, they thought of the Concert of Europe as an institution for the preservation of governments rather than frontiers.

Carl Vogt, a professor of zoology who took an active interest in politics, was an exception. He was born in Giessen in Hessen, sat on the left of the Frankfort Assembly and afterwards lived in exile in Switzerland. In his view, the fundamental ideological issue of European politics was between the idea of territorial stability and the principles of nationality and self-determination.[127] It was a conflict between the dead letters of the Vienna treaties and the living word of the peoples.[128] On the one side was Francis Joseph's Austria, who kept up the old notion of the sanctity of treaties concluded by sovereigns and persisted in treating the peoples as if they were flocks of sheep;[129] on the other side was Napoleon III, who seemed to him to be in many respects a necessary expression of those modern forces which resisted the fetters that the Holy Alliance had imposed on the spirit of the peoples.[130] For Vogt, as for his opponent Schweitzer,[131] the organization of the great powers was in the first place an instrument for the prevention of territorial revision.[132] His view of European politics was a sign of the general change from liberalism to nationalism which took place in Germany during the last decades before the foundation of the *Reich*. His ideas were closer to those of the national liberals in Prussia than to those of the radicals in the south and west.

127. Vogt: *Andeutungen zur gegenwärtigen Lage,* p. 87.

128. Ibid., p. 74.

129. Ibid., p. 43.

130. Ibid., p. 77.

131. See pp. 42–3 above.

132. In his analysis of the Schleswig-Holstein issue of 1864 he presented the five great powers, 'in their totality, as a collective notion', as protectors of the treaty law of Europe (Vogt: *Andeutungen,* p. 34).

The national liberals

In south and west Germany critical thought about the Concert of Europe was conditioned by the geographical and political situation of the secondary and the minor members of the Confederation. While the ideas of the moderate reformers in the 'Mittelstaaten' were influenced by a desire to acquire an independent voice in foreign affairs, the thought of the radical liberals throughout the south and the west tended to reflect an anxiety to avoid Austrian and Prussian domination. Similarly, Prussian criticism of the Concert was conditioned by the place of Prussia within Germany and in Europe. The ideas of the earlier Prussian national liberals derived from a determination to put an end to the state of subordination to Austria and a wish to improve the position of Germany abroad.

Christian Carl Josias von Bunsen was a diplomatist and philologist, whose interests centred on the history of Christianity and philosophy of history. He directed his criticism of the Concert of Europe at Austria. After the Congress of Vienna Austria, together with Russia, had taken the leading part in Castlereagh's system of congress politics and, during the years 1820, 1821 and 1822, had introduced 'the absolutist policy of legitimism' in Europe.[133] In 1859, he observed, it was still fear of revolution and the idea of solidarity of all legitimate governments which guided the Austrian approach to European politics.[134] Bunsen rejected the postulate of the existence of an international revolutionary conspiracy. His attitude to the revolutionary movement is described in Ranke's edition of the correspondence of Frederick William IV and Bunsen. In radicalism, Ranke explained, Bunsen saw 'a corrective against the encroachments of extreme catholicism and Jesuits which the sluggishness of the liberals had made indispensable. Yet he does not hesitate to describe radicalism as the "moral cholera" of the day. He does not hold it to be contagious through infection from outside, but to be epidemic. The fear of radical conspiracies he did not share: conspiracy was out of the question; it was only a case of air pollution.'[135] When, in

133. *Christian Carl Josias Freiherr von Bunsen. Aus Seinen Briefen und nach eigener Erinnerung geschildert von seiner Witwe,* ii, 397 (letter of 24 October 1847).
134. Ibid., iii, 546.
135. Ranke: *Sämmtliche Werke,* xlix-l, 453, *Aus dem Briefwechsel Friedrich Wilhelms IV. mit Bunsen.*

the year of revolutions, the King reproached him for describing the conspiracy as an apparition[136] and accused him of suffering from the disease of liberalism, he retorted, in Ranke's paraphrase, 'The spinelessness, which the King has attributed to liberalism, he will find in France, where there has been no power of resistance. The opposite of that is lockjaw, of the type that has been prevalent in Austria.'[137]

In a seven-volume work, published in an English translation under the title *Christianity and Mankind, their Beginnings and Prospects*, Bunsen set forth his belief in an inevitable development towards a Christian society of mankind, in which the principles of universality and harmony would replace those of nationality and conflict. Here he demonstrated his liberal faith in a universal moral order and a final triumph of the better qualities of human nature.[138]

Bunsen criticized the assumptions of the theory of social preservation. But Johann Gustav Droysen attacked the Metternichian Concert of Europe root and branch. Born in 1808, he held chairs at Kiel, Jena and Berlin in turn and founded the Prussian school of historians. The fusion of history and politics by the agency of patriotic passion, the chief characteristic of that tradition of scholarship, can be studied in those of his writings in which he presented the Prussian case against the political system of post-Napoleonic Europe.

In an article entitled 'Die politische Stellung Preussens', published in 1845, he denied that the Pentarchy was an institution of international law and insisted that it was 'merely a theory, a pretext, a usurpation'.

> Are these five powers perhaps delegates of the rest of the European states? Their authority is nothing but their interest and their power to encroach. Have they been able to protect the peace of Europe? Just look at unfortunate Spain, at the misery of the Christian subjects of the High Porte, at Russia's campaign in the Balkans. Do they secure the existence of the smaller states? Poland has been swallowed up by Russia; and the kingdom of the Netherlands, which was created on the pretext of the European balance of power, has been allowed to dissolve. The truth is that the five great powers, though very far from

136. Ibid., p. 462.   137. Ibid., p. 464.   138. See especially vols iii and iv.

agreeing when it came to acting for the good of everybody, always found themselves in agreement when it was a matter of denying the lesser states a voice, preventing them from joining each other, and keeping their interests in a permanent state of tension.[139]

Not only had the practice of the Concert reduced the weaker states of Europe to political passivity and wounded the feelings and aroused the opposition of those who esteemed sovereignty. It had also restricted the freedom and provoked the antagonism of the new social movements.[140]

In a memoir on the state of German affairs in April 1848 he returned to the charge and attacked the theory of the Concert of Europe. The political system that the great powers had imposed on Europe and Germany in 1815 was

nothing but the artificially shaped head stone of the edifice of international law known as the Holy Alliance, of which the catchwords were legitimacy and the monarchical principle, the goal mutual insurance of princely interests against the so-called revolution, and the constitution, if one can call it that, the *oligarchy of the five great powers,* administered through congresses, conferences, interventions etc. This dual system for Germany and Europe served above all to guarantee the alleged juste repartition des forces—this mechanical division of the peoples and countries of Europe—and, thus, to kill the deepest impulse of the movement for freedom, even though it was to this that the debt for the most glorious victories was owing. It meant that every public *right* was pronounced subordinate to politics and their requirements; it meant that the interpretation of the so-called 'interests of Europe' was left in the hands of just those great powers, who naturally concerned themselves only with their own advantage and paid the least attention to the right and freedom of the peoples. Above all, Germany, instead of 'joining the ranks of the European powers as a collective power ("Gesammtmacht")', was formally organized as a political vacuum in the centre of Europe.[141]

139. Droysen: *Politische Schriften,* pp. 50–1.
140. Ibid., pp. 51–2; Droysen: *Vorlesungen über die Freiheitskriege,* pt ii, p. 723; see also Droysen: *Pol. Schriften,* p. 291, on the conflict between the idea of the territorial state and the essence of the antirevolutionary union of European monarchs.
141. Droysen: *Pol. Schriften,* p. 122; see also pp. 217–19, 'Preussen und das System der Grossmächte' (1849).

It was clear to him, however, that the system was breaking down rapidly. Growing disagreements among the great powers had disrupted their unity, while the steady pressure of the liberal and national forces had undermined the foundations of the oligarchy.[142] Furthermore, changes in the power relationships of the great powers, particularly in the ratios between Prussia and her neighbours, together with a rise in the influence of some of the secondary powers, such as Spain, Sweden and Belgium, were altering the character of the states system radically.[143]

In Droysen's view, the political and territorial arrangements of the Vienna Congress were obsolete and due for overthrow. Since they were based on the particularist organization of Germany, they should be abolished through a reorganization of Germany. He rejected the idea of a sixth great power made up of the lesser states of Germany, which was championed by his fellow historian Schaumann,[144] because it rested on the assumption that the European states system also in the future would be directed by great powers.[145] The task of breaking through the Vienna treaties and rearranging Germany belonged to Prussia, the state that in 1815 had accepted the oligarchic system in order to be counted a great power.[146] It was her mission now to assume alone the position in Germany that since 1815 she had shared with the catholic, cosmopolitan and anti-German Austria, and to create a united, independent Germany under Hohenzollern leadership.[147] The new Germany that he had in mind was not a great power of the traditional type but a nation state devoted to safeguarding the prosperity and freedom of the people and maintaining peace and law in Europe.[148] The establishment of this peace state in the centre of Europe would mean the end of the oligarchy of great

142. Ibid., p. 123, 'Denkschrift, die deutschen Angelegenheiten in Monat April 1848 betreffend' (1848).

143. Ibid., pp. 227–8, 'Preussen und das System der Grossmächte'.

144. See above p. 46.

145. Ibid., pp. 50–3, 'Die politische Stellung Preussens' (1845). Droysen argued that such a solution would weaken Germany and endanger her future, and pointed to a development of the 'Zollverein' as the best way to German unity.

146. Ibid., p. 58, 'Die politische Stellung Preussens' (1845); pp. 226–7, 'Preussen und das System der Grossmächte' (1849).

147. Ibid., p. 136, 'Denkschrift etc.' (1848); pp. 227–9, 'Preussen und das System der Grossmächte' (1849).

148. Ibid., pp. 58 and 62–3, 'Die politische Stellung Preussens' (1845); p. 136, 'Denkschrift etc.' (1848); p. 165, 'Rückschau II' (1848); p. 229, 'Pressuen und das System der Grossmächte' (1849).

powers and a fundamental change in the nature of European politics. 'The time of powers, of dynastic issues, is past; the principle of states, of citizenship in states, takes their place.'[149]

Droysen's contribution to the theory of the Concert of Europe comprised all the elements of the German case against the school of Gentz and Metternich. It contained the arguments of those who objected to the arbitrary rule of the stronger members of the states system, of those who opposed the policy of intervention and repression, and of those who rejected the principle of territorial stability. But it was more than a compendium of the critical thought of a generation. By refuting the conservative theory and rejecting the old Concert so completely he helped to clear the way for new ideas of the Concert of Europe. In stressing the development from dynasties to nation states he fixed the starting-point and indicated the general direction of the new way of thinking. However, Droysen did not belong to the school of thought that gained ascendancy in Germany in the second half of the century, because he was content to see Germany as a nation state and did not want her to become a European power.

The revolutionaries

The revolutionary view of the conservative Concert of Europe found its best expression in the journalism and political correspondence of Karl Marx and Friedrich Engels. Most of their observations on the political system that had prevailed in Europe between the Napoleonic and the Crimean Wars appeared in the articles on the European situation that Marx, with the occasional help of Engels, contributed to the *New York Daily Tribune* during the eighteen-fifties. The system of balance of power and maintenance of the *status quo* was to their minds a source of decay.[150]

---

149. Droysen: *Pol. Schriften,* p. 59, 'Die politische Stellung Preussens' (1845); see also p. 136, 'Denkschrift etc.' (1848), and p. 229, 'Preussen und das System der Grossmächte' (1849).

Though in his vision of the future Germany and Europe Droysen was a liberal, in his analysis of the existing state of affairs he was a Hegelian. Power, he observed, had always been the most important element in political life; and only the power of Prussia and Germany could bring about a new and better world. Droysen's thoughts on the state and power are discussed briefly in Heller: *Hegel und der nationale Machtstaatsgedanke in Deutschland,* (1963 reprint of 1921 edn), pp. 176–82, and in Meinecke: *Weltbürgertum und Nationalstaat,* pp. 308–11.

150. Karl Marx: *The Eastern Question,* p. 3 (letter of 22 March 1853).

The impotency of legitimate, monarchical government, ever since the first French Revolution, has resumed itself in the one axiom; Keep up the *status quo*. A *testimonium paupertatis,* an acknowledgement of the universal incompetence of the ruling powers, for any purpose of progress or civilization, is seen in this universal agreement to stick to things as by chance or accident they happen to be. Napoleon could dispose of a whole continent at a moment's notice; aye, and dispose of it, too, in a manner that showed both genius and fixedness of purpose. The entire 'collective wisdom' of European legitimacy, assembled in Congress at Vienna, took a couple of years to do the same job; got at loggerheads over it, made a very sad mess indeed of it, and found it such a dreadful bore that ever since they have had enough of it, and have never tried their hands again at parcelling out Europe. Myrmidons of mediocrity, as Béranger calls them; without historical knowledge or insight into facts, without ideas, without initiative, they adore the *status quo* they themselves have bungled together, knowing what a bungling and blundering piece of workmanship it is.[151]

The treaty of Vienna formed 'one of the most monstrous *fictiones juris publici* ever heard of in the annals of mankind'.[152] The society that rested on it, 'conservative Europe—the Europe of "order, property, family, religion"—the Europe of monarchs, feudal lords, moneyed men, however they may be differently assorted in different countries',[153] was ripe for revolution.

Neither Marx nor Engels attached great importance to the Concert of Europe.[154] Looking at the European scene from

151. Ibid., p. 2–3 (letter of 22 March 1853).
152. Marx and Engels: *On Colonialism,* p. 199 (letter of 17 December 1858 to N.Y.D.T.).
153. Marx: *The Eastern Question,* p. 452 (Leader, 17 August 1854).
154. In their correspondence on the Eastern Question they once referred to the idea of collective action by the powers, and described the European Areopagus as 'that joint-stock company disappearing before one word of the Austrian Minister, as it had been conjured up by him' (the reference was to Count Buol's declaration that the time for collective action had passed) (ibid, p. 135; letter of 23 September 1853).

Contrary to most of the radicals, Marx and Engels distinguished between the Concert of the five great powers and the Holy Alliance. In their correspondence to N.Y.D.T. the latter institution appeared as a reactionary, interfering union of the three eastern powers. For references to the Holy Alliance in the correspondence between Marx and Engels, see *Karl Marx Friedrich Engels, Historisch-kritische Gesamtausgabe; Werke/Schriften/Briefe,* ed. D. Rjazanov and V. Adoratskij, part 3, vol. i, 183, 311 and 456 and part 3, vol. iii, 163 and 185–6.

England, they saw but two real powers on the Continent. On the one side was Tsarist Russia, the instigator of the conspiracy of princes against peoples, the fortress of absolutism and reaction. On the other was the European Revolution, 'the explosive force of democratic ideas and man's native thirst for freedom'.[155] The revolutionary movement was the sixth power in Europe. It was greater than all of the five so-called great powers, they believed, and capable of asserting its supremacy and upsetting all traditional balance of power calculations.[156]

Marx and Engels, who spent the greater parts of their lives abroad, viewed European affairs in a cosmopolitan light. Their theory of the political system of Europe was not so closely connected with a particular approach to the German question as were the thoughts of the south German and Prussian opponents of the Concert of Europe.[157] In their conception of European politics these revolutionaries were more akin to the radical liberals in the smaller states than to the other two groups of German critics of the conservative Concert. The moderate reformers in the secondary states, finding the oligarchy of great powers oppressive, concerned themselves with the hierarchy of the states system. The nationalists in Prussia and elsewhere, rejecting the doctrine of territorial immutability, concentrated on the political geography of the states system. But the south and west German radicals as well as the international revolutionaries, both conceiving of the organization of the great powers as a means of denying the peoples their rights, thought in terms of the layers of the society of Europe.[158] In basing their European theory on class and

155. *The Eastern Question*, p. 18; see also Engels and Marx: *The Russian Menace to Europe*, pp. 25 and 39–40, 'The Foreign Policy of Russian Czarism' (1890, by Engels).
156. *The Eastern Question*, pp. 220–1 (Leader, 2 February 1854).
157. A passage in a letter from Engels to *The Northern Star*, of 18 November 1845, characterizes the revolutionary attitude to the German question: At the Congress of Vienna 'Germany was cheated on all hands, and mostly by her own so called friends and allies. This I should not much care for myself, as I know very well that we are approaching to a reorganization of European society, which will prevent such tricks on the one hand, and such imbecilities on the other . . .' (*Hist. krit. Gesamtausgabe,* part i, vol. iv, 489). Whereas most of the other opponents of the conservative Concert saw European politics in the light of their German ideas, Marx and Engels saw German politics in the light of their cosmopolitan philosophy.
158. Marx's account of the situation in 1871 is an example of the horizontal interpretation of European politics: 'While the European governments thus testify, before Paris, to the international character of class rule, they cry down the International Working Men's Association—the international counter-organization of

society, instead of nation and state, Marx and Engels shared the fundamental characteristic of the reactionary defenders of the conservative theory of the Concert of Europe.

The events of 1848 and the Crimean War, the fall of Metternich and the rise of Bismarck put an end to the old Concert of Europe. While the school of Gentz and Metternich went into decline and other ideas of European politics came to the fore, the early traditions of critical thought petered out. After the defeat of German liberalism in the middle of the century and the reorganization of Germany under Bismarck, the radical liberals in the south and the west and the 'reindeutsche' school in the secondary states had little influence on German politics and made few contributions to European theory. With the expansion of Prussian power and the establishment of the German *Reich*, the national liberals in Prussia identified themselves with the new Germany and became an important influence on German thought about the Concert of Europe in the later period. The disciples of Marx and Engels remained a force in the *Reich* but concentrated their attention on the domestic scene instead of the European situation, devoting their minds to the class struggle rather than the political relations of the great powers. In the second half of the century after 1815 German criticism of the conservative Concert of Europe was largely retrospective and academic.[159]

labour against the cosmopolitan conspiracy of capital—as the head fountain of all these disasters' (Marx and Engels: *Selected Works*, i, 490, 'The Civil War in France', dated 30 May 1871).
159. Brockhaus's *Das Legitimitätsprincip. Eine staatsrechtliche Abhandlung* is an instance of this type of contribution to the theory of the Concert of Europe. The author, writing in 1868, traced the development in the theory of legitimacy and analysed critically the principles of the 'Holy Alliance'.

Chapter Two

THE PROGRESSIVE THEORY

1. DEVELOPMENT

In Germany, contrary to England, there were few liberals who
supported the Concert of Europe. German liberals—even those in
the south who preferred liberal constitutions to national unification when they could not have both—were national liberals in
the sense that they desired some kind of unification of the German
lands. Those among them who took an interest also in European
affairs, and shared the aims of liberal internationalists in the
western countries, believed that the creation of a liberal international society presupposed a solution of the national problems
of Europe.[1] Hence their European as well as their German
thought tended to become a search for an answer to the national
question. To most of them the Concert of Europe, the traditional
enemy of both liberal institutions and national unification, seemed
unfit to play a useful role in the unification of Germany and the
reorganization of Europe.

Yet, there was a small number of Germans, including conservatives as well as liberals, who thought that the Concert of
Europe had a part to play in the formation of a more developed
and better organized international society. In both the earlier and
the later part of the period between the Congress of Vienna and
the foundation of the *Reich* the idea that linked the existing
Concert to the goal of international organization found exponents.
It is just possible to trace a development of a weak tradition of
progressive thought about the Concert of Europe.

As early as September 1814 Karl Friedrich von dem Knesebeck,
Frederick William III's Generaladjutant, saw the new structure of
European politics as the germ of a legal community of states. 'For

1. Heinrich von Gagern is a leading case in point: see, e.g., his speech in the *Landtag*
of Hesse-Darmstadt on 18 May 1836, in *Deutscher Liberalismus im Vormärz. Heinrich
von Gagern. Briefe und Reden 1815–1848*, p. 162.

the first time *Europe appears as a community of states. May it maintain itself in that form'*, he wrote in one of the memoirs that he prepared for the Congress of Vienna. The great powers of the victorious alliance, joined by France and Spain, would represent the community of states. If they could preserve and guarantee the independence and the boundaries of the states sanctioned by the Congress of Vienna, could deliberate in a friendly fashion on the general welfare and could arrange regular meetings of the first ministers or the sovereigns themselves, the foundation-stone 'for a future co-existence of states, governed by the rules of international law', would have been laid.[2] His own contributions to the edifice included a scheme of counterbalances for the states system, in which Germany had the part of the pivot,[3] and a plan for a 'Völkerbund', a league of European nations, which included also second rank powers.[4]

But most of the members of this group of thinkers were international lawyers. Johann Ludwig Klüber had been professor of law at Erlangen and had gained some political experience before he became secretary in the Foreign Office in Berlin in 1816. In the postwar decades he kept up the belief in progress and the faith in the rulers which had inspired the earlier writings of his contemporary, Professor Krug.[5] Among his publications were a survey of the negotiations and a collection of the documents of the Congress of Vienna, several books on international law and a history of the rebirth of Greece. In the preface to his history of Greece, written in 1835, he surveyed the record of the Concert and contemplated the future of Europe. Though as yet no general 'Völker–Tribunal' for the preservation of peace had been set up, a system had been introduced which, 'as one of the greatest steps forward that human reason had taken on the straight path of civilization', could not be rated highly enough. Already it had

2. Knesebeck: *Denkschrift, betreffend die Gleichgewichts-Lage Europa's, beim Zusammentritte des Wiener Congresses,* pp. 6–8. This memoir, which was sent to Stein with a letter of 28 September 1814, is printed also in Pertz: *Das Leben des Ministers Freiherrn vom Stein,* 1849–55, iv, 640–54. See also extract from 'Über die Folge in dem Geschäftsgange', a memoir which Knesebeck sent to Hardenberg during the Congress of Vienna, quoted in Wünsch: *Die politische Ideenwelt des Generaladjutanten Karl Friedrich von dem Knesebeck,* p. 26.
3. Knesebeck, pp. 9–11.
4. This memoir, entitled 'Ideen zu einem europäischen Völkerbunde', was prepared during the Congress of Vienna and is discussed in Wünsch, p. 47.
5. See above pp. 38–9.

proved its beneficial qualities, not only by various acts of conciliation and mediation, by the diplomatic work of congresses and conferences and by the introduction of alliances for defence or of reconciliation, but also through actions of intervention and occupation. In the future it would, 'not without due regard for the rights of also the less powerful sovereign states, gradually develop and establish itself through the steadily more pronounced liberal, meaning just and humanitarian, outlook of the rulers, their advisers and subjects, through popular representation in the central governments and through the beneficial controlling influence of reason and the power of habit, the latter of which can quench even bloodthirstiness'. Klüber believed that the new political system, by protecting Europe against the old sins of wantonness, jingoism, pride, anger, bloodthirstiness, vindictiveness and passion for conquest and by uniting the powers in a 'moral-political society of states', would usher in an age of fewer wars, less civil war and general disarmament.[6]

Karl Salomo Zachariä, who was born at Meissen and educated at Leipzig University, held his first chair of jurisprudence at Wittenberg. In 1807 he left Saxony for Baden, where he became professor at Heidelberg and, later, member of the First Chamber. His political philosophy was made up of aristocratic principles, with an admixture of liberal ideas. In international politics it was the organization of the society of Europe that interested him most. His *Vierzig Bücher vom Staate* included books on 'Völkerrecht', 'Weltbürgerrecht' and 'Staatenrecht', which were published in a revised edition in 1841. In these he examined the legal and political structure of the new Europe and compared it with the arrangements of earlier ages. Europe constituted a political society of nations, a 'Völkerstaat'.[7] Its 'Grundgesetz', fundamental law, was the final act of the Congress of Vienna, by which the lands of Europe were distributed and the boundaries of states laid down, and its 'organisches Gesetz', structural law, the protocol of the Congress of Aix-la-Chapelle.[8] The form of its constitution was aristocratic.[9] The five great powers, who had

6. Klüber: *Pragmatische Geschichte der nationalen und politischen Wiedergeburt Griechenlands, bis zu dem Regierungsantritt des Königs Otto,* pp. x–xiii.
7. Zachariä: *Vierzig Bücher vom Staate,* v, 220. 'Völkerstaat' is defined in vol. iii, p. 11.
8. Ibid., v, 217–19.
9. Ibid., v, 220. The society of European nations had now tried all the simple forms of constitution: in the Middle Ages, when the European 'Völkerstaat' came

made the law and guaranted the political and social peace, formed an exclusive society, the Pentarchy, at the head of Europe. Its members had '*jointly* and equally as a corporation the supreme management of European affairs, the Directorium Europae', and were associated collectively with the rest of the states through a 'Schutzgenossenschaft', a protective association.[10] This constitution was superior to the one that had obtained in Europe between the Peace of Westphalia and the French Revolution in that it presupposed a balance of power of the Pentarchy only, corresponded better with the territorial partition of Europe, and was simpler and more practical in use.[11] That Europe had had twenty-five years of almost undisturbed peace was a sign of its excellence.

But this success Zachariä ascribed also to other factors. Various changes in the condition of European mankind had curtailed some of the forces conducive to war: religious hatred had decreased; the evil effects of colonial policies had diminished; foreign travel and cultural intercourse had expanded and national antipathy consequently declined; investments had risen and war become less profitable; the number of small states had dropped; the influence of public opinion had increased; and knowledge and learning had advanced. Furthermore, the establishment of a balance of power between the eastern absolute monarchies and the western constitutional monarchies had consolidated the relations of states.[12] So, although the nature of man remained warlike and although not all the powers had an equal interest in preserving peace,[13] some progress could be detected in international relations. For Zachariä Europe was a developing body of nations and the Concert of Europe its vital organ.[14]

The most substantial contribution to this set of ideas also came

into being, it was a monarchy with the Pope at the head; the Reformation was a revolution; the system of the balance of power after the Peace of Westphalia was democratic; the French Revolution was also a European revolution; Napoleon tried to turn Europe into a monarchy; but after 1815 it became an aristocracy. As for the future, Zachariä's own preference was for a composite constitution (ibid., v, 173–234).

10. Ibid., v, 220–1.
11. Ibid., v, 221–2.
12. Ibid., v, 222–7.
13. Ibid., v, 222–30. Among the sources of tension he included the trade war of nations.
14. In the frequency with which the principle of non-intervention—a doctrine of natural law, not of public law—was violated in modern Europe he saw a sign of the advancing integration of the society of nations (ibid., v, 167–8).

from a lawyer. Johann Caspar Bluntschli was born in Zürich in 1808 and studied in Bonn and Paris. Subsequently he returned to Switzerland, where he entered politics and became a professor at the university of his native town. But in 1848 he was appointed professor at the University of Munich; and in the following years, when he took an active part in the liberal movement, he identified himself with the German national cause. However, it was mainly as one of the foremost international lawyers of Bismarck's Germany that he became known. In a considerable number of books and articles, most of them written during the last few years before and the first decade after the foundation of the *Reich*, he examined the structure of the society of Europe.

He regarded the Concert of the great powers as the first practical attempt to organize Europe. In spite of all the lingual and national differences that divided the European peoples and despite the many struggles in which they involved each other, he wrote in an article in *Die Gegenwart* in 1878, there still was a general feeling of common kind and common interests, which united all the nations of Europe into a steadfast society of states. Since the negotiations at Münster and Osnabrück, which had led to the Peace of Westphalia, many European congresses had assembled in order to regulate the relations of states and strengthen the peace of Europe. All Christian states had participated in the 'European Concert', which both presupposed and expressed a certain harmony in the normal relations of the states of Europe. Towards the end of the second and in the beginning of the third decade of the nineteenth century the five European great powers had even made an attempt to found a firm organization of great powers, meeting in annual congresses to settle important issues between and within states.[15] Elsewhere he discussed the legal position of this Pentarchy. The union arranged at Aix-la-Chapelle in 1818 did not constitute a legally established senate for Europe, he pointed out, but only expressed the fact that these states possessed the power at the moment and recognized it as their common function to regulate European affairs.[16] Since no detailed delimitation of the competence and scope of this institution had

15. Bluntschli: *Gesammelte kleine Schriften*, ii, 279–80, 'Die Organisation des europäischen Statenvereines'.
16. Bluntschli: *Das moderne Völkerrecht der civilisirten Staten als Rechtsbuch dargestellt*, p. 100.

been reached and no firm principles of consultation and co-operation with the lesser states had been established, it did not represent the completion of the organization of Europe, but merely the beginning.[17]

Sixty years after the Congress of Aix-la-Chapelle, when the practice of holding regular congresses had long since died out and the community of interests among the great powers had dissolved, the Pentarchy existed no longer.[18] But the idea had survived that there was a small number of great powers in Europe who could not be ignored in the settlement of European questions, and who were called upon to look after the peace and protect the law. Since 1871 the German *Reich* had taken the place of Prussia; and the new Italian state, too, had begun to look upon herself as a great power and taken steps to join this highest circle.[19] Though Bluntschli admitted that these states enjoyed considerable authority when they had reached agreement on particular issues and the measures to be adopted and accepted that they were the only states capable of discharging the executive functions of the society of Europe,[20] he found this survival of the earlier organization as imperfect as the old Pentarchy:

... an organization of the European association of states which will guarantee the peace of the world and the efficacy of international law is still lacking. Although the great powers may be the only ones qualified and called upon to ensure implementation, all European states which deserve to exist are naturally entitled to participate in decisions to do with the general international legal order and with the management of common European interests and arrangements. Moreover, regard for the peoples also requires that a representative body, which the legislative bodies of the European states would place next to the representatives of the governments, be drawn into the process of international legislating.[21]

17. Ibid., p. 100: 'The so-called pentarchy may be viewed as the beginning of an organization of Europe, but not as its completion'; *Deutsches Staats-Wörterbuch,* ed. Bluntschli and Brater, iii, 462.
18. Bluntschli: *Ges. kleine Schriften,* ii, 280, 'Die Organisation des eur. Statenvereines'.
19. Bluntschli: *Deutsche Statslehre und die heutige Statenwelt,* p. 448.
20. Bluntschli: 'Völkerrechtliche Briefe', *Die Gegenwart,* No. 52 (23 December 1876), p. 423; Bluntschli: *Das mod. Völkerrecht,* p. 264.
21. Bluntschli: *Deutsche Statslehre,* pp. 448–9.

When Bluntschli discussed the merits and shortcomings of the old and the new Concert of Europe he did not dispute the need for great power leadership but stressed the rights of the smaller states. In the project for the organization of Europe that he prepared himself the leading role of the six principal powers was clearly defined and the sovereignty of the other states carefully protected.[22]

Primarily, however, it was his internationalism which distinguished Bluntschli. 'The one-sidedness of the national policy', he believed, 'needed the complement and the correction of the *international* or, more correctly, of the *humane* policy. *Nationality* and *humanity* are not irreconcilable; for the nations all have within themselves the *common human nature*. Thereby they are united into *one mankind*; and mankind, in turn, takes manifold forms in the nations.'[23] Whereas the states, mindful of their separate interests and jealous of their independence, had moved farther apart, the nations were drawing closer to each other. With the progress of science and the new developments in the means of transport and communication had come a fresh awareness of the community of mankind.[24] As Christianity joined the nations in a universal religion and made for the religious satisfaction of mankind, so 'the natural rights of man' united all men and led up to 'the future world law', which would secure the peace and welfare of humanity and protect the free and natural development of all peoples.[25] While a world confederacy of states, a 'Gesammtbund' or a 'Gesammtreich', was the goal of progressive mankind, and international organization, initially of Europe and eventually of the world, was the way,[26] the Concert of Europe was the first step.

With Bluntschli the progressive tradition of thought had reached its most advanced position in Germany. In the following years it was swept away by more powerful ideas. In his time it was

22. In his article for *Die Gegenwart*, 'Die Organisation des eur. Statenvereines', he discussed Sully's and Professor Lorimer's ideas on European organization and set forth his own scheme (Bluntschli: *Ges. kleine Schriften*, ii, 279–312).
23. Bluntschli: *Lehre vom Modernen Stat*, iii: *Politik als Wissenschaft*, p. 76; see also his speech in the Baden First Chamber of 14 May 1866 in *Denkwürdiges aus meinem Leben*, iii, 152.
24. Bluntschli: *Ges. kleine Schriften*, ii, 280–1, 'Die Organisation des eur. Statenvereines'; *Lehre vom Modernen Stat*, i: *Allgemeine Statslehre*, p. 33.
25. Bluntschli and Brater, *Deutsches Staats-Wörterbuch*, xi, 184.
26. Ibid., xi, 185; Bluntschli: *Lehre vom Modernen Stat*, i: *Allgemeine Statslehre*, p. 27; *Ges. kleine Schriften*, ii, 281, 'Die Organisation des eur. Statenvereines'.

still possible to perceive a harmony between national and international pursuits, and to combine pride in the rise of Germany with faith in the advance of international organization. [27] But in the decades between the foundation of the *Reich* and the outbreak of the World War it became more and more difficult to reconcile the dominant concerns of the German nation with the quest for an international community. Then the national liberals, no longer able to assume that national unification would lead to international harmony, had to choose between nationalism and internationalism. Most of them embraced the former.

The few who adhered to the creed of internationalism and rejected the ideology of the *Reich* did not see in the Concert of Europe a harbinger of the future world order. The leading example of this group was Theodor Mommsen, the national liberal historian of classical Rome. In the middle years of his life he wholeheartedly supported Bismarck's efforts at national unification, hoping and believing that Europe was settling 'firmly and happily upon the principle of the unification of the great nations, maintained and balanced by the system of political equilibrium'. [28] In his old age, when the development of the *Reich* had disappointed him deeply, he sternly criticized both the domestic and the foreign policy of Germany. Till he died, in 1903, he kept up his faith in 'the holy alliance of the nations'—the lodestar of his life, as he described it. [29] But the Concert of the great powers never played an important part in his international thought. Some years before the foundation of the *Reich*, when he still thought that Germany would become a pacific and constructive influence in Europe and the world, he expressed great satisfaction at seeing Prussia pluck up enough courage and self-confidence to throw off her old role of 'the fifth wheel on the wagon of Europe' and exert her will in a congress of the powers. [30] Like most national liberals of that generation, he was more interested in the place of Prussia

27. In a speech delivered after the Prussian victories over France, Bluntschli expressed the conviction that the new Germany would fulfil her obligations to Europe and the world and become a guardian of the peace, law, order and freedom of the world (Bluntschli: *Das moderne Völkerrecht in dem französisch-deutschen Kriege von 1870*, pp. 30–1).

28. Mommsen *et al.*: *Letters on the War between Germany and France*, p. 33.

29. Mommsen: 'A German's Appeal to the English. Ein Deutsch eran die Engländer', *The Independent Review*, i (1903), 165.

30. Mommsen: *Reden und Aufsätze*, p. 377. 'Die Annexion Schleswig-Holsteins' [1865]. The reference was to the London Conference after the war with Denmark.

within the Concert than in the role of the Concert in international society. Once Germany had secured her position among the great powers he gave little thought to the Concert of Europe.

Internationalism just survived in the *Reich*. But the notion of the European Concert as a forerunner of an organized international society lost its place in German thought.[31] Paradoxically, it was the improvement in Germany's position in the Concert of Europe which put an end to her progressive tradition of thought.

Three developments may be distinguished in German progressive thought between the Congress of Vienna and the Congress of Berlin. Firstly, the view of the European states system broadened. Though the earlier international lawyers did not ignore the problem of the relationship between the powers of the Concert and the other states, Bluntschli gave more thought to it than any of his predecessors. The fact that he used the term 'the European Concert' to refer to all sovereign members of the states system of Europe is an indication of his regard for the lesser states.[32] Secondly, the conception of the society of Europe became more democratic. The places occupied by sovereigns and states in the earlier ideas were taken in the later thought by peoples and nations. Politics between sovereigns were replaced by international relations. Finally, the theory of the Concert in Europe began to develop into a theory of the Concert in the world. Knesebeck, Klüber and Zachariä, always inclined to identify the geographical limits of the states system with the borders of Europe, could still think in purely European terms. But Bluntschli, conscious of the expansion of the political world, speculated about a society comprising all mankind. By presenting the Concert of

31. The Concert of Europe did not play an important part in the theory of the German Peace Movement. See, e.g., the lecture published under the title *Krieg und Frieden,* in which R. L. C. Virchow, prominent in the campaign for disarmament, pressed for an international court of arbitration with machinery for collective enforcement, and the contribution to *Staatsrechtliche Abhandlungen*; *Festgabe für Paul Laband,* i, entitled 'Die Organisation der Welt', in which Walther Schücking, a leading member of the Peace Societies, demanded international organization. In neither place was the Concert of Europe presented as a step towards the goal.

32. Turkey had been admitted to the Concert of Europe in 1856, he wrote in 1876, but had failed to live up to the 'Aryan-European concept of law' (Bluntschli: 'Völkerrechtliche Briefe', *Die Gegenwart,* No. 50 (9 December 1876), 378). Montenegro, Serbia and Rumania had been brought into the European Concert through the Berlin settlement of 1878, he wrote in 1880 (Bluntschli: 'Le Congrès de Berlin et sa portée au point de vue du droit international', *Revue de Droit international et de Législation comparée,* xii (1880), 276).

great powers as an attempt to organize Europe and European organization as a stage towards world organization,[33] he linked the Concert to the idea of universal international organization.

The assumptions at the root of the progressive theory, whether in its most developed or in its more rudimentary forms, resembled those made by the liberal internationalists in the western countries. It was an optimistic view of the intellectual and moral qualities of human nature which led these Germans to pin their faith on first the rulers and then the peoples, belief in an advancing integration of the society of Europe which induced them to concentrate upon organization of the states system, and confidence in the progress of civilization which encouraged them to anticipate a more peaceful and just world. Their assumptions about man, society and history were not in harmony with the spirit that gained predominance in the German *Reich*.

Both the conservative and the progressive set of ideas about the Concert of Europe were social theories in the sense that they rested on notions of society, order and law. But the contents of these notions were not identical in the two theories. While the European society of the conservative theory was made up of dynasties and held together by personal ties, that of the progressive theory, in its more advanced form, was composed of nations and united by bonds between peoples; while order in the conservative theory was the existing dynastic and territorial arrangements, in the progressive theory it was the developing international organization; and while law according to the conservative theory consisted of the established titles of sovereigns and the general treaties of Europe, according to the progressive theory it was derived from the natural rights of man.[34] The difference was between a philosophy of preservation and stability and a philosophy of creation and growth. Some thinkers managed to bridge the gap. By combining the principles of positive and of natural law, certain international lawyers were able to see the Concert, on the one hand, as a tribunal upholding the law of the great

33. Bluntschli and Brater, *Deutsches Staats-Wörterbuch*, iv, 352; Bluntschli: *Lehre vom Modernen Stat*, i, *Allgememeine Statslehre*, p. 33: 'The European spirit is already turning its gaze towards the globe, and the Aryan race feels itself called upon to order the world.'

34. The difference between the two conceptions of law was brought out in Bluntschli: *Das mod. Völkerrecht*, pp. 47–9, where the author attacked the principle of dynastic legitimacy, which had guided the great powers in the restoration period.

European treaties and, on the other, as an agent in the integration of the society of Europe.[35]

2. THE HEGELIAN ANTITHESIS

The great adversary of the Concert of Europe and international organization was Hegel. To the European institutions introduced by the statesmen of the Congress of Vienna he reacted as negatively as to the idea of eternal peace put forward by Kant. 'Although several states leagued together can, as it were, exercise jurisdiction over others, and although alliances of states, such as the Holy Alliance, can occur, these arrangements are always only relative and limited, as is eternal peace', he wrote in a book which was intended to guide the students who attended his lectures at the University of Berlin in the early postwar years.[36]

He did not deny the existence of the traditional political and legal systems of Europe. In the balance of power he recognized a means of protecting individual states against the violence of an overwhelming power, which had its historical origin in the wars of conquest that had followed the formation of the states system and its political basis in the common interest of preserving the independence of each state.[37] In international law he saw an influence modifying the practice of mutual infliction of harm, a system rooted in the life of nations which, 'according to the general principles of their legislation, their customs, their culture', constituted a family.[38] But he did not believe that the states could develop relations of lasting stability. They had no praetor to settle their issues, only war to decide their disputes.[39] Each state, facing the others in sovereign independence, was an autonomous

35. Professor Berner, a contributor to *Deutsches Staats-Wörterbuch* (ed. Bluntschli and Brater), is an example. In his article on International Law he wrote about the Pentarchy: 'For a long time the *five great powers* have in fact formed some kind of international tribunal and have watched over the observance of the great states-treaties and of the customs of international law' (xi, 79). Elsewhere, in his article on Congresses and Conferences, he expressed faith in the advancing integration and organization of the society of Europe (v, 662–3).
36. Hegel: *Sämtliche Werke*, vii: *Grundlinien der Philosophie des Rechts; oder Naturrecht und Staatswissenschaft im Grundrisse*, p. 337 (par. 259). For his views of eternal peace and the Holy Alliance, see also ibid., pp. 435–6 (par. 324) and p. 443 (par. 333).
37. Hegel, *S.W.* xi: *Vorlesungen über die Philosophie der Geschichte*, pp. 540–1; *Hegel: Die Verfassung des Deutschen Reichs*, pp. 111–12.
38. Hegel, *S.W.* vii: *Grundlinien*, p. 446 (par. 339); see also vi: *Enzyklopädie der philosophischen Wissenschaften im Grundrisse*, p. 298 (par. 447).
39. Hegel, *S.W.* vii: *Grundlinien*, p. 443 (pars. 333 and 334) and p. 446 (par. 339).

individual employing its power in the pursuit of its interests.[40] All states were 'to that extent in a state of nature vis-à-vis each other'.[41]

The life of the state, not the organization of international society, provided the inspiration of his political thought. 'The state is no work of art; it exists in the world, hence in the sphere of caprice, of chance and of error; evil conduct can disfigure it in all directions. However, the ugliest man, the criminal, the invalid and cripple is always still a living human being: the affirmative element, life, exists in spite of the defect; and this is what concerns us here'.[42] It is characteristic of his type of realism that he was able to accept the state in its darkest nature and at the same time make an idol of it. The state was to him 'God moving through the world'.[43] 'In world history', he wrote in the introduction to *Vorlesungen über die Philosophie der Geschichte,*

> one can only take account of those peoples which form states. For it should be known that the state is the realization of freedom, i.e. of the absolute end purpose, that it exists for its own sake; furthermore, it should be known that all value man has, all spiritual reality, he has solely through the state. ... The state is the divine idea as it exists on earth. Thus the state is in general the more specific object of world history, in which freedom maintains its objectiveness and lives within this objectiveness.[44]

This deification of the state was essential to his system of thought. For it was by attributing transcendent power to the state and adding a spiritual side to its life that he linked together his theory of politics and his philosophy of history. In addition to the actual existence of the states, in which they were independent of each other and only externally related, he conceived of a higher, abstract sphere, in which they were united. The bond was 'Geist'— reason or spirit. Each nation possessed its own 'Volksgeist'; and above them all, as judge and praetor, was the 'Weltgeist'.[45] On

40. Ibid., p. 337 (par. 259), p. 432 (par. 322) and p. 441 (par. 331).
41. Ibid., p. 442 (par. 333).
42. Ibid., p. 336 (par. 258).
43. Ibid., p. 336 (par. 258).
44. Hegel, *S.W.* xi: *Vorlesungen,* p. 71.
45. Hegel, *S.W.* vi: *Enzyklopädie,* pp. 298–9 (pars 448, 449) and vii: *Grundlinien,* p. 337 (par. 259) and p. 446 (par. 339).

the notion of a world spirit rested his philosophy of history. The world spirit was the directing force of history, and world history a progressive self-realization of the world spirit. The process of realizing itself through history took place by the agency of individual nations who, in turn, acted as bearers of the respective stages of development of the world spirit. [46] At any particular time the nation carrying the charge was 'the *dominating one* in world history for this epoch—*and there it can be epoch-making only once*. As against this its absolute right to be the bearer of the current developmental stage of the world spirit, the spirits of the other peoples are devoid of rights; and these peoples, like those whose epochs are past, no longer count in world history.' [47]

Friedrich Meinecke—who saw Hegel's system as a great synthesis of the old cosmopolitan and the modern national ideas, of rationalism, absolute values and universal beliefs on the one hand and realism, the empirical approach and the historical view on the other—described this philosophy of history as a theory of marionettes. [48] About the 'eigenen Selbst', the selfhood, of the state and nation he wrote that Hegel, 'with the strange duplicity which runs through his entire philosophy, had acknowledged and at the same time denied it, that he had given it all imaginable freedom in the sphere of conscious reality in order afterwards to chain it closely in the higher sphere of the absolute. With him, the state and the historical world in general lead a double life of apparent freedom in the real world and real servitude in the spiritual sphere.' [49] Franz Rosenzweig, too, pointed to this paradox of the freedom of the state. Making a distinction between what he called the invisible and the visible spheres of Hegel's world, he observed that 'the invisible law which holds this invisible community of nations together, the law of universal history, is the same as the one that for ever divides the visible nations. History springs only from antagonism between independent states; and history alone is the bond that unites these independent "individuals".' [50]

A fundamental issue of Hegel interpretation is between those

46. Hegel, *S.W.* vii: *Grundlinien,* p. 449 (par. 347).
47. Ibid., p. 449 (par. 347).
48. Meinecke: *Machiavellism; the Doctrine of Raison d'État and its Place in Modern History,* pp. 364 and 368.
49. Meinecke: *Weltbürgertum und Nationalstaat,* p. 280.
50. Rosenzweig: *Hegel und der Staat,* ii, 183-4.

who present the invisible as the essence of his system and those who treat it as an ideological cloak for the visible. The former interpreters stress the element of spiritual universalism, and insist that national culture was the end of the power policy of the state. The latter concentrate on the quality of brutal state egotism, and maintain that power itself was the highest aim of the pursuits of the state. If Meinecke represents the first type of scholar,[51] Hermann Heller is an example of the second. 'Hegel's "Weltgeist" is nothing but the expression of the moral justification of the nationalist world power', he wrote in *Hegel und der nationale Machtstaatsgedanke in Deutschland*.[52] 'In fact, no one has drawn up a bolder metaphysics of national imperialism than Hegel has.'[53] Meinecke thought of Hegel primarily as the final product of an older tradition of thought, and saw in him the link between the universalists of the previous generation and the nationalists of the nineteenth century.[54] But Heller studied him as a source of the political ideas of the German *Reich*, and recognized in him the father of imperialism.[55]

It was the physical rather than the metaphysical part of Hegel's system which appealed to the next generations of Germans, the doctrine of the real freedom of the state rather than the idea of its spiritual bondage which fired their imaginations. Three elements may be distinguished in the Hegelian tradition of European thought: emphasis on the power of the state, acceptance of war and rejection of international organization.

In *System der Staatslehre*, published in 1857, Constantin Rössler, philosopher, pamphleteer and politician, compared the relationship between a weakened state and its stronger neighbours to that between warm and cold air. 'As soon as a nation presents symptoms of an incurable weakness, in its internal or its external life, its stronger neighbours must take away its independence, until either

51. For Meinecke's position, see especially *Weltbürgertum und Nationalstaat,* p. 280 and *Machiavellism,* p. 367. In the latter he attacks Heller's position. Another adherent of the spiritual and cultural interpretation is Gerhardt Giese. In his *Hegels Staatsidee und der Begriff der Staatserziehung,* he supports Meinecke against Heller (pp. 106–14).
52. P. 130.
53. Heller, p. 129; also p. 124: Hegel, contrary to the natural-law theorists, 'hypostatizes the legal reality ['Rechtswirklichkeit'], which is established through political power, into metaphysical legal values ['Rechtswert'], national imperialism into the standpoint of the world spirit'.
54. Meinecke: *Weltbürgertum und Nationalstaat,* ch. xi.
55. Heller, p. 131.

its dormant strength awakens to liberation or it disappears, spiritually as well as politically, from the ranks of living nations' (pp. 553–4). Count Helmuth von Moltke, Chief of first the Prussian and then the German General Staff, warned his compatriots that only small states could rely on neutrality and international guarantees: 'a great state exists only through itself and by means of its own energy; it justifies its existence only if it is resolved and armed to assert its existence, its freedom and its rights; and to leave a country defenceless would be the greatest crime of its government'.[56] Especially the German *Reich*, which was unfavourably placed both historically and geographically, needed strength. As an upstart and intruder in the European family of states she had aroused the suspicion of the older members. Occupying the centre of Europe, she had to face in all directions, while her neighbours in east and west needed to face one way only.[57] The prospect of a general increase in the strength of the principal governments of Europe, which was the consequence of his doctrine, did not worry him, because he believed that the sources of instability and war were popular passions and party ambitions and that the only reliable defenders of order and peace were strong monarchical governments.[58] Friedrich Naumann, Lutheran pastor and political writer, expressed the view characteristic of his generation when he wrote, *'Learning, culture, custom are of no use whatever in world history if they are not protected and carried by power!* . . . Whoever wants to live must fight. This applies to the individual, to the class, to the nation.'[59]

Though the stress was on survival, the case for the power state contained arguments reminiscent of the higher sphere of Hegel's world. Rössler thought that it could be said of the Christian 'Kulturvölker' 'that they realize one ideal, one concept, by means of diverse energies'.[60] In a speech on defence bills Count von Caprivi, the general who succeeded Bismarck as Chancellor, once told the *Reichstag*,

56. Moltke: *Gesammelte Schriften und Denkwürdigkeiten*, vii, 106–7 (speech in *Reichstag*, 16 February 1874).
57. Ibid., vii, 126 (speech in *Reichstag*, 1 March 1880); v, 210 (letter of 21 January 1889).
58. Ibid., vii, 125–6 (speech in *Reichstag*, 1 March 1880) and 138 (speech in *Reichstag*, 14 May 1890); v, 200–1 (letter of 10 February 1881).
59. Naumann: *Demokratie und Kaisertum*, pp. 206–7.
60. Rössler, *System der Staatslehre*, p. 553.

It must be clear in our minds that we have to carry on a struggle for existence—for political, material and cultural existence. It must be clear in our minds that it is our duty to do everything of which we are capable to go through this struggle. It is our duty firstly towards *God*. Each nation must take its place within the civilization of the world. No other nation could replace the loss of the German. States, contrary to men, do not have a duty to sacrifice themselves for others out of charity; their first duty is to maintain themselves. Only when a state maintains itself can it still remain God's tool.[61]

Lofty ideas of the state and history had been translated into German power policy. The *Reich* had become the bearer of Hegel's spirit.

The idea which represented war as a natural and inevitable phenomenon and a healthy activity[62] was widely received during the last years before and the first decades after the foundation of the German *Reich*. The old phrase 'der Kampf ums Dasein', the struggle for existence, became a popular quotation in the speeches and writings of the contemporaries and successors of Bismarck.[63] In 1868 Adolf Lasson, political philosopher and international lawyer, published a pamphlet, *Das Culturideal und der Krieg,* in which he expressed the opinion that eternal peace had no place in the world of realities. 'Man, state, war are connected concepts; it is not possible to think of one without the other' (p. 68). But the frankest observations on the nature and role of war were made by Moltke. He thought with Clausewitz that war was the continuation of policy by other means.[64] Far from being always a crime, it was 'an *ultimate* but completely legitimate means of upholding the existence, the independence and the honour of a state'. In common with human life and indeed the entire natural world, the life of

61. *Die Reden des Grafen von Caprivi im Deutschen Reichstage, Preussischen Landtage und bei besonderen Anlässen, 1883–1893,* p. 269 (23 November 1892).
62. That this idea was Hegelian may be seen in Hegel, *S.W.* vii, *Grundlinien,* p. 436 (par. 324): 'It is not only that the peoples emerge strengthened from war, but also that nations afflicted with domestic conflict gain internal peace from war abroad. Certainly, war brings insecurity to property; but this *real* insecurity is nothing but a movement which is indispensable.'
63. Vitzthum von Eckstädt, the Saxon diplomatist, is an example. Writing in 1885, he observed that Austria had stood for the negative in politics, namely 'the sweet habit of life', but Prussia for the positive, 'der Kampf ums Dasein' (*Berlin und Wien in den Jahren 1845–1852. Politische Privatbriefe,* p. xxvi).
64. Moltke, *Ges. Schriften,* vii, 49 (speech in *Reichstag,* 15 June 1868).

nations was 'a struggle of the developing against the existing'.[65] The internationalist and the Hegelian conceptions of war were confronted when Bluntschli sent Moltke a manual of the law of land warfare, and the soldier answered the lawyer, 'Eternal peace is a dream, and not even a beautiful one; and war is an inherent part of God's world order. The noblest virtues of human beings, courage and renunciation, loyalty and spirit of self-sacrifice with one's life at stake, are brought out in war. Without war the world would stagnate in materialism.'[66]

Projects for international organization were met with scepticism and hostility. Lasson had faith neither in the traditional machinery of congresses of sovereigns and diplomatic negotiations as a means of solving problems of international politics nor in the new device of a 'Völkerareopag' as an instrument for averting war. 'States cannot have a tribunal over them, and a tribunal cannot judge states.' States yielded only when coerced, he believed.[67] Moltke was of the opinion that if it was at all possible to dispel the mutual distrust which kept the nations in arms against each other it would be done by means of agreements between strong governments and not through 'the Babylonian confusion of international fraternization, international parliaments and whatever is being proposed in that direction'.[68] Hence he much preferred a diplomacy guided by insight and backed by power to the Areopagus of nations sponsored by some international lawyers.[69] Otto Pfleiderer, the Rector of the University of Berlin, insisted in a speech, delivered at that institution in 1895 and published under the title *Die Idee des ewigen Friedens,* that it would be irresponsible frivolity for German statesmen to ignore the experience of their nation and hope to win peace 'from the justice and energy of a European Areopagus of peoples, instead of from our nation's own strength and readiness for war' (p. 14). Strictly anarchist views of international society were widely accepted in influential circles of the post-Bismarckian *Reich.* When, at the time of the First Hague Peace Conference, the Russians suggested the setting up of machinery for compulsory arbitration Friedrich von Holstein, the most powerful of the civil servants,

65. Ibid., v, 200 (letter of 10 February 1881).
66. Ibid., v, 194 (letter of 11 December 1880).
67. Lasson, *Das Culturideal und der Krieg,* pp. 67–8.
68. Moltke, *Ges. Schriften,* vii, 125 (speech in *Reichstag,* 1 March 1880).
69. Ibid., v, 200–1 (letter of 10 February 1881).

argued against it on the grounds that the great powers were not disinterested enough to play their parts in the proposed institution.

For the state—the larger, the more so—regards itself as an end in itself [he instructed his superiors], not as a means of attaining higher goals beyond itself. For the state there is no higher goal than the protection of its own interests. In the case of great powers, however, the latter will not necessarily be identical with the maintenance of peace, but much rather with doing violence to enemies and competitors through a correctly composed stronger group.[70]

Hegelian doctrines were diametrically opposed to those of internationalism. The internationalists had faith in the reason and good will of the peoples, believed in a steady development of international relations and took a broad and inclusive view of the European states system. But the Hegelians relied on the force of monarchical government, thought in terms of power politics among states and concentrated in a narrow and exclusive fashion on the interests of their own state. The internationalists hoped that the progress of civilization would result in a more peaceful and just world. But the Hegelians saluted war as an intrinsic element of European politics and a useful instrument of foreign policy. The internationalists, who perceived an advancing integration of the society of states, aimed at international order. But the Hegelians, who saw only anarchy, concentrated upon national survival. The Hegelian theory of European politics, with its pessimistic assumptions about the nature and condition of man, suited a nation which had gained unity by force and security through war. It pervaded the minds of statesmen and scholars, eclipsed the optimistic notions of liberal internationalism and cut short the nascent tradition of progressive thought.

But Hegelian doctrines played an even more important part in the history of German ideas of the Concert of Europe. Mingling with the ideas of Ranke's disciples in the German *Reich* and merging in the balance of power tradition of international theory, they perverted the major school of thought about the Concert of Europe.

70. Lepsius *et al.* ed.: *Die Grosse Politik der Europäischen Kabinette, 1871–1914*, xv, 189 (9 May 1899). Bülow incorporated this passage in a subsequent despatch to Münster in Paris (ibid., pp. 191–2).

Chapter Three

THE BALANCE OF POWER THEORY

1. DEVELOPMENT

It was Austrian and Prussian statesmen who upheld the conservative doctrines, and international lawyers who developed the progressive notions of the Concert of Europe. The balance of power ideas drew support from a wide circle. Men as different as Baron Hans Christoph von Gagern, Karl Heinrich Ludwig Pölitz and Johann von Türckheim were among their defenders.

Gagern, who had been Dutch plenipotentiary at the Congress of Vienna, spent his later years preparing memoirs and writing commentaries on politics, law and morality. The balance of power was in his view a system 'which only fools and ignorant people deny or seem to regard as of little value, but true statesmen always keep in view'.[1] Its essence was barriers against encroachment.[2] As it had been the highest aim of the Quadruple Alliance against Napoleonic France, so the balance of power remained one of the principal ideas of the Great Alliance of the postwar years.[3]

Pölitz, a liberal teacher at Leipzig University who wrote a book on the history and politics of the European and American states systems, was a political scientist rather than a historian. His major work was *Die Staatswissenschaften im Lichte unsrer Zeit*, of which an enlarged edition appeared in 1827–28. Here he described the system set up by the five great powers as a new balance of power system, and observed that it had given Europe the character of a 'Staatenverein', an association of states, led by the great powers.[4] In the absence of an international tribunal, the balance of power remained the highest aim of statecraft.[5] The system of the power balance was the best safeguard for the state of possessions and the

1. Gagern: *Mein Antheil an der Politik*, v, *Der zweite Pariser Frieden*, pt 1, p. 426.
2. Gagern: *Critik des Völkerrechts. Mit practischer Anwendung auf unsre Zeit*, p. 203.
3. Gagern: *Der Einsiedler oder Fragmente über Sittenlehre, Staatsrecht und Politik*, ii, 52 and 31.
4. Pölitz, *Staatswissenschaften* . . ., pt v, p. 57.
5. Ibid., pt i, p. 600.

sanctity of treaties, 'since it is only through this that an accurately calculated *counterpoise* to all selfish interests and against all attempts at dictatorship and supremacy is possible'.[6]

Türckheim, who published a work under the title *Betrachtungen auf dem Gebiet der Verfassungs- und Staatenpolitik,* had taken part in the political life of Baden and had held the post of minister of foreign affairs in the early eighteen-thirties. The Areopagus system of European politics was in his view 'nothing but an application of the old balance of power system to contemporary conditions'. The fundamental principle was still oscillation, 'which should serve to prevent an excess of force from tilting disruptively to one side', and the only real difference that the number of scales had been reduced to five and the system thus made less elastic.[7]

But Gagern, Pölitz and Türckheim were minor characters. The principal champions of balance of power ideas were north German historians, who found it difficult to accept the views of Metternich and his disciples. In the doctrines of territorial and dynastic conservation they saw not only a cloak for the interests of the Habsburgs but also a digression from traditional European thought. By returning to the idea of the balance of power, the essence of the classic theory of European politics, they developed a system of thought which suited the ambitions of Prussia and the needs of Germany. The rise of the balance of power theory, which became Germany's principal contribution to speculation about the Concert of Europe, may be traced in the political and historical writings of the postwar decades.

In the years after 1815 writers on European politics were naturally inclined to compare the system introduced at the Congress of Vienna with the one that had existed before the French Revolution. Gentz and Ancillon, both of whom had reacted to the Napoleonic upheaval by praising the structure of prerevolutionary Europe and extolling the merits of the old balance of power system, were among those who drew distinctions and traced similarities between the old and the new Europe. While Gentz found the postwar system a superior alternative, Ancillon pronounced it the perfection of the traditional ways of the balance of power. Both of them adopted the conservative theory of the new system.[8]

6. Ibid., pt v, p. 62.   7. Türckheim, *Betrachtungen . . .*, ii, 12.
8. For fuller expositions of the ideas of Gentz and Ancillon, see above, Ch. One, pp. 16–23 and 36–7.

Arnold Herrmann Ludwig Heeren, the Göttingen historian, bridged the gap between the French Revolution and the Congress of Vienna with a Manual of the history of the states system from its formation till its restoration. One of the main foundations of the prerevolutionary states system, he observed, had been 'the accepted principle of the *maintenance* of the so-called *political balance of power,* i.e. the principle of preserving mutual freedom and independence by preventing any individual state from gaining superiority and encroaching'.9 Without it the states system could never exist. When, in the last decades of the eighteenth century, the principle of egotism had replaced it, the states system had disintegrated.10 The restoration of Europe after the defeat of Napoleon had gone hand in hand with the reinstatement of the balance principle.11 The postwar system, too, though it presented the novel feature of an aristocracy of great powers,12 was a paragon of states 'which, for all the external and internal inequality, still in their mutual relations regard themselves as free and independent of each other, and intend to maintain this freedom and independence'.13

With the idea of the balance of power he coupled the principle of legitimacy. While the former was intrinsic to any free system of civilized states, the latter, he considered, was fundamental to the European system of the postwar years.14 So closely did he adhere to the maxims of dynastic and territorial legitimism that he in 1817 was satisfied with the structure of the German Confederation and opposed to all plans for unification.15 Gentz, Ancillon and Heeren speculated about the balance of power, and related, in different

9. Heeren: *Historische Werke,* 4th edn, viii, *Handbuch der Geschichte des Europäischen Staatensystems und seiner Colonien, von seiner Bildung seit der Entdeckung beider Indien bis zu seiner Wiederherstellung nach dem Fall des Französischen Kaiserthrons, und der Freiwerdung von Amerika,* p. 13. Other foundations of the old states system were the law of nations and the rise of naval powers (pp. 11 and 14).

10. Heeren: *H.W.* ix, *Handbuch der Geschichte,* 168–9.

11. Ibid., pp. 442–3.

12. Ibid., pp. 443–4. Whilst recognizing the inevitability of the rise of the aristocratic system, Heeren pointed to its dangers as well as its advantages.

13. Heeren: *H.W.* ii: 'Der Deutsche Bund in seinen Verhältnissen zu dem Europäischen Staatensystem' (written 1817), p. 429.

14. Heeren: *H.W.* viii, *Handbuch der Geschichte,* 13–14 and ix, 411. Also ii, 'Der Deutsche Bund', p. 427: 'For a states system such as that of Germany and Europe there is, however, only one firm basis, namely the sanctity of the possessions recognized as legitimate.'

15. Heeren: *H.W.* ii: 'Der Deutsche Bund', 430–6.

ways, the new constitution of Europe to the classic system of politics. But none of them went so far as to reject the conservative ideas of the Concert and to put in their place a balance of power theory. That step was taken by Leopold von Ranke.

In 1831 when Ranke, after some years of research in Austria and Italy, returned to his chair at the University of Berlin he accepted an invitation to edit *Historisch-Politische Zeitschrift*, a journal designed to counter democratic and anti-Prussian propaganda. For the next four years he was engaged in the current debate. 'The line that I took,' he explained when nearly half a century later he looked back at those years, 'was neither revolution nor reaction. I had the bold idea of advocating a course in between these opposed tendencies, one which, by being bound up with the present, rested on the past and yet opened the way for those of the new ideas which contained truth.'[16] The extremism of the camps dominating the postwar world, the revolutionary movement and the monarchical union, repelled Ranke, who rejected the idea of popular sovereignty as well as the doctrine of absolutism. Nor was he attracted by the constitutional ideas of the southern liberals or moved by the nationalist passion of the national liberals. In common with the Gentz who had translated Burke, he adhered to the principles of a moderate conservatism.

But it was not the moderation of his politics so much as a fundamental disagreement with the political philosophy of the men of the restoration which prevented Ranke from supporting the theory of social preservation. In 'Politisches Gespräch', one of the most significant of his contributions to *Historisch-Politische Zeitschrift*, he let two characters discuss the nature of politics. The one who expressed the author's views laid down the rule that no trend of opinion, however dominant, can break the force of political interest. The antagonism in the internal life of the state between revolution and reaction, he taught his friend, was altogether secondary to the great issues of power politics and external relations.[17] This doctrine determined Ranke's attitude

16. Ranke: *Werke*, liii–liv, *Zur eigenen Lebensgeschichte*, 50 ('Dictat vom December 1875'). Ranke's attitude to the social issue can be studied also in *Werke*, xlix-l, *Zur Geschichte Deutschlands und Frankreichs im neunzehnten Jahrhundert*, and *Ueber die Epochen der neueren Geschichte*.
17. Ranke: *Werke*, xlix-l, 332 (a translation of this dialogue can be found in Von Laue: *Leopold Ranke; the Formative Years*). It was Dilthey who coined the phrase 'Primate der auswärtigen Politik' and first used it about Ranke's doctrine (see Meinecke: *Aphorismen und Skizzen zur Geschichte*, p. 79).

to the cosmopolitan ideology of the legitimists. The postwar union of the great powers, he declared, was no stronger than the interests that had brought them together.[18] In due course these states, which had been unable to arrange a common defence against Napoleon until France had threatened the independence of all and Europe had faced annihilation, would revert to their traditional state of disunion. Before the French Revolution 'each state was engaged in its own particular development, and each, I have no doubt, will return to that as soon as the after-effects of the revolutionary wars come to an end'.[19] By exposing the age since the French Revolution as a break in the history of the states system—'a kind of intermezzo of European-universalistic politics' in Meinecke's paraphrase[20]—he cut to the root of the philosophy of those who persisted in discussing European affairs in social terms and in thinking of the Concert of Europe as a counteragent to revolution. Thus he prepared the ground for a theory which presented the diplomatic system of the great powers in the setting of power relations between the members of the states system.

The picture that Ranke drew of the states system had two sides. Firstly, he emphasized the individuality of the states. States were unique individuals, analogous one to another but essentially independent of each other—thoughts of God, he called them.[21] 'Why, after all, are there several states?' he wondered. 'Is it not because there are several and equally good possibilities? God expressed the idea of mankind in the various peoples. The idea of the state is expressed in the various states. If there were only one flawless possibility for the state, if there were only one proper form of it, then only universal monarchy would be reasonable.'[22] Secondly, Ranke, like Hegel, drew attention to the unity of Europe. The geographical proximity, continuous relations and parallel development of the Latin and Teutonic countries had produced a community of nations with a distinct history, common religion and shared values.

18. Through conversations with Gentz in Vienna in 1827 and 1828 Ranke had learnt much about the disagreements that divided the great powers in the postwar years. Caemmerer: 'Rankes "Grosse Mächte" und die Geschichtschreibung des 18. Jahrhunderts', in *Studien und Versuchen zur neueren Geschichte,* pp. 310–11).
19. Ranke: *Werke,* xlix–l, 329, 'Pol. Gespräch'.
20. Meinecke: *Weltbürgertumund Nationalstaat,* p. 301.
21. Ranke: *Werke,* xlix–l, 328–9, 'Pol. Gespräch'.
22. *Ibid.,* 72–3, 'Frankreich und Deutschland'.

ception of the state, had been overwhelmed by the social tension of the postwar world and driven to set aside their earlier theory of balance of power, and to embrace the conservative doctrines of European politics. Ranke, inspired by the idea of nationality, was able to uphold the principle of state individuality against the cosmopolitan tendencies of restoration thought, and to put forward a regenerated balance of power theory of the political relations between the great powers.

The balance of power of Ranke's system of thought was thoroughly different from the equilibrium of Metternich's philosophy. Metternich's was a state of relaxed repose accompanied by stability and order, Ranke's a situation of tense harmony pregnant with movement and change. The difference can be traced to a contrast in their attitudes to tension. While Metternich treated it as a sign of emergency and an obstacle to orderly progress, Ranke accepted it as normal and creative. 'It was one of the characteristic habits of Ranke's mind and temperament,' Theodore H. Von Laue writes in his *Leopold Ranke: the Formative Years,* 'to conceive all human situations in terms of a creative equipoise of tensions.' Everywhere he detected sharpness of impact as well as basic harmony. [28] This combination was manifest in the life of the great powers. The five principal powers of Europe were like the branches of a tree or celestial bodies, he observed in a series of lectures which he delivered in 1854. Though each followed its own course, together they formed a system.

> Such was the formation the great powers had assumed in the middle of the eighteenth century: they could be compared to so many celestial bodies incessantly moving together and side by side, sometimes in a certain conjunction and sometimes in a certain divergence from each other. In this epoch they never were at one; they always moved autonomously, following their own inner drives, which is altogether the fundamental principle of being a great power—it can join another power temporarily, which often happened in that age, when each of these powers was looking for an alliance; but a great power must never allow itself to be subjected to the inclinations of another. [29]

The essence of this system was the balance of power. By regulating

28. P. 49.   29. Ranke: *Ueber die Epochen,* pp. 204-5.

the struggle among states, it sustained the duality of individuality and unity.

The term 'Concert of Europe', or any of its synonyms, rarely appears in Ranke's writings. Rather than analyse it separately, he simply identified the diplomatic system of the great powers with the balance of power. 'Which, after all, is really the controlling force in our Europe?' he asked the year after the Congress of Berlin. 'It is the agreement among the great powers, which precludes the domination of any one power and comprises all of them. War starts when it is no longer possible to attain this agreement.'[30] To him the Concert of Europe was a group of great powers involved in the operations of the balance of power.

In politics Ranke was a European rather than a German or a Prussian. His nationalism was not of the exclusive and militant type which became dominant in Bismarckian Prussia and the German *Reich*. The ideas of national unification and German power did not rouse his enthusiasm. For him the German nation was a cultural more than a political notion.[31] Though born in Saxony, he spent most of his life in Prussia. But loyalty to his adopted country never developed into passion. With regard to the rivalry between Austria and Prussia for the leadership of Germany he remained a dualist until Bismarck's success convinced him of the need for Prussian hegemony. When he advocated a strengthening of Prussia it was not so much for reasons of German politics as out of concern for the European balance of power. The preponderance of Napoleonic France had been closely connected with the weakness and consequent defeat of the Prussian state, he pointed out.[32] Yet the statesmen of the Congress of Vienna had failed to remedy this defect in the political structure of Europe. 'By the peace settlement of 1815 Prussia has undoubtedly been made too weak to fulfil her European functions. Not only is she without continuity of territory, which in emergencies has led to very unpleasant conflicts, but she also lacks seclusion for each of

---

30. Ranke: *Werke,* xliii–xliv, *Serbien und die Türkei im 19. Jahrh.,* p. VII.
31. See a passage in Ranke: *Ueber die Epochen*: '. . . so these two concepts, the coining of nationalities and their organization into states, are not necessarily connected. However, it is now no longer practicable to isolate the nationalities from each other; they all belong to the great European Concert ['grossen europäischen Concert'], (p. 236).
32. Ranke: *Werke,* xlviii, *Hardenberg und die Geschichte des preussischen Staates von 1793-1813,* p. 331.

her parts. For how is it possible to ward off foreign influence over these territories?' Since 1815, he argued at the time of the Crimean War, Prussia's position in Europe had become even weaker. While the resources of the other great powers had expanded considerably, hers had remained at their low level.[33] That situation was changed completely by Bismarck. Though Ranke disliked the passion and the aggressiveness of this statesman, he approved of his results. Through the wars with Denmark, Austria and France Prussia had liberated herself from the pressure of her neighbours and had established Germany as an equal among the great powers. 'The highest gratification to a nation's self-esteem comes from knowing that no one on earth is above it.'[34] In the German *Reich* he gave his support to the policy of power balance and peace which Bismarck pursued after 1871.[35] Till his death, in 1886, he remained a moderate German and a good European.

Ranke's great contribution to the theory of the Concert of Europe consisted in regenerating the eighteenth-century idea of the balance of power and applying it to the nineteenth-century system of great-power politics. Dissociating himself from the reactionaries on the one side and the liberals on the other, he presented an interpretation of European politics distinct from both the conservative and the progressive ideas. This system of thought gained considerable following among his contemporaries in Prussia and his successors in the *Reich*. By applying it first to European and then to world politics, Ranke's disciples turned it into the principal German tradition of thought about the Concert of Europe.

In the second half of the century the Rankean school outrivalled the established tradition of conservative thought and eclipsed the emerging tradition of progressive ideas. In the rivalry with these it received support from the two leading schools opposed to the Concert of Europe. From the one came the passionate ideas of the Prussian national liberals, from the other the harsh doctrines of the Hegelians. Both contributions merged in the principal system of European thought, but neither without causing a transformation.

33. Ranke: *Werke,* liii–liv, 673, 'Pol. Denkschrift aus der Zeit des Krimkrieges'.
34. Ranke: *Das Briefwerk,* p. 590 (letter of 1 May 1885).
35. Ranke's attitude to the political issues of his age has been analysed by Otto Diether, in his *Leopold von Ranke als Politiker.*

While the influence of national liberalism nationalized the balance of power tradition, the impact of Hegelian thought brutalized it. The confluence of ideas in the last decades of the nineteenth century swelled the central stream of European thought, but changed the course. Heinrich von Treitschke stands where the national-liberal tributary met the main stream and Otto von Bismarck where the Hegelian current joined, while the imperialists of the early twentieth century mark the final course.

Treitschke's contribution to the theory of the Concert of Europe was a synthesis of national-liberal criticism and balance of power thought. While his views on the national question and the Metternichian Concert resembled Droysen's, his conception of European politics and the Concert of Bismarck's times was in certain respects similar to Ranke's.

The twin objects of Treitschke's passion were national unification and German power. 'One thing is still wanting—the State,' he declared in 1863 in an oration delivered on the occasion of the fiftieth anniversary of the battle of Leipzig. '. . . Our people is the only one which has no general legislation, which cannot send representatives to the great concert of the Powers. No salvo salutes the German flag in a foreign port. Our fatherland at sea has no flag—like the pirates.'[36] This state of affairs was the work of the Congress of Vienna. In a series of lectures on politics, which he delivered regularly at the University of Berlin in his later years, he fiercely criticized the territorial settlement and political system that Metternich and his contemporaries had imposed on Europe. The statesmen of 1815, whose conception of states and peoples had been far too mechanical, had failed, he said, to take account of the latent conflicts between Prussia and Austria in Germany, and between national efforts and foreign occupation in Italy. The outcome of their negotiations had been mutilation of Germany and Italy. Yet their decisions had been treated as *ratio scripta* in the postwar years. The free life of the peoples of Europe had been suppressed by the police force of the 'Vierbunde' of the Holy-Alliance powers. As a result Germany and Italy had remained dismembered till well into the second half of the century.[37]

By 1860 Italy was on her way to unity. Treitschke was con-

---

36. Quoted in Guilland: *Modern Germany and her Historians,* p. 268.
37. Treitschke: *Politik,* i, 76, and ii,535–7.

vinced that before Germany could set out on the same course and gain national freedom, she would have to make a clean break with the past. In the particularism of liberals and princes in the south German states he recognized the greatest enemy of the nation, and in the power of Prussia the best hope for Germany. From an early stage he championed the policy that Bismarck later put into practice. Though Saxon by birth and upbringing, he was fanatically anti-Austrian and pro-Prussian.

The doctrine of primacy of foreign policy was fundamental to Treitschke's theory of European politics. With Ranke he shared the opinion that the men of the restoration had exaggerated the unity of the society of Europe and had paid too little attention to the sovereignty of states.[38] They had entertained the unreasonable view 'that the international differences should be determined by internal politics'—in his experience always a sign of political doctrinairism.[39] Though he did not deny that the activities of certain cosmopolitan movements with international ramifications occasionally made it necessary to intervene in the party strife of neighbouring countries,[40] he insisted that conflicts between parties and between ideologies were less important in European affairs than power struggles among states and nations.

Both Ranke and Treitschke gave prominence to the idea of struggle. But Treitschke embraced it with an enthusiasm suggestive of the Hegelians rather than of Ranke. States and war go together, he declared. 'Without war no State could be. All those we know of arose through war, and the protection of their members by armed force remains their primary and essential task. War, therefore, will endure to the end of history, as long as there is multiplicity of States.'[41] But war was not merely unavoidable and necessary. As a tonic for sick peoples, an agent of creation and a means of cultural progress, it was also highly desirable. Only in times of exhaustion, dejection and languishment, such as the period following the defeat of Napoleon, did the idea of eternal peace gain influence over the minds of men.[42] In the

38. Ibid., ii, 534.
39. Ibid., ii, 536; see also Treitschke: *Historische und Politische Aufsätze,* ii, 5th edn, p. 207, 'Bundesstaat und Einheitsstaat' (1864).
40. Treitschke: *Politik,* ii, 537.
41. Ibid., i, 72 (the translations on this and the following pages of extracts from *Politik* are taken from Dugdale's and de Bille's translation); see also i, 30.
42. Ibid., i, 72–6.

Germany of his own times, he noted with deep satisfaction, the oversensitive, philanthropic temperament had given place to the spirit of Clausewitz. [43]

But Treitschke did not think of international life as an anarchy completely devoid of order. Though the states habitually engaged in brutal strife, they constituted in his view a society. Indeed, to war itself there were two sides: 'Moreover war is a uniting as well as a dividing element among nations; it does not draw them together in enmity only, for through its means they learn to know and to respect each other's peculiar qualities.' [44] There were other bonds as well: 'Religion, science, and commerce bind the nations to each other, and, although each State is the supreme power within its own sphere, these forces lead it beyond itself to take its place in the international mosaic [Staatengesellschaft].' [45] However, the idea of a society of states was not nearly so important to Treitschke as to Ranke. By recognizing also the integrating influences at work among states he just managed to preserve the duality of Ranke's system. But by responding with his deeper emotions only to the separating factors of international life he upset the balance between the principles of individuality and unity.

In *Deutsche Geschichte im Neunzehnten Jahrhundert*, his *opus magnum*, as well as in the lectures on politics, Treitschke dealt with the history and structure of the European states system. He traced it to the Seven Years War, the first truly European war. By raising Prussia to the rank of the great powers Frederick the Great had fused the two old states systems, east and west of central Europe, and turned them into one single, indivisible community ('Gemeinschaft'). In the process the importance of second- and third-rank powers had dwindled. No longer able to meet the demands of great-power warfare and to bring influence to bear in coalitions, they had had to leave the management of European affairs to the principal powers. Thus the system had gained the aristocratic character of the Pentarchy. [46] Since the Seven Years War this 'Fünfherrschaft', had developed in accordance with the needs of European politics, and had reached a stage where all other states,

43. Ibid., ii, 361.
44. Ibid., i, 73.
45. Ibid., ii, 518.
46. Treitschke: *Deutsche Geschichte im Neunzehnten Jahrhundert*, i, 60–1. The same points are made in Treitschke: *Politik*, ii, 531–2.

except those directly involved in issues, were excluded from every negotiation of European importance.[47] In the course of the nineteenth century two great changes had taken place in the structure of the states system. Italy had emerged as a candidate for the position of a sixth great power, and Prussia had given place to a unified Germany.[48] The latter event had caused a revolution in the political system of Europe.

Prussia's victory over France in 1871 had turned the old system upside down.

> From then onwards the map of our Continent has been much more in accordance with nature. The middle was strengthened, and the brilliant idea which put Europe's centre of gravity in its right place, was made a reality. The founding of the German Empire works automatically for the calm of the system of States, inasmuch that the ambition of Prussia may now be soothed . . .[49]

In speeches in the new *Reichstag* Treitschke repeatedly extolled the change that Germany had wrought in the relations of the states. In a characteristic manner he sometimes added the warning that anyone who dared attempt to pull down the pillars of the new balance of power and upset the existing European order would have to deal with a united and proud people and to face a nation equipped and determined to defend its work.[50]

The notion of the balance of power was not the most important part of Treitschke's idea of the Concert of Europe. The classic conception of the European balance, the development of which he traced in the lectures on politics, he found too mechanical.

> The whole idea is crude, and as thoroughly unpolitical as the notion of an eternal peace, for, as we have already seen, the frontiers of States must be continually liable to fluctuation, and may not be thrust into narrow fetters. Nevertheless the point of view was wholesome for that period [after the Peace of Westphalia], for it acted as the only check upon the encroachments

47. Treitschke: *Deutsche Geschichte,* ii, 118–19; *Politik,* i, 42.
48. Italy's position as a great power is discussed in Treitschke: *Politik,* ii, 541.
49. Ibid., ii, 540.
50. *Reden . . . im Deutschen Reichstage 1871–1884,* pp. 77–8, 14 April 1874, and p. 169, 1 March 1880.

of some one powerful State, which were otherwise un-restrained.[51]

But the idea was not without an element of truth, because there could be no states system without an at least approximate power balance among the leading members. 'We cannot think of it as a *trutina gentium* with its scales exactly suspended, but any organized system of States must assume that no one State is so powerful as to be able to permit itself any licence without danger to itself.'[52] Normally, however, it was from a national rather than a European point of view that he regarded the balance of power. In the years of unification he subordinated concern for European balance to pursuit of national power. After 1871, when Prussia had satisfied her ambitions and Germany consolidated her position, he recon-ciled national with European considerations by appointing the German *Reich* the watchdog of the rearranged balance of power.[53] He never achieved the calmness and detachment characteristic of Ranke's attitude to the balance of power. Ranke, seeing the balance of power as the system that maintained the duality of European unity and state individuality, placed it at the centre of his theory of European politics. But Treitschke, perhaps hardly conscious of any such duality of principles in the states system, subordinated the balance of power to the interests of Germany. His view of the Concert of Europe was as narrow and patriotic as his attitude to the balance of power. To him the Concert was little more than the aggregate of the great powers, the body on which Prussia had imposed her will, the group in which the *Reich* had secured hegemony.[54]

51. Treitschke: *Politik,* ii, 527.
52. Ibid., ii, 547–8.
53. See, for example, a passage in Treitschke: *Rede, gehalten zur Feier der fünfund-zwanzigjährigen Regierung Seiner Majestät des Kaisers und Königs Wilhelm I,* in which Treitschke referred to Germany's new role in Europe: 'Foreign countries, too, are beginning to feel that this strengthening of the centre of Europe is a blessing for the civilization of the world. . . . where the army is the people in arms war becomes an enormously risky undertaking. Europe can thank the strong armament of Germany and the wise restraint of her statecraft for the fact that, despite so many occasions for strife, for fifteen years no general war has disturbed the peace of this part of the world' (pp. 8–9; speech, 4 January 1886).
54. For the Concert of Europe, i.e. the Concert of the great powers, Treitschke normally used the name 'the Pentarchy'. In an article on Turkey and the great powers of 1876 he discussed the terms on which Turkey had been admitted 'zum europäischen Concert' (Treitschke: *Zehn Jahre Deutscher Kämpfe,* 2nd edn, p. 695). But in the use of this term he apparently followed the practice, quite common in his

In his antagonism to the principle of territorial immutability and passion for the idea of the national state, in his antipathy against Austria and faith in Prussia, Treitschke followed Droysen. But in his conception of the character of the new Germany and of its role in European politics he differed radically from the earlier national liberal. While Droysen believed it possible to dispense with the power state and wanted to do away with the oligarchy of great powers, Treitschke identified the nation state with the power state and accepted the aristocratic order of the states system. In stressing the primacy of foreign policy and concentrating on the relations of great powers Treitschke was in agreement with Ranke. But in his attitude to Germany and Europe the national liberal contrasted with the conservative historian. While Ranke accepted the doctrine of particularism for the arrangement of Germany and upheld the idea of unity in diversity for the European system of states, Treitschke, frankly rejecting the one and half ignoring the other, devoted himself to national unity and German power. If Ranke can be criticized for limiting his field of vision to the old European countries and failing to perceive the growing importance of non-European states, Treitschke can be accused of lacking in sympathy for foreign nations and seeing little beyond Germany.[55]

The influence of national liberalism on balance of power thought was to replace the notion of the European balance with the idea of the German nation. Nationalizing the balance of power theory was the first stage in transforming it into a set of ideas opposed to the Concert of Europe. The second stage of the process was to graft Hegelian ideas on the Rankean theory. Here Bismarck played an important part.

day, of letting it refer to all the sovereign members of the European society of states.

55. Treitschke's attitude to the world was as narrowly European as Ranke's: 'Contrary to the hopes of the dreamers, it has been shown that the other continents are not able to create a civilization equal in quality to that of old Europe. Colonial life is a tree without roots; so Europe is still the heart of the world; and, knowing the world, we can predict that so it will remain' (*Politik,* ii, 533); 'Just as our small earth, as far as we can tell, will remain the noblest star in the planetary system, so this old, diversiform Europe, too, no matter how splendidly world communications may develop, will still remain, in any foreseeable future, the heart of the world, the home of all creative culture and, therefore, the place where the great power-issues between the states of the world are ultimately settled. All colonies are grafts; they have been deprived of youth, of natural growth from the root' (*Deutsche Kämpfe, Neue Folge* . . . ('Die ersten Versuche deutscher Kolonialpolitik' (1884), pp. 336–7).

For Bismarck, as for Hegel, states were autonomous individuals. The basic principle of his political philosophy was always the self-interest of the state. 'The only sound basis for a great state—' he said in 1850, 'and it is essentially this which distinguishes it from a small state—is political egotism, not romanticism; and it is not worthy of a great state to contend for something which does not concern its own interests.'[56] 'Any great power', he insisted a few years before the close of his career forty years later, 'which goes beyond its sphere of interests in trying to exert pressure and influence on the politics of other countries and to direct affairs, which periclitates beyond the area allocated to it by God, which practises power politics and not the politics of interests, is busying itself with prestige.'[57]

In the spiritual sphere, Bismarck implied, the states were part of a universal order and subject to divine laws. But on the worldly level they lived in a state of nature. 'The political relations between two neighbouring great states can be compared to the situation between two travellers in a desolate forest who do not know each other and neither of whom quite trusts the other; if one puts his hand in his pocket, the other already cocks his revolver; and if he hears the click of the other cock, he already fires.'[58] The normal physical condition of international politics was fluid, he believed. Alliances were merely strategic positions and could never have permanent validity. Neither the Holy Alliance, the German Confederation nor any of the alliances arranged after the foundation of the German *Reich* could give exemption from the principle *toujours en vedette*.[59] The demands of the 'Kampf um's Dasein' took precedence of all treaty obligations.[60]

For the idea of Europe Bismarck had only scorn. In contradiction to those who presented Europe as a united power, a kind of federal state, he called it simply a 'notion géographique'. 'Who is Europe?' he could ask in his earlier years when representatives of other great powers used the word. 'I have always found the word "Europe" on the tongues of those politicians who demanded something from other powers which they did not dare to ask for

56. Bismarck: *Die politischen Reden*, i, 264–5 (speech, 3 December 1850).
57. *Die pol. Reden,* xii, 477 (speech, 6 February 1888).
58. Ibid., xii, 217 (speech, 11 January 1887).
59. Bismarck: *Gedanken und Erinnerungen,* ii, 258–9.
60. Ibid., ii, 249.

in their own name,' he observed on one occasion.[61] Nor did he show much respect for the diplomatic concert of the great powers when he viewed its performance in retrospect. In the speeches of his later years he liked to recall the crucial stages of his early career, and to remind his listeners how he had outwitted the great powers when they had threatened collectively or attempted individually to put obstacles in the way of Prussian expansion and German unification. There were notes of triumph and traces of irony in some of his references to the 'europäischen Senioren-convent'.[62]

Bismarck, too, adhered to Ranke's doctrine of the primacy of foreign policy. In the earlier part of his career he was generally ready to adjourn domestic matters in order to pursue national ambitions in the foreign field. 'For me foreign affairs are an end in themselves and are more important than the others,' he declared in 1866.[63] In the later years he showed relatively little interest in the political parties and the *Reichstag*.[64] The position of Germany in Europe remained his dominant concern. God had placed Germany in a situation more exposed than that of any other power, he pointed out. With France in the west and Russia in the east, both warlike nations, she was threatened from two sides and could not afford to relax. 'The pikes in the European fish-pond prevent us from becoming carps by letting us feel their spines in both of our flanks; they force us to make an effort which we might not have made voluntarily; they also force upon us a solidarity which is against the innermost nature of us Germans. . . .'[65] For Bismarck politics was essentially a struggle for national existence.

But Bismarck's national egotism was not of the exclusive kind. Though war and clever diplomacy were the means by which he founded and secured the *Reich*, he was not unconcerned with the

61. Bismarck: *Die gesammelten Werke,* iv, ed. Thimme, 1927, p. 58; *Grosse Politik,* ii, 87–8.
62. For examples of his use of this term for the European Concert, see *Die pol. Reden,* ix, 235; xi, 418; xii, 452; xiii, 140 and 316; and Bismarck: *Ged. u. Er.,* i, 335. The term 'der diplomatische Areopag von Europa' appears in *Die pol. Reden,* xii, 445.
63. A. v. Brauer; 'Bismarcks Staatskunst auf dem Gebiete der auswärtigen Politik' in Poschinger, ed., *Neues Bismarck-Jahrbuch,* i, 319; see also Bismarck: *Ged. u. Er.,* ii, 56.
64. Bismarck: *Ged. u. Er.,* ii, 182, for his attitude to the parties. His speeches in the *Reichstag* on foreign affairs were aimed at foreign governments rather than the German public.
65. *Die pol. Reden,* xii, 455–6 (speech, 6 February 1888).

rights and safety of other states. This was true especially in the years after unification, when to see the new Germany accepted as an honest and peaceable member of the states system was among his highest aims.[66] Appreciating that the national interest not only demanded but also restricted the pursuit of power, he avoided the excesses of his imperialistic successors and resisted the temptation to try to break through the European system. In both theory and practice he acknowledged the unity of the states system and accepted the principle of power balance. To remain 'selbstdritt' was the precept of his foreign policy after 1871: 'As long as the world is governed by the uncertain balance of power among five great powers, all there is to policy may be summed up in the formula: try to be one of three. That is the only real protection against coalitions.'[67]

Thus the anti-European element in Bismarck's philosophy, dominant particularly in the age of national unification, was matched with a pro-European component, which was more apparent after 1871 than before. But there was also a third strand in his European thought. At the height of his career he evoked the political principles that had prevailed in Germany and Europe in Metternich's time. In German affairs he had always been a staunch supporter of the Prussian monarchy and a determined opponent of revolutionary movements.[68] After 1871 he became a conservative also in European politics. The German *Reich*, he decided, was what the old Austrian Chancellor had called a saturated state.[69] Through the war with Austria, Prussia had thrown off the inferior role which she had endured since the Congress of Vienna; and in the war with France, Germany had established her position among the powers. The system of 1815 had been corrected at last. Henceforth his aim was to preserve what had been achieved, and his policy to keep down all forces which threatened to unsettle the internal and external relations of the states. As Metternich had done half a century before, he directed attention from international conflict to social tension in

66. Bismarck: *Ged. u. Er.*, ii, 267. 'Honesty, frankness and placability' were the means of gaining the confidence of foreign governments, he wrote.
67. Bismarck: *Deutscher Staat*, p. 145. For other references to the European balance of power, see *Die pol. Reden*, xii, 216 and 467, and Bismarck: *Ged. u. Er.*, ii, 253.
68. See his correspondence with Leopold von Gerlach, especially letter of 30 May 1857 (Bismarck: *Ged. u. Er.*, i, 175).
69. *Die pol. Reden*, xii, 177 (speech, 11 January 1887).

an endeavour to foster monarchical solidarity in defence of conservative interests. The old Continental monarchies had tasks more important than rivalling each other in Balkan politics, he wrote in the chapter of his memoirs in which he dealt with the period after the Franco-Prussian War.

> If the monarchical governments have no understanding of the need for keeping together in the interests of political and social order, but make themselves subservient to the chauvinistic impulses of their subjects, I fear that the international revolutionary and social struggles which will have to be fought out will be all the more dangerous, and will take such a form that victory on the part of monarchical order will be more difficult.[70]

In one of his speeches he presented the League of the Three Emperors, arranged after the defeat of France, as a renewal of the Holy Alliance of the eastern monarchies, which had perished in the Crimean War, and expressed the hope that it would give Europe another age of peace.[71]

But Bismarck did not commit the dogmatic excesses characteristic of the men of the restoration.[72] The idea of international anarchy and the doctrine of primacy of foreign policy, which had dominated his political thought during the period of national unification, mingled with the conservative ideas of his later years and restrained him from overestimating the cohesion of the society of Europe and exaggerating the importance of the social issue. Bismarck's theory of European politics was a blend of Hegelian anarchism, Rankean balance of power thought and Metternichian conservatism, stamped with the mark of an aggressive and self-assertive character. 'Now I drive Europe four-in-hand from the box', he is said to have answered when the civil servants in the Foreign Office congratulated him on the success of the Congress of Berlin, his zenith as a European statesman.[73]

Bismarck's lasting contribution to the theory of the Concert of

70. *Ged. u. Er.,* ii, 229–30.
71. *Die pol. Reden,* xii, 178–9 (11 January 1887).
72. See his letter to Gerlach of 30 May 1857: I do not find it possible 'in policy to carry through the principle [of struggle against revolution] to the extent that its remotest consequences transcend every other consideration, that it in a way becomes the only trump suit in the game, the lowest card of which still covers the highest of every other suit' (Bismarck: *Ged. u. Er.,* i, 175).
73. See Luckwaldt: 'Das europäische Staatensystem 1850–1890', in *Liberalismus und Nationalismus 1848–1890,* p. 358.

Europe was not so much to restore Metternichian doctrines as to channel Hegelian ideas into the main stream of German thought. Whereas the conservative theory went out again with his retirement, the anti-European power-political ideas survived to become a major element in the international thought of his successors.

Treitschke, who attacked the old Concert of Europe and rejected the principle of territorial stability, championed the nation against cosmopolitanism. But Bismarck, who overrode the new Concert and scorned the idea of international organization, upheld the state against internationalism.[74]

While Treitschke, concentrating on the power of the German nation, denigrated the system of the balance of power, Bismarck, devoting himself to the establishment of the German *Reich*, slighted the institution of the Concert of Europe. Between them they undermined the balance of power tradition and prepared the way for a nationalism opposed to the Concert of Europe.

Like the age of unification, the period between 1890 and 1914 was a time of anti-European thought. In those years Germans speculated less and less about the role of the Concert in international politics and more and more about the standing of the *Reich* among the great powers. Bismarck had been content to maintain the position that Germany had secured in Europe; but those who followed him wanted to enter the competition for a place in the world. 'We do not want again to become, in the words of Friedrich List, the servants of mankind,' Prince Bernhard von Bülow, Secretary of State from 1897 and Chancellor from 1901, declared in a *Reichstag* speech at the end of the century, '. . . in the next century the German people will be either the hammer or the anvil.'[75] His reflections on Germany's international situation, which were characteristic of the men of his generation, found their clearest expression in *Deutsche Politik*, a book published two years after the outbreak of the First World War. Reviewing the history of the *Reich*, he observed that the other powers had regarded Germany, the *Homo novus* in the family of nations and the youngest of the great powers, as a troublesome intruder in the European Areopagus. The truth, he insisted, was that the *Reich* ever since its foundation had been a full member, possessing both

74. Bismarck's attitude to state and nation, which resembled Ranke's, is discussed by Hans Rothfels in his introduction to Bismarck: *Deutscher Staat* (see especially pp. xxxi/xxxii).

75. Bülow: *Reden, nebst urkundlichen Beiträgen zu seiner Politik*, i, 96 (11 December 1899).

the will to participate in the negotiations and the strength to join in the actions of the high council.[76] Since the end of the nineteenth century Germany had gone a step further. As her national life had assumed world dimensions and her foreign policy had burst the limits of the old Europe, Germany had followed the leading powers and entered the path of world politics.[77] 'For the sake of our interests as well as for the sake of our dignity and honour we had to take care to win for our world policy the same independence as we had secured for our European policy.'[78]

The problem of reconciling the imperialistic ambitions of the post-Bismarckian *Reich* with the traditional principles of the balance of power system was tackled by the professors of history at the University of Berlin.[79] The Bismarck historian Max Lenz made one of the first attempts. In *Die grossen Mächte, Ein Rückblick auf unser Jahrhundert,* a small book published in 1900, he brought Ranke's famous essay up to date and extended his ideas of European politics to world politics.[80]

Also Lenz's contemporary Hans Delbrück, historian of the art of war and Treitschke's successor at the University of Berlin, applied the theory of the European balance of power to the relations of the great powers in the world. The Latin and Teutonic nations, in spite of their numerous differences and incessant rivalry, constituted in his view one great 'Kulturfamilie'.[81] For four hundred years they had been engaged in subduing the rest of the world and drawing it into their cultural sphere. They had pursued this enterprise with increasing success and rising intensity. It is of decisive importance to the future of mankind, he

76. Bülow: *Deutsche Politik,* pp. 3–5. See also his *Reichstag* speech of 8 February 1898, in which he touched upon Germany's role in the Concert and presented what must be the most elaborate version of the obvious pun about 'das europäische Konzert' (*Reden,* i, 24–6).

77. Bülow: *Deutsche Pol.,* p. 14. Friedrich List is said to have coined the word 'Weltpolitik' and to have used it for the first time as early as 1846 (Rein: 'Über die Bedeutung der überseeischen Ausdehnung für das europäische Staaten-System', *Historische Zeitschrift,* cxxxvii (1928), 87).

78. Bülow: *Deutsche Pol.,* p. 29.

79. Ludwig Dehio clarified the intellectual relationship between Ranke and the imperialistic historians in his *Deutschland und die Weltpolitik im 20. Jahrhundert,* (English trans. *Germany and World Politics in the Twentieth Century*).

80. Ranke's influence can be seen also in an article written by Lenz in 1900, 'Ein Blick in das zwanzigste Jahrhundert', see his *Kleine Historische Schriften,* 2nd edn.

81. Delbrück: *Vor und nach dem Weltkrieg. Politische und historische Aufsätze 1902–25,* p. 13, 'Deutschlands Stellung in der Weltpolitik' (1902).

warned in *Preussische Jahrbücher* in 1899, 'that a certain balance of power among the great nations be preserved or restored in this process. If all territories outside Europe go to only one or two nations, then one day these will crush all others with this preponderance of power.' The spiritual richness of the epoch depended on the coexistence of many large and small civilized nations, which allowed each to develop its particular qualities and all to influence each other. So Germany, he concluded, must adopt a large-scale colonial policy. By extending German nationality, language and culture to vast territories outside Europe she should seek to make up for centuries of neglect.[82] Though German world policy was a challenge to British world hegemony, its aim was not to defeat and overthrow Britain, he emphasized in his later prewar writings, but to substitute a balance of rival powers for the supremacy of one power.[83]

Otto Hintze, historian of Prussia, presented the imperialistic movement as the introduction to a new epoch in the history of the balance of power. The essence of this movement, he wrote in 1907, was struggle for position in the new world system of states, which was taking the place of the old European system.

> The goal of modern imperialism is not *one* empire, but a number of empires, coexisting with the same independence and in a similar power balance as the great powers did in the old European states system. Striving for supremacy is not irreconcilable with this. Though it hitherto in the history of the states has been, as it were, the motor of political progress, it has not led to absolute dominance by one power but to reinforced counterefforts, which always have succeeded in restoring and maintaining the balance of power system.

He saw no conflict between the aims of German world policy and the principles of the balance system.[84]

The professors concentrated on the goal of world policy and left it to more popular writers to discuss the obstacles. Since the role that Germany coveted in the world transcended the part that she played in Europe, she could not satisfy her imperialistic ambitions without breaking through the European system.

82. Delbrück: *Erinnerungen Aufsätze und Reden,* pp. 486–7.
83. Delbrück: *Vor und nach,* pp. 97–8, 133 and 211.
84. Hintze: *Staat und Verfassung,* p. 459.

Prominent among the men who concerned themselves with the restrictions imposed on Germany by the system of the European balance of power was Paul Rohrbach. In the dozen years preceding the First World War he published a stream of passionately imperialistic literature. In *Deutschland unter den Weltvölkern*, of which the first edition appeared in 1903 and an enlarged version in 1908, he observed that the old system of six great powers maintaining a power balance in Europe, which had reached its highest point with the Congress of Berlin in 1878, was changing character radically. Two of the states, Britain and Russia, were developing into world powers; and an outside power, the United States of America, was joining them. While Italy and Austria-Hungary had been left behind as purely European powers, Germany and France were in positions in between. 'What prospects do we, as a nation, have of decisively swinging across to the side of those peoples who are going to shape world history in the twentieth and, as far as one can see, probably also in the following centuries?' was the question he set out to answer.[85] Germany was no longer saturated. The growth of her population and expansion of her industry and trade had created a need for colonies and given her new interests in the world. To look after them she needed more power.[86] But in the endeavour to strengthen her position she encountered the opposition of Britain. The British scheme of 'encirclement' confronted the German policy of expansion.[87] So Germany, it may be concluded from Rohrbach's analysis, in attempting to join the principal powers of the 'Konzert der Weltpolitik'[88] had come up against the system of the European balance of power. For when Britain, the traditional guarantor of the Continental power balance, was seeking to arrange a counterweight to a dominant and expansionist power in the centre of Europe, she was acting in accordance with the established principles of European balance politics. The conflict between Germany's ambitions in the world and her situation within Europe brought the idea of a new balance of world powers into opposition to that of the European balance of power.

The historian who has studied Ranke's influence on German

85. Rohrbach: *Deutschland unter den Weltvölkern, Materialen zur auswärtigen Politik,* p. 31.
86. Ibid., pp. 14–15, 23–6 and 345; Rohrbach: *Der deutsche Gedanke in der Welt*, p. 161.
87. Rohrbach: *Deutschland*, p. 176.
88. Rohrbach used this term in *Deutschland*, p. 319.

imperialism and analysed the relation between European balance and world policy writes that the imperialistic historians threw a great bridge from the peaceful days of Ranke's lifetime into the crowded age of modern imperialism.[89] This bridge, it could be said, led from balance of power thought about the Concert of Europe to balance of power thought opposed to the Concert of Europe. From accepting the ideas of the Rankean imperialists to rejecting the balance theory of the Concert was a short step. It was taken by a soldier.

Friedrich von Bernhardi, general of the cavalry, was a Pan-German. Guided by Hegelian ideas inherited from his father[90] and dominated by a nationalist passion reminiscent of Treitschke, he combined in his thought the two principal tendencies opposed to the Concert of Europe. It was as a writer on military and political affairs that he became best known. His *Deutschland und der nächste Krieg,* which appeared in 1912 and became notorious throughout Europe for its militant tone,[91] was a vigorous attack on the European system. Since the Congress of Vienna, the author observed, the idea of the balance of power had been an almost sacrosanct principle in the political system of the great powers. But, because Britain enjoyed preponderance of power through control of the seas, there was no real power balance in Europe. Attempts to establish it had resulted only in preventing the free development of states, especially Germany, and in facilitating the rise of world powers, particularly Britain. A complete break with the obsolete notion of a European balance was now necessary, he insisted. This did not mean that the idea of a states system with common cultural interests should be dropped, but that it should be developed on a new and truer foundation.

> Today there can be no question of a *European* states system but only of a *world states system,* in which the balance of power rests on real power factors. In this states system we must strive to gain, at the head of a central European confederation, a position of equal rights, by in one way or another reducing the

89. Dehio: *Germany,* p. 42.
90. See Heller, *Hegel,* pp. 204–5.
91. The motto of the book, printed on the title page, was from Nietzsche's *Also sprach Zarathustra*: 'War and courage have achieved more great things than charity has. It was not your compassion but your bravery which up till now saved the victims. What is good? you ask. To be brave is good.'

alleged European balance of power to its true value and correspondingly increasing our own power.[92]

After the outbreak of world war the professors joined the popular writers in denouncing the European balance of power.[93] The balance of power theory of the Concert of Europe was essentially political. Its emphasis was on state and power. According to the conservative theory, the Concert of Europe was a union of sovereigns which maintained the existing order by guaranteeing the legal structure of the society of Europe. According to the progressive theory, it was an organization of nations which was advancing towards international order through a strengthening of the bonds of civilization. According to the balance theory, it was a system of powers which ensured the survival and safeguarded the security of sovereign states by preserving a balance of power. The theme of the conservative theory was conflict between the rulers of Europe and the movements of revision and revolution, of the progressive theory relations among nations and peoples, but of the balance theory struggle between states. In the case of the conservative theory there was a tendency to include the lesser sovereigns of Europe in the idea of monarchical solidarity, in the case of the progressive theory an inclination to embrace all the nations of the world in the notion of international organization, but in the case of the balance theory a habit of concentrating exclusively on the great powers in the conception of political system. The balance of power theory had less in common with the other theories of the Concert, than with the principal strands of anti-European thought.

The bond with the two great sets of ideas opposed to the Concert of Europe was common opposition to cosmopolitan conceptions of European politics. In Hegelian anarchism and in national liberal nationalism no less than in the Rankean philosophy of power politics the accent was on the vertical divisions of the society of Europe. This consonance between pro-European and anti-European ideas made possible the great confluence of trends which marked German international thought in the last half of the century. The convergence of the three traditions might be expressed diagrammatically:

92. Bernhardi: *Deutschland und der nächste Krieg,* pp. 117–19.
93. Dehio: *Germany,* p. 103n.

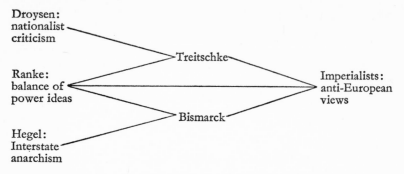

Droysen:
nationalist
criticism

Treitschke

Ranke:
balance of
power ideas

Imperialists:
anti-European
views

Bismarck

Hegel:
Interstate
anarchism

However, the antithesis between pro-European and anti-European ideas prevented a harmonious coexistence of the trends, and turned the later history of German international theory into a struggle between the leading tradition of pro-European thought and the twin schools of criticism. Here four periods may be distinguished. In the quiet years before 1848 pro-European thought predominated: while the anti-European schools still were gathering strength, the conservative and the balance of power tradition confronted each other. In the violent and venturesome age of war and unification anti-European thought gained the upper hand: the national liberal and the Hegelian school first helped to eclipse the conservative tradition and then came to dominate the alliance with the Rankean tradition. The years of saturation and stability between the foundation of the *Reich* and the retirement of Bismarck were a period of synthesis: Bismarck, satisfied with his achievements and determined to maintain Germany's position in Europe, chained anti-European to pro-European thought. In the age of ambition and expansion, which culminated in the First World War, the anti-European strand broke loose and wiped out its pro-European rival: by extending Ranke's European ideas to world politics and projecting a Concert of rival world powers, the imperialists gave the final twist to the balance of power theory and turned it against Europe.

The balance of power tradition was extinguished through gradual transformation. It lost its character through a process which could be described as debasement by fusion. While the national liberal and Hegelian trends merged in the Rankean tradition, the spirit of German nationalism and the philosophy of interstate anarchism subverted the principles of balance thought.

Thus moderate and noble ideas about European politics degenerated into selfish and brutal doctrines of anti-European policy. The measure of the perversion of the balance of power theory is the difference between Ranke's request that the power of Prussia be expanded for the sake of European balance and Bernhardi's demand that the balance of Europe be eliminated for the sake of German power.

2. DISSENT

Though by far the most important politically, the imperialists were not the only opponents of the European balance system. Both before and after the foundation of the *Reich* there were writers who voiced objections and advocated alternatives to the balance of power Concert of Europe. Among them were international lawyers in pursuit of a legal community, south Germans bent on a reorganization of Europe, and liberal nationalists with a vision of a Europe of free nations.

An early example of an international lawyer who censured the European system was Johannes Baptista Fallati, from 1842 professor of political history at Tübingen. The essence of his criticism was that the system placed power before right. In 'Die Genesis der Völkergesellschaft. Ein Beitrag zur Revision der Völkerrechtswissenschaft', an article published in 1844, he wrote:

> The basic idea of the political balance of power is simply that of balancing and weighing the power of the various states in such a way that the predominance of one does not endanger the security of the rest. It presupposes the recognition of the right of each state to individual existence [Persönlicheit]; but to restore this if violated is not its goal. Because if it were, the balance of power would have no regard for power, since right is indifferent to power, and could beget only defensive and never real offensive alliances.[94]

He believed that the natural inequality of the states made it impossible for the system of the balance of power to exist in a democratic form, but rejected the aristocratic one of post-1815 Europe.[95] Instead of the 'Pentarchie' he wanted a 'Völkermonarchie', a monarchy of nations.[96]

94. *Zeitschrift für die gesammte Staatswissenschaft*, i, 320.
95. Ibid., pp. 593–5.
96. Ibid., p. 601.

The south German criticism of the European system was that it excluded the secondary states. Julius Fröbel, who was born in Schwartzburg-Rudolstadt, sat on the extreme left of the Frankfort Assembly, lived in exile in America in the fifties, and held posts in the governments of Austria and Württemberg in the sixties, made this complaint. The European powers that had been left out, he wrote in 1864, rightly recognized in the Pentarchy 'an oligarchic usurpation, the destruction of which must be desired by *all*'. Germany, who as a political power had been divided between Austria and Prussia, could see in it only 'the alliance of its murderers'.[97] However, the pentarchic system had broken down already.[98] As early as the Crimean War Fröbel, then in America, had detected the shift from a European to a world balance of power. 'High politics have become world politics.'[99] He advocated a federation comprising all the states of western Europe. A United States of Europe could join America and Russia in a world triarchy, which would include the entire higher civilization.[100] As will be seen, there was much common ground between Fröbel and Constantin Frantz; but the conservative Frantz did not include France and Britain in his plan for a European federation.

The liberal nationalist view was expressed by Heinrich Bernhard Oppenheim, a publicist with a revolutionary background. At the time when Bismarck was founding the German *Reich* Oppenheim charged the European system with ignoring the claims of the peoples. The various forms of the 'Concert européen' and the amphictyonic arrangement of great powers had developed from the mechanical system of the balance of power, he observed. 'Since, according to the spirit of this diplomatic-dynastic system, the boundaries of states up to modern times have been carved out with insufficient regard for the substance of the life of peoples . . ., most modern wars appear as a reaction of the right of nationality to the encroachments of diplomacy.'[101] He believed that a Europe organized on the principle of nationality would be more peaceful.

However, one man stands out from the rest of this group of

---

97. Fröbel: *Theorie der Politik, als Ergebniss einer erneuerten Prüfung demokratischer Lehrmeinungen,* ii, 209; see also p. 203.
98. Ibid., ii, 192–3.
99. Fröbel: *Kleine Politische Schriften,* i, 50.
100. Fröbel: *Kleine Pol. Schriften,* i, 51–6; *Amerika, Europa und die politischen Gesichtspunkte der Gegenwart,* pp. 208–9; *Theorie,* ii, 197.
101. Oppenheim: *Friedensglossen zum Kriegsjahr,* p. 115.

critics. Constantin Frantz not only attacked the institution of the Concert of Europe and criticized the principle of the balance of power, but opposed the whole mainstream of German thought about European politics. The son of a Protestant pastor, he was born in 1817 near Halberstadt, and educated at Halle and Berlin. After many years of service in the Prussian government he left Berlin in 1873 and settled in Saxony. He was repelled by the political philosophy that had developed in Prussia and fructified in the *Reich*. In several of his books he dealt severely with Ranke's and Hegel's ideas and Bismarck's achievements. The Rankean conception of European politics, he complained, led to cult of power. Ranke, always interested in the diplomatic history instead of the social and moral condition, thought of the peoples in outworn terms, he held. 'He is not a man of the *future*.'[102] Hegel, who had made the state an end in itself, was guilty of 'deification of the state'. Without his preparation of the Prussian mind the events of 1866 could not have happened.[103] Bismarck's attempt to make Prussia an effective great power had resulted in catastrophe. The defeat of Austria and the destruction of the German Confederation had introduced an age of 'blood and iron': 'European international law has lost its last support; *power*, though in itself without standard, has taken the place of *right*. Thus only the accomplished *fact*, the product of power, counts. . . . ' There was no real peace, only a certain tranquillity which was maintained through fear and fearfulness.[104]

The idea of the great power, which Ranke, Hegel and Bismarck in their different ways had helped to sustain, was the primary target of Frantz's attack. It was embodied in the great power system of European politics. Though now in decay, this system still bedevilled diplomatic practice and political theory, he thought. Even from its name, 'great power system', it was clear 'that it centres on the idea of naked *power* and thereby ignores historical and moral foundations as well as higher civilizing aims'. It meant that the five great powers continually were striving for more

102. Frantz: *Die Weltpolitik unter besonderer Bezugnahme auf Deutschland*, pt ii, p. 172.
103. Frantz: *Das neue Deutschland*, pp. 334-9.
104. Frantz: *Die Religion des Nationalliberalismus*, pp. 251-2; *Deutsche Antwort auf die orientalische Frage*, p. 77; *Der Föderalismus, als das leitende Princip für die sociale, staatliche und internationale Organisation, unter besonderer Bezugnahme auf Deutschland*, p. 381.

military and economic power, and that the lesser states, with the exception of those which had chosen to aim at great power status, had to struggle simply to survive. Since the members of the Pentarchy, in pursuit of their own interests, had arrogated to themselves all decisions of European importance, the smaller states, the real promoters of freedom and culture, were sinking into insignificance and heading for annihilation.[105] Abolition of the entire 'great power bugbear' was his negative aim.[106]

In *Untersuchungen über das Europäische Gleichgewicht,* a substantial work published anonymously in 1859, as well as in later books, Frantz examined the record of the Pentarchy and investigated the circumstances of its decline. Evoked by the common interest of the powers in defeating revolutionary and Napoleonic France and reinforced by the spiritual bond of the Holy Alliance, the new institution had set out to maintain the restoration in accordance with the treaties of 1815. It had had some success. By begetting a generation of peace and stability, it had moved the nations a little closer to each other and brought international law a step forward. But the system had failed to awaken great spiritual principles and even to consolidate international law. The peace had been armed. Already by the eighteen-thirties the postwar community of interests and principles had given place to discord between the Holy Alliance of the three absolutist monarchies in the east, who upheld the maxims of legitimism, and the alliance of the two constitutional monarchies in the west, who championed the principle of non-intervention. A balance of power between these groups had allowed the Pentarchy to present the appearance of life for another few decades. But the transition from armed peace to open war had put an end to that. After the Crimean War it was vain to expect the 'great power board' to maintain the balance of power. 'There is no longer a European Pentarchy, just as there no longer is a balance or power, and woe be to the state that might rely on the European balance of power or on the Pentarchy.'[107] A new pattern was taking shape. The rise of world powers on the fringes of Europe and beyond and the growing importance of secondary states pointed towards a system of tetrarchy in world

105. Frantz: *Der Föderalismus,* pp. 379–80.
106. Ibid., p. 386.
107. Frantz: *Untersuchungen,* p. 118 (erroneously numbered 117).

politics and polyarchy in European politics.[108] Frantz believed that this system held such great dangers for central Europe that they could be met only by a reorganization of the European states system.

In an age of world politics, he argued, Europe could not hold her own between Russia and America, and remain the centre of civilization and history, without a federation of the 'Abendländer', the Christian countries once part of the Roman Empire. Dreaming of a revival of the Holy Roman Empire, he advocated a pacific federation based on Christianity and international law. It would exclude Tsarist Russia, who had different ideas of religion and law, and Napoleonic France, a persistent source of revolutionary propaganda and nationalist inspiration, as well as liberal Britain and overseas states, and would centre on Germany. A German 'collective power' could serve as clamp to the wider federation.[109] Austria and Prussia should take the first step towards the new order by treating the great power system as a relic of the past and abandoning the notion of the great power. That was his alternative to the policy of 'blood and iron'.

Frantz's European thought, which was Germany's principal contribution to the federative thinking that arose in his generation in many parts of the Continent,[110] ran counter to all of the three leading trends in German speculation about European politics. While his rejection of the traditional system of rivalling great powers contravened Rankean balance of power ideas, his advocacy of a supernational and superstate organization conflicted with national liberal nationalism and Hegelian interstate anarchism. By opposing the cosmopolitan idea of a legal community of Christian peoples to the prevailing political views of international relations, he resisted the movement towards anti-European

108. Ibid., p. 96. Here he included France among the states capable of conducting world policy (ch. iv, pp. 5–8). In the books of his later period he counted only North America, Russia and Britain world powers: see, e.g., Frantz: *Der Föderalismus*, pp. 399–400.

109. Frantz: *Die Wiederherstellung Deutschlands*, p. 421: 'If such a clamp is lacking, i.e. if there is no such third party, in which the political element can join that of international law, the principle of exclusivity, inherent in every state, will soon gain absolute influence. Then the states will face one another in the form of *powers*, strange and harsh to each other, which soon will lead to a pure power system, as was the case in Napoleon's time, when Germany just did not exist politically.' In this passage one may detect signs that the passionate opponent of Hegelian political philosophy had once been a Hegelian himself.

110. See Binkley: *Realism and Nationalism 1852–1871*, p. 158.

thought. But he found only few supporters[111] and gained no influence in the new Germany. He was a romantic visionary in an age of realist thought, and his ideas were a reminder of Germany's distant past rather than an inspiration for her future.

In Germany it was the traditions of thought that emphasized the social unity of Europe which foundered, and the ones that stressed the political divisions between the states which survived. While the conservative tradition went into decline after the revolutions of 1848 and the Crimean War, the progressive one came to an early end with the rise of Bismarck and the establishment of the *Reich*. While the moderate, the radical and the revolutionary criticism of the conservative system died out in the reorganized Germany, the various protests against the balance of power system failed to constitute a tradition of thought. Only the balance of power tradition of pro-European and the national liberal and the Hegelian school of anti-European thought remained.

Three positions mark the trend of German thought about the European Concert. The conservative doctrines, which were formulated by the men of the restoration and introduced in 1815, rested on the notion of European unity. The power balance theory, regenerated by Ranke and reinstated in the years before 1848, stood on the principle of balance between European unity and state individuality. The nationalist and the anarchist ideas, advanced by national liberals and Hegelians in opposition to conservative and progressive views and brought to a head in twentieth-century imperialism, stood for the doctrine of state individuality. Between the end of the Napoleonic Wars and the beginning of the First World War Germany moved from European cosmopolitanism to anti-European nationalism.

This drift of ideas reflected the course of history. The doctrines of monarchical solidarity in defence of the existing order were fostered by the tranquillity in international relations which followed the wars against France and the Congress of Vienna. The revival of the theory of power balance was promoted by the

111. One was Ottomar Schuchardt, who developed Frantz's federalist ideas along constitutional lines. The direction of his thought is indicated by the titles of his books: Frantz and Schuchardt: *Die deutsche Politik der Zukunft*; Schuchardt: *Umrisse einer Staatsverfassung für das mittlere Europa. Eine Ergänzung zur Politik der Zukunft,* and Schuchardt: *Der mitteleuropäische Bund.*

return of alliance politics after the years of congress diplomacy. The spirit of national ambition and the philosophy of state egotism were encouraged by the deterioration in international relations, which started with the Crimean War and culminated in the First World War, and by the decline of the European system, which went hand in hand with the rise of world powers.

Political thought, it may be concluded, is produced by the forces of history working on the minds of individuals. But ideas themselves are historical factors. The conservatism of the statesmen in Vienna and Berlin facilitated the partnership of Austria and Prussia in German affairs and cemented the alliance of the three autocratic monarchies in European politics. The balance of power thought of north Germans acted as an inspiration to the strengthening of Prussia and as a guide in the bolstering of Bismarck's *Reich*. And the anti-European ideas of the national liberals and the Hegelians in Prussia and Germany prepared the ground for national unification and charted the course into world politics. The shift from pro-European to anti-European thought sped Germany on a path which led, from defiance of Austria and integration of Germany, to challenge to Britain and disintegration of Europe. The German contribution to the theory of the Concert of Europe was the product of historical experience and political ambition.

Part Two

BRITISH IDEAS OF THE CONCERT OF EUROPE

INTRODUCTION

British thinkers about the Concert of Europe, like the Germans, may be divided into three broad groups, which for convenience may be called conservative, balance of power, and progressive. Each had resemblances to its German counterpart but developed distinct characteristics and took a separate course. The competition between the three had an outcome very different from that between the German thinkers.

The smallest was the conservative group. The idea of maintaining the existing dynastic order of Europe, which played so large a part in Continental conservatism, never appealed to more than a very few Englishmen. The essence of British conservatism was the principle of preserving the territorial settlement of the Vienna Congress; but that began to lose support already within a decade or two of 1815. The conservative thinkers were always outnumbered by their opponents. In the postwar period both Tories and Whigs censured the antirevolutionary activities of the congress system; and in later years Radicals attacked the policy of maintaining the Vienna settlement. Tory, Whig, and Radical ideas about the conservative Concert of Europe led up both to balance of power and to progressive thought.

The balance of power view of the Concert of Europe had roots in territorial conservatism and Tory criticism of dynastic conservatism. Those who saw the Concert of Europe as an instrument for maintaining the balance of power in Europe started by accepting the principle of territorial preservation and rejecting the doctrine of antirevolutionary intervention. Their ideas, though strongly opposed by the leaders of the Manchester School, dominated till late in the eighteen-seventies. In the Eastern crisis of those years they made way for progressive thought.

Those who may be called progressive thinkers fell into two groups. On one side were the men who saw the Concert of

Europe as an agent in the reform and civilization of the community of nations. They were the descendants of the Whig opponents of dynastic and the Radical critics of territorial conservatism. Their leading notion, of joint intervention in aid of subject peoples, had in it both the idea of political freedom, which the Whigs had set against the doctrine of repression, and the idea of national liberty, which the Radicals had opposed to the principle of immutable boundaries. Their contribution to progressive thought is here called the humanitarian set of ideas. On the other side were the thinkers who saw the Concert of Europe as a means of pacifying international society and the germ of its organization. Here their set of ideas is named the organizational version of progressive thought. Humanitarian notions dominated in the first years after the Congress of Berlin, organizational ones in the last few decades before the First World War. Though nationalists and imperialists opposed both the earlier and the later version, progressive thought established itself as the leading British tradition.

The British pattern of thought was quite different from the German. German thinkers on the whole began by upholding the Concert and then turned against it; British writers did the reverse. In Germany the nationalist and Hegelian schools of anti-European thought overpowered their conservative and progressive opponents and corrupted the balance of power tradition. In Britain the critics of conservative ideas prepared the way for balance of power and progressive thought. There the progressive tradition expired prematurely with the foundation of the German *Reich*; here it survived to inspire the establishment of the League of Nations.

Chapter One

THE CONSERVATIVE THEORY

1. SUPPORT

Dynastic conservatism

Not many British statesmen or writers saw the Concert of Europe as a union of sovereigns for the protection of thrones. England had no Gentz. But among British statesmen, especially those in close touch with Continental monarchs, there were some who gave occasional support to Metternich's ideas.

Foremost among them was Castlereagh. In the years before the conflict between Britain and her partners in the congress system had become manifest he occasionally revealed sentiments closely resembling those of the principal rulers on the Continent, with whom he was on so intimate terms.

> The immediate object to be kept in view [he wrote late in 1815] is to inspire the States of Europe, as long as we can, with a sense of the dangers which they have surmounted by their union, of the hazards they will incur by a relaxation of vigilance, to make them feel that the existing concert is their only perfect security against the revolutionary embers more or less existing in every State of Europe; and that their true wisdom is to keep down the petty contentions of ordinary times, and to stand together in support of the established principles of social order.[1]

In later years, when British opinion of the European policy of the Continental rulers had become hostile, he showed more sympathy than most. In a debate in the House of Commons in 1821 he extenuated the allied monarchs' offence of intervention by pointing to the anarchist spirit and subversive tactics with which they had to deal:

> There was now a conspiracy abroad which menaced the existence of every regular government. When that was the case, he

1. Castlereagh: *Memoirs and Correspondence*, ed. Vane, xi, 105.

was not prepared to say how far general principles like those contained in the declarations of the sovereigns might not be defended, as the means of preventing evils with which all governments were threatened. A system of universal subversion existed throughout Europe, and one revolution was made the means of giving birth to another. [2]

But though he subscribed to the notion of a revolutionary conspiracy, Castlereagh rejected the Continental doctrine of intervention. [3]

Not till revolution had moved closer to British shores did that doctrine find advocates. After the July Revolution in France and the subsequent outbreak in Belgium, Aberdeen demanded concerted action by the great powers to put an end to the state of anarchy in the Netherlands. [4] Sir Richard Vyvyan, in a debate in the House of Commons in 1831, went so far as to maintain that in cases of revolution in foreign countries intervention ought to be the rule and non-intervention the exception: 'When they beheld such a revolution as that which had taken place in Belgium, it was high time that those Powers which were anxious to preserve their own dynasties, and to maintain the tranquillity of Europe, should interfere.' [5] But it was fear of French aggression and European war, rather than horror of revolution, which inspired this doctrine in Britain.

On a few occasions English monarchs paid tribute to the notion of a union of sovereigns entertained by Continental rulers. In 1825 George IV, who often showed admiration for Metternich and veneration of the Austrian Emperor, expressed his fear of the possible effects on the revolutionaries in Europe of the intended recognition of the South American provinces: 'The King has too much reason to apprehend that the separation from our Allies, so justly and so honestly referred to by the Emperor of Austria, will very soon lead to consequences that will end in disturbing the tranquillity of Europe.' He came close to contradicting the official British interpretation of the principles of the postwar system of politics when he opposed the Quadruple Alliance to 'the Jacobins

2. *Hansard*, 2nd ser., v, col. 1257 (21 June); see also *Memoirs and Corres.*, xii, 404 and 443.
3. See below pp. 124–6.
4. F. Balfour: *The Life of George Fourth Earl of Aberdeen*, i, 281.
5. *Hansard*, 3rd ser., vi, col. 238 (18 August).

of the world (now calling themselves the Liberals)'.[6] When Victoria, at the time of the Crimean War, appealed to the Prussian king not to separate himself from the Concert of Europe in the conflict with Russia she referred to the divine responsibility and heavy obligations associated with the sacred offices of the sovereigns of those great powers 'which, since the peace of 1815, have been guarantors of treaties, guardians of civilisation, defenders of the right, and real arbiters of the Nations'.[7] George and Victoria, sharing the aristocratic notion of European politics, participated in the spirit of monarchical solidarity. But they did not subscribe to the rest of the theory of the Concert of Europe entertained by Metternich's master and Frederick William IV.

Each of the major elements in dynastic conservatism—the idea of a revolutionary conspiracy, the doctrine of antirevolutionary intervention and the notion of a close union of principal sovereigns—received occasional sympathy from British statesmen. But the complete theory found no exponent. So the Continental school of conservative thought cannot be said to have had a branch in England. Favoured with stability in her social structure and political institutions and protected against revolutionary contagion by the Channel, she was in a position to champion other ideas of the Concert of Europe.

Territorial conservatism

The interpretation that held the Concert of Europe to be an instrument for conserving the boundaries of the Vienna settlement was more dominant in British than in German conservative thought. The reduction of international and the rise in social tension in postwar Europe shifted the emphasis in Austrian conservatism from the antirevisionist to the antirevolutionary strand. Dissatisfaction with the particularist order imposed on Germany restricted the influence in north German conservatism of the principle of territorial preservation. But the British conservative thinkers, less interested than the Austrian in the social condition of the Continent and more concerned than the Prussian

6. Wellington: *Despatches, Correspondence, and Memoranda*, ii, 402 (paper of 27 January 1825).
7. *The Letters of Queen Victoria*, ed. Benson and Esher, iii, 22–3 (Letter of 17 March 1854); see also *Further Letters of Queen Victoria. From the Archives of the House of Brandenburg-Prussia*, ed. Bolitho, p. 53. In the last letter she used the term 'the Concert of Europe'.

about the territorial sovereignty of states, gave priority to maintaining the distribution of territory made in 1815. The principal advocates of this line of thought were the foreign secretaries of the postwar decades.

Castlereagh argued repeatedly that the principle of the new system of politics was territorial conservation. The Quadruple Alliance, he wrote in the circular despatch of 1 January 1816, 'could only have owed its origin to a sense of common danger; in its very nature it must be conservative; it cannot threaten either the security or the liberties of other States'.[8] The quintuple combination arranged at the Congress of Aix-la-Chapelle he defined as 'l'union et le concert pacifique qui va s'établir avec la France pour le maintien de la paix et des traités existants'.[9] The attempt of the Continental powers to turn the alliance into an anti-revolutionary institution led him to state his position more sharply. In the state paper of 5 May 1820 he wrote:

> In this Alliance as in all other human Arrangements, nothing is more likely to impair or even destroy its real utility, than any attempt to push its duties and obligations beyond the Sphere which its original Conception and understood Principles will warrant:—It was an union for the Reconquest and liberation of a great proportion of the Continent of Europe from the Military Dominion of France, and having subdued the Conqueror it took the State of Possession as established by the Peace under the Protection of the Alliance:—It never was however intended as an Union for the Government of the World, or for the Superintendence of the Internal Affairs of other States:[10]

After Castlereagh's death this position was maintained by Canning.[11] 'I was—I still am—an enthusiast for national independence . . .,' he declared in 1823.[12] 'The rule I take to be,' he wrote with regard to the Congress of Verona, 'that our engagements have reference wholly to the state of territorial possession

8. Webster: *The Foreign Policy of Castlereagh 1815–1822,* Appendix A, p. 510.
9. Wellington: *Desp., Corr. and Mem.,* vii, 168.
10. *Foundations of British Foreign Policy from Pitt (1792) to Salisbury (1902),* ed. Temperley and Penson, p. 54.
11. See *Hansard,* 2nd ser., viii, cols 873–4.
12. Temperley: *The Foreign Policy of Canning 1822–1827,* pp. 464–5.

settled at the peace; to the state of affairs between nation and nation; not . . . to the affairs of any nation within itself.'[13]

It was the Continental challenge to the British interpretation of the principles of the Concert which had induced Castlereagh and Canning to state their case for the idea of territorial preservation. A threat to the territorial order itself led a later foreign secretary to reiterate it. After the July Revolution in Paris Aberdeen reviewed the European situation in the light of the treaty of the Quadruple Alliance and the protocols and declarations of the Congress of Aix-la-Chapelle. In a dispatch to his ambassadors he wrote:

> Under these conditions there is nothing clearer than that the Great Powers must act in perfect union and concert, founded on their determination to preserve the state of territorial possession as settled in the Treaties of Vienna and Paris. The very dangers of the Revolution in France, with all its accompanying circumstances, point to the propriety of union, and acting promptly so as to avert approaching danger. The spirit of the Treaty appears to justify and to require this concert.[14]

This idea of the Concert of Europe evolved in opposition to the dynastic conservatism of the Continental rulers. Its affinity was with the balance of power theory of the Concert of Europe, its offspring, rather than with its rival twin. It was about an alliance of great powers established by treaties and formal declarations, not a union of principal sovereigns founded in common sentiments and interests; about the external freedom of the members of the states system, not the internal condition of the parts of the society of Europe; about the threat of aggression, not the danger of revolution. But the essence of the idea was conservative: preservation of the boundaries that the statesmen of 1815 had drawn in an attempt to balance the powers of Europe. It was the experience of French expansion and European war which had given rise to the idea, and fear of a recurrence which kept it up. When the danger of aggression by France receded, and new problems came to the forefront, it gave way to other ideas of the Concert of Europe. Gradually freeing themselves from the treaties of 1815 and the settlement of Vienna, British statesmen

13. Phillips: *The Confederation of Europe,* p. 275.
14. F. Balfour, *Earl of Aberdeen,* i, 262.

came to regard the Concert of Europe as an instrument for maintaining a more elastic balance of power.

2. CRITICISM

Tory criticism of dynastic conservatism

In the postwar decade British critics of the conservative theory concentrated on the dynastic strand. Both Tories and Whigs censured the antirevolutionary tenets of the Metternichian school. While members of the government attacked the doctrine of intervention, leaders of the opposition went a step further and inverted the idea of a European conspiracy.

Castlereagh, though sensitive to the dangers of revolution and sympathetic to the views of sovereigns, rejected the dynastic idea of intervention. At the time of the Congress of Troppau he told the Russian ambassador that, on viewing the spectacle presented by that meeting, he found it impossible 'not to consider the right which the Monarchs claim to judge and to condemn the actions of other States as a precedent dangerous to the liberties of the world'.[15] In the circular of 19 January 1821 he pointed out that the antirevolutionary measures proposed by the representatives of the three eastern powers at Troppau were repugnant to the fundamental laws of England. But, he continued,

> even if this decisive objection did not exist, the British Government would, nevertheless, regard the principles on which these measures rest, to be such as could not be safely admitted as a system of international law. They are of opinion that their adoption would inevitably sanction, and, in the hands of less beneficent Monarchs, might hereafter lead to, a much more frequent and extensive interference in the internal transactions of States, than they are persuaded is intended by the August Parties from whom they proceed, or can be reconcilable either with the general interest or with the efficient authority and dignity of independent Sovereigns[16]

In the House of Commons he declared that he 'could not recognize the principle that one state was entitled to interfere with another, because changes might be effected in its government in a way which the former state disapproved'.[17]

15. Webster: *The Foreign Policy,* p. 299.
16. Ibid., p. 321.
17. *Hansard,* 2nd ser., v, cols 1256–7 (21 June 1821).

To the Continental doctrine he opposed the British theory of intervention. According to this, neither trivial matters nor speculative dangers but only direct threats to national security or vital interests were valid grounds for interfering in the domestic affairs of other states. Britain could not act upon abstract and speculative principles of precaution, he asserted in the state paper of May 1820, but would be found in her place 'when actual danger menaces the System of Europe'.[18] It should be clearly understood, he emphasized in the circular of January 1821, that no government could be more prepared than the British to uphold the right of any state or states to interfere, 'where their own immediate security, or essential interests, are seriously endangered by the internal transactions of another State'. But, he continued, since only the strongest necessity could justify the assumption of this right, its exercise would always be an exception to general principles.[19] This contribution to the theory of intervention became known as the principle of non-intervention. For half a century it remained the proclaimed doctrine of most British statesmen.

In 1823 Peel, who had become Home Secretary in Liverpool's administration, protested in the House of Commons against 'that doctrine maintained by what was called the Holy Alliance, of its right of interference with the liberty of nations, by the establishment of a sort of European police for the prevention of the success of revolution wherever it might be found, and under whatever circumstances'.[20] His principle was that 'every state was sovereign and independent, and was the only judge of the reforms and modifications which were necessary in its government'. There was a qualification, however: the rights of states, like those of individuals, were subject to the interference of other states if the exercise of them tended to the general injury; but that injury 'ought not to be of an imaginary or speculative kind—it ought to

18. Temperley and Penson: *Foundations*, p. 63. See also Webster: *The Foreign Policy,* p. 283: 'All speculative policy is outside her powers. It is proposed now to overcome the *revolution*; but so long as this revolution does not appear in more distinct shape ... and do not attack materially any other State—England is not ready to combat it' (Castlereagh speaking to Lieven in October 1820).

19. Webster: *The Foreign Policy,* p. 322. See also *Hansard,* 2nd ser., iv, col. 54 (23 January 1821); and Castlereagh: *Memoirs and Correspondence,* xii, 444: ' ... the principle upon which we must always act as a State is that of non-interference pushed even to an extreme ...' (letter of 14 December 1821 to Bagot).

20. *Hansard,* 2nd ser., viii, cols 1419–20 (29 April).

be of a nature clear to the feelings and palpable to the sight of every man'; and of the necessity of making such an interference each state ought to be the chief judge. [21]

Canning, too, followed Castlereagh in opposing to what he called 'the doctrine of an European police' [22] the principle of non-intervention. 'Intimately connected as we are with the system of Europe,' he remarked after the French invasion of Spain in 1823, 'it does not follow that we are therefore called upon to mix ourselves on every occasion, with a restless and meddling activity, in the concerns of the nations which surround us.' [23] In his view, it was essential to a legitimate interference in the internal affairs of other countries 'that our interests should have been, in some way or other, affected by their condition, or by their proceedings'. [24]

But in dissociating himself from the 'areopagitical spirit' [25] of the Continental allies Canning went further than Castlereagh. Aversion to the very idea of involvement in Europe led him to oppose the entire system of diplomacy by congress. As early as the Congress of Aix-la-Chapelle he had objected in a Cabinet meeting to the system of periodical meetings of the four great powers to deal with the general affairs of Europe, foreseeing clearly that it necessarily would 'involve us deeply in all the politics of the Continent, whereas our true policy has always been not to interfere except in great emergencies, and then with a commanding force'. [26] After he had become Foreign Secretary he did more than any other man in Europe to put an end to the system. To extricate Britain and restore her independence—'for Europe . . . now and then to read England' [27]—was his aim. Britain should neither help to bolster up despotism on the Continent nor engage in a 'wild crusade' [28] to force her own system upon Europe. She should stand 'neutral not only between contending nations, but between conflicting principles'. [29]

Canning, in common with Castlereagh, combined support of the British with opposition to the Continental version of con-

21. *Hansard,* 2nd ser., viii, col. 66 (4 February 1823).
22. Ibid., viii, col. 1485 (30 April 1823).
23. Canning: *The Speeches* . . . , vi, 422.
24. Temperley: *Foreign Policy of Canning,* p. 217.
25. *Hansard,* 2nd ser., viii, col. 1483 (30 April 1823).
26. Castlereagh: *Memoirs and Corres.,* xii, 56–7.
27. Phillips: *The Confederation,* p. 278.
28. *Hansard,* 2nd ser., x, col. 82 (3 February 1824).
29. Ibid., viii, col. 1523 (30 April 1823).

servative thought about the Concert. But the stress was on the latter. It was for his criticism of dynastic rather than for his defence of territorial conservatism that he was remembered. The idea of British aloofness from Continental politics constantly reappeared in later thought.

Whig criticism of dynastic conservatism

The Whigs went further than the Tories. For the ministers, who generally were inclined to observe neutrality in the social issue, to advocate dissociation from the autocratic governments was the limit. But for the leaders of the opposition, who sided with the struggling peoples, hostility towards the oppressors was the rule. They inverted Metternich's favourite theory, and presented the union of sovereigns as a conspiracy against the peoples.

The first round of attack on dynastic principles was touched off by the publication of the peace treaties. Within months of the signing of the treaty of Quadruple Alliance Francis Horner described the new institution as an 'anti-jacobin confederacy' of powers.[30] Its aim, he wrote in a private letter, was

> to suppress by arms any appearance in future of what they call revolutionary principles, that is of whatever they may choose to call so, that is of any attempt in any country to check the abuses of royal authority, or to mend political institutions. If this is submitted to, and can be put in force, there will soon be an end of the very shadow of liberty, and of all that can be called civilization in Europe.[31]

A union of the sovereigns of three or four great military powers might be almost as dangerous, he suggested in the House of Commons, as the despotism of Napoleon, which it had replaced.[32]

The second round of criticism was touched off by the transactions of the Congress of Aix-la-Chapelle. In an open letter to Lord Holland the young John Russell compared the new system of politics with the traditional balance of power. The union of the chief sovereigns of Europe, he found, was in several important respects inferior to the system of checks and balances which it had

30. Horner: *Memoirs and Correspondence,* 2nd edn, ii, 302 (letter of 2 December 1815).
31. Ibid., ii, 303–4 (letter of 2 December 1815).
32. *Hansard,* 1st ser., xxxii, col. 780 (20 February 1816).

superseded.[33] One great evil was its readiness to interfere in the internal affairs of states: '. . . should any of these provinces, which have fallen under the sway of legitimate Monarchs, attempt to improve the form of their government, or revolt against the abuses of power, there can be no doubt that the Amphictyonic council of Sovereigns would take cognizance of the offence.' One of the principal objects of the old balance had been to protect the weaker states in the full and free enjoyment of their civil and political rights against external attacks. Internal institutions had never entered into its composition. The object of the new system was, in this respect, directly the reverse: 'Internal interference alone, . . . and with no reference to equality of territorial power, is the chief end of the new settlement. All the treaties and conventions entered into among the Sovereigns, since 1814, have this purview. In all essential matters of internal policy, things must remain as they are; otherwise the Sovereigns will interpose to keep them so.'[34] He wanted Britain to stand aloof from meetings of sovereigns. Whilst the other powers derived many advantages from this Amphictyonic council, England, who used to hold the balance in Europe, was losing her honourable name and becoming the follower and tool of the great Continental monarchs.[35]

The declarations of principles and acts of intervention issuing from the congresses in the early eighteen-twenties brought Whig criticism to culmination. But the fact that Britain by then was dissociating herself from the theory and practice of the Continental allies resulted in a tendency among the Whigs to exonerate their own country and concentrate the attack on the 'Holy Alliance' of the three eastern powers. In the House of Lords the protagonists were Grey, Holland and Lansdowne.

In the debate on the address in reply to the King's speech at the opening of the session in 1821 Grey, referring to the treatment of the King of Naples by the recent assembly of despots, complained about the arrogance of the powers of the so-called Holy Alliance. No encouragement should be given, he demanded, to 'what was called the "monarchical principle", by which it was pretended that henceforth there should be no improvement in government

33. Russell: *A Letter to the Right Honourable Lord Holland, on Foreign Politics,* 4th edn, pp. 2, 4, 7 and 46.
34. Ibid., pp. 5–6.
35. Ibid., pp. 45–7.

except what came from thrones; which was plainly saying, that the shackles of despotism should be for ever riveted on mankind'.[36] A few years later he expressed the fear that 'the grand confederacy of monarchs allied against the liberties of mankind' was about to arrange a conspiracy more formidable and dangerous than any previously seen.[37]

After the Congress of Laybach Holland referred to the new system of politics as a case of five powers confederating together 'for the express purpose of guaranteeing every government, good or bad, against the resentment of the people', and described the project as a 'diabolical attack' on the general freedom and independence of nations.[38] In 1824, when he again criticized the policy of conserving the monarchical principle, he excluded Britain and limited his attack to the Holy Alliance of the eastern powers.[39] Later the same year Lansdowne observed that all the great military powers of Europe were engaged in a confederacy on a principle which never could be acceptable to Britain. It involved 'the most despotic control over every one of the minor powers'.[40]

In the House of Commons the attack was led by Mackintosh, Brougham and Russell. After the Congress of Laybach Sir James Mackintosh referred to the sovereigns of the three eastern powers as 'imperial commissioners for exercising the office of dictator of Europe', and accused them of treating 'monarchs as their vassals, and nations as their slaves'.[41] In a debate on Naples he spoke about 'the self-constituted, usurping, tyrannical, and insolent tribunal at Laybach'.[42] Was it not true, he asked with reference to the Austrian invasion of Italy, 'that the allied sovereigns had entered into a conspiracy against the laws of nations? Was it not true that the attack on Naples was an attack on all states that attempted a reformation of the abuses of government? Could there, in the whole range of history be found conspirators against

36. *Hansard,* 2nd ser., iv, cols 9–10 (23 January); see also cols 744–5 (19 February 1821).
37. Ibid., ix, col. 189 (12 May 1823).
38. Ibid., iv, col. 1058 (2 March 1821).
39. Ibid., x, cols 39–40 (3 February).
40. Ibid., x, col. 985 (15 March).
41. Ibid., iv, col. 840 (21 February 1821).
42. Ibid., iv, col. 1378 (20 March 1821).

the peace, the repose, and the rights of nations, if these military despots were not?'[43]

An equally outspoken attack on the legitimist ideas of the allied monarchs was Brougham's speech in the debate on the address in reply to the King's speech at the opening of the session in 1823. Discussing the Congress of Verona and the disturbances in Spain, he introduced a series of quotations from various declarations of principles extracted from the past notes of Russia, Prussia and Austria with the suggestion that 'to produce any thing more preposterous, more absurd, more extravagant, better calculated to excite a mingled feeling of disgust and derision, would baffle any chancery or state-paper office in Europe'.[44] In another speech he described the doctrine of international interference, 'whenever and wherever the three despots should think fit to attack the rising liberties of the nations of Europe', as monstrous.[45]

Russell elaborated his earlier criticism. The natural selfishness of kings and the absence of a remedy against their joint encroachment made the postwar association of the great powers peculiarly liable to abuse, he explained in a speech in the House of Commons in 1824.[46] The sovereigns of the Holy Alliance were opponents of 'the glorious cause of humanity, of civilization, of science, of freedom, of every thing that dignified and adorned our common nature'. They were 'conspirators against the moral dignity of human nature', aiming 'to subdue in man all that connected him with a superior state of being, and to degrade him to a level with the brute creation'.[47] What is called the monarchical principle, he wrote in a book published the same year, is 'an expedient for closing all bright prospects of improvement to the human race, a provision for perpetual despotism, a law for eternal ignorance, a decree on the part of the sovereigns of Europe to prevent all hope of redemption from the rule of tyranny, bigotry, and vice'.[48]

The breakdown of the congress system reduced the anger of the Whigs. But their idea of a conspiracy of sovereigns took long to disappear. It remained a part of English thought as long as the Holy Alliance of the eastern governments was an influence in

43. *Hansard,* 2nd ser., v, col. 1259 (21 June 1821).
44. Ibid., viii, col. 49 (4 February).
45. Ibid., viii, col. 1531 (30 April 1823).
46. Ibid., x, col. 1234 (18 March).
47. Ibid., x, col. 1246.
48. Russell: *Memoirs of the Affairs of Europe from the Peace of Utrecht,* i, 59.

European politics. Even in the second half of the century the inverted conspiracy doctrine made an occasional reappearance, in the shape of a warning against a revival of the Holy Alliance and an outbreak of a war of principles between autocrats and democrats.[49]

Both of the ideas that British politicians opposed to the conservative doctrines of the Continental rulers survived in later thought about the Concert of Europe. While the Tory principle of non-intervention became an element in the balance of power theory, the Whig conception of the political rights of peoples found a place in the progressive theory.

Radical criticism of territorial conservatism

Compared with Germany, where a particularist constitution frustrated nationalist ambitions, Britain produced little criticism of the principle of territorial preservation. Her own boundaries had not been touched by the peace congresses and could not give rise to a demand for revision. But sympathy with the various European peoples struggling for nationhood inspired some opposition to the system of permanent frontiers. While a number of Whigs strongly objected to the principles underlying the Vienna settlement, a few Radicals assailed the doctrine of perpetuating it.

The sporadic criticism with which the parliamentary opposition greeted the territorial clauses of the peace treaties in 1816 found its way into some of the writings and speeches of the postwar generation of Whigs. Russell complained that the five confederates had calculated the limits and divisions of the territory of Europe 'for the immediate purpose of indemnifying themselves, and not with the prospective view of forming a balance for others'.[50] The pacification of Vienna seemed to him 'a compact of a few feudal lords transferring their slaves' rather than the long promised deliverance of Europe.[51] He did not think it possible to maintain the partitions agreed upon. While there was nothing in the spirit or letter of these treaties to stop any two great sovereigns from arranging an exchange of territory and thus unsettling the balance of power for the other parties to the alliance, the fear of

49. See Stratford de Redcliffe's speech in the House of Lords on 22 July 1864 (*Hansard*, 3rd ser., clxxvi, cols 1879–84).
50. Russell: *A Letter*, p. 7.
51. Ibid.: *Memoirs of the Affairs of Europe*, i, 55.

revolution would prevent the others from hazarding a war to redress that disturbance of the balance.[52]

Grey attacked the Vienna settlement on the same grounds. The revolt in Belgium led him to accuse the statesmen of 1815 of having set aside the principle of balance and ignored the wishes of the peoples. 'Instead of acting on the principle of the balance of Europe, which would protect the weak against the strong,' he said in the House of Lords in 1830, 'we have departed from that principle, and formed alliances upon principles of confiscation and division, in accordance with which we have transferred one kingdom to another, without regard to the sentiments or to the interests of those who were transferred. From the first moment, those transfers have never allowed to Europe an hour's security.'[53] It was on the traditional principle of the balance of power rather than the novel idea of the national rights of peoples that the Whigs based their criticism of the new order.

The Radical case against conservation of boundaries rested on the idea of nationality. The Belgian revolt, a national challenge to the existing order, drew a sharp attack on the principle of immutability from Joseph Hume, a Radical member of the House of Commons. In a debate in 1830 he spoke about the disgraceful parcelling out of Belgium which had taken place in 1815. Inveighing against the idea 'that those treaties which it was said were to pacify Europe, and which had been found to have exactly the opposite effect, were, notwithstanding, still to be maintained', he asked, 'Was it not time for the House to hesitate, to doubt that policy which might formerly have appeared wisdom, but which was now proved not to be so?'[54]

The Radical leaders of the next generation were equally critical of territorial conservatism, but concentrated their attack on the balance of power. The following generation, however, produced a Radical who had something to say about the Vienna settlement and the Concert of Europe. In 1887 the historian Edward Freeman delivered two lectures at Oxford in which he surveyed the past fifty years of European history. It was a period of national revolts against the settlement of 1815, he found. The events of 1830 were 'the first great and successful revolt, the first assertion on a great

52. Russell: *A Letter,* pp. 7 and 46–7.
53. *Hansard,* 3rd ser., i, col. 39 (2 November).
54. Ibid., i, col. 82, incorrectly numbered 88 (2 November); see also ii, col. 695 (18 February 1831).

scale of the doctrine that it is not for certain sovereigns or diplomatists to meet together and settle the destinies of nations, but that it was for the nations to settle their destinies for themselves'. The events of 1848, 1859–60, 1866 and 1871 were assertions of the same doctrine on a still larger scale.[55]

The target of Freeman's attack was the Concert of Europe, which had imposed the original settlement and persistently tried to keep it up:

> In the whole history of political language it would be hard to find a stranger use of a word than that use of the word 'Europe' to which we have been some years past daily accustomed. 'Europe', the 'will of Europe', the 'mandate of Europe', the 'concert of Europe', are phrases which have been of late in every mouth. What do they mean? Certainly not an agreement among the nations of Europe, not even an agreement among the princes of Europe. What 'Europe' means in these now every-day phrases is simply six powers—five nations and a family—who have received no commission to act in the name of their fellows, but who speak and act as if they were so commissioned, who expect their will to be obeyed, simply because they have the physical strength to make men obey it.

He denied that the physical strength of the body of powers that some people called the 'European Aeropagus' was accompanied by any moral force. Though the despots and diplomatists of the great powers were inclined to think that their signatures to a document bound, by some legal force, those who had never signed it or been consulted about it, right was on the side of the rising nations. So, in the last resort, was might. Over and over again within the last fifty years

> have we seen the wisdom and the will of 'Europe' give way to the higher wisdom, the stronger will, of the nations for whom 'Europe' sought to lay down the law. We need not despair of hearing the word some day formally go forth that the nations are to be free to act for themselves, as the word went forth not so long ago that Europe was to do everything for or against

55. Freeman: *Four Oxford Lectures, 1887: Fifty Years of European History and Teutonic Conquest in Gaul and Britain,* pp. 3–4.

them, and that they were not to lift a hand or speak a word in their own cause.[56]

The Radical conception of an antirevisionist was as different from the Whig notion of an antirevolutionary Concert of Europe as territorial from dynastic conservatism. In the Radical view, the Concert was a body of great powers determined upon maintaining the existing boundaries, rather than a union of principal sovereigns bent on upholding the established governments; an oligarchy of states opposed to rising nations, rather than a conspiracy of monarchs against struggling peoples; a brake on territorial revision along national lines, rather than an obstacle to political reform on constitutional principles. But between the idea that the Radicals set against territorial conservatism and the principle that the Whigs opposed to dynastic conservatism there was affinity. In the second half of the century the Radical notion of national liberty joined the Whig principle of political freedom in the humanitarian conception of the Concert of Europe.[57] Both ideas became important elements of the progressive tradition of thought.

The pattern of British ideas

There was a spectrum of British thought about the conservative Concert. On the extreme right was dynastic conservatism, supported occasionally by a few Tories; next to that territorial conservatism, advocated by foreign secretaries; in the middle Tory criticism of dynastic conservatism; then Whig criticism of dynastic conservatism; and on the extreme left Radical criticism of territorial conservatism. The division between the thoughts advanced in support and those developed in opposition to the Concert of Europe ran between the second and the third part of the spectrum. But there was no break in continuity at this point. Both Castlereagh and Canning straddled the dividing line between territorial conservatism and Tory criticism of dynastic conservatism, the former leaning to the right and the latter to the left.

56. Freeman: *Four Oxford Lectures*, pp. 55–8. The family that together with five nations made up 'Europe' was the Habsburgs.
57. Freeman himself demonstrated the connection between Radical criticism and progressive thought. In the two lectures of 1887 he launched a retrospective attack on territorial conservatism. In an earlier work he illustrated the progressive theory: the deliverance of the subject nations of Turkey, he wrote in the preface of his *The Ottoman Power in Europe, its Nature, its Growth, and its Decline*, 'ought to be, if possible, the work of all Europe' (p. xii; see also pp. 286–7 and 311).

These sets of ideas, like any two adjacent parts of the spectrum, complemented each other.

The chronological order of the various ideas followed roughly the spectrum from right to left. The earliest contribution was Castlereagh's partial support of the antirevolutionary and the latest Freeman's passionate criticism of the antirevisionist Concert of Europe. This development from one extreme to the other reflected a progression from sympathy with sovereigns and interest in the security of states to respect for peoples and concern for the freedom of nations.

Except for the scattered dynastic notions, which hardly amounted to a coherent view of the Concert of Europe, each of these groups of ideas sprang from aversion to established doctrines of conservative thought. Territorial conservatism was advanced as an alternative to the Continental theory of dynastic conservatism. The Tory and the Whig criticism were directed at the dynastic, the Radical at the territorial version of European conservatism. The dissent and protest which made up most of the early English speculation about the Concert of Europe acted as seed beds for the later thought. Each of the ideas that these groups of thinkers set against the doctrines of their rivals or opponents became an element in one of the two traditions that gained ascendancy later in the century. The notion of the integrity of states, which was inherent in territorial conservatism, joined the principle of non-intervention, which was the essence of Tory criticism, in the balance of power tradition. The Whig idea of political freedom met the Radical doctrine of national liberty in the progressive tradition. The connection between thoughts about the conservative Concert of Europe and the ideas of the balance of power and the progressive thinkers might be expressed diagrammatically:

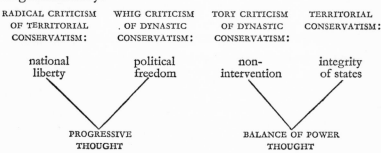

RADICAL CRITICISM OF TERRITORIAL CONSERVATISM:	WHIG CRITICISM . OF DYNASTIC CONSERVATISM:	TORY CRITICISM OF DYNASTIC CONSERVATISM:	TERRITORIAL CONSERVATISM:
national liberty	political freedom	non-intervention	integrity of states

PROGRESSIVE THOUGHT

BALANCE OF POWER THOUGHT

Chapter Two

THE BALANCE OF POWER THEORY

1. DEVELOPMENT

While in Germany balance of power ideas of the Concert of Europe arose as a reaction, in Britain they evolved in succession to conservative thought. The German balance of power theory started off as a challenge to the dynastic conservatism of the post-war decades, and established itself as a rival interpretation of European politics but ended up succumbing to the schools of thought opposed to the Concert of Europe. Its British counterpart was at first closely intertwined with the territorial conservatism of the earlier Tories but gradually liberated itself from the tie with the Vienna settlement and eventually made way for the progressive theory. For more than half a century the balance of power ideas dominated British speculation about the Concert of Europe. They were developed by statesmen and endorsed by a number of international lawyers.

It was Castlereagh who applied the old British principle of maintaining the European balance of power to the new system of politics, and so linked the traditional theory of the balance to the emergent Concert of Europe. In the Treaty of Chaumont, largely his work, the link was established formally. Article XVI, the basis of the Quadruple Alliance and one of the sources of the Concert of Europe, defined the aim of the Treaty as 'the maintenance of the Balance of Europe, to secure the repose and independence of the Powers, and to prevent the invasions which for so many years have devastated the world'.[1] Castlereagh's idea, which he developed in the last years of the war and subsequently put into practice, was one of general security. Its essence was the notion of a body of great powers always ready to defend the established balance of power by combining against any state which was determined to disturb the existing territorial order. Though the

1. Quoted in Phillips: *The Confederation,* p. 78.

possibility of French aggression was uppermost in his mind, the system of combination was in principle directed against any state 'whose perverted policy or criminal ambition shall first menace the repose in which all have a common interest'. [2] The characteristic elements of this idea were the principle of solidarity of the great powers and the doctrine of conservation of the boundaries of 1815. Both reflected Castlereagh's peculiar experience of European politics.

Solidarity implied British involvement in Continental politics. The French challenge and the coalition war had drawn Britain into Europe and convinced her Foreign Secretary of the need for some form of lasting commitment. 'The wish of the Government is to connect their interests in peace and in war with those of the Continent,' he wrote from Chatillon in 1814. Now that Britain might look forward to a return to ancient principles, 'she was ready to make the necessary sacrifices on her part to reconstruct a Balance in Europe'. [3] The engagement he had in mind was not partnership in an exclusive connection with any particular state for the pursuit of special interests, but participation in a general system of great powers to safeguard the repose and preserve the peace of Europe. [4] This idea of solidarity and involvement found expression in his advocacy of the Quadruple Alliance and the congress system.

The other distinctive element of Castlereagh's conception was equally closely connected with the part he had played in European history. It was inevitable that, after his exertions at the Congress of Vienna, he should wish to preserve the territorial settlement contained in the peace treaties. Till his death he rested his balance policy on the Vienna arrangements. Maintaining a balance to him meant upholding the existing boundaries. It was this identification of European balance of power with the established distribution of territory which enabled him to combine the balance of power theory with the conservative theory of the Concert of Europe.

One of the virtues of the peacetime alliance of great powers, he explained in the House of Commons in 1821, was 'that it was hardly possible for the human mind to conceive any system of

2. Webster: *The Foreign Policy,* Appendix A, p. 512 (circular despatch of 1 January 1816).
3. Phillips: *The Confederation,* footnote, pp. 68–9.
4. Castlereagh: *Memoirs and Corres.,* ix, 460. Webster: *The Foreign Policy,* Appendix A, p. 512.

territorial aggrandizement which did not find in it a counter-action to its own impurity [*sic*]'.⁵ The idea of security against aggression through a system of common defence of a stable territorial order was Castlereagh's contribution to the balance of power theory of the Concert of Europe. Later statesmen, with less or no experience of coalition war and European reconstruction, had other ideas.

Palmerston's references to the doctrine of the balance of power were more explicit than Castlereagh's. In the age of European war and peace congresses, when the idea enjoyed general acceptance, it was possible to take its meaning for granted. Castlereagh could let it pervade his European thought without attempting to extract it for definition and analysis. Later in the century, when Radical criticism of the notion forced it into the open, statesmen were compelled to clarify their use of the term. A passionate attack by John Bright in the debate of 31 March 1854 on the declaration of war provoked Palmerston to define and defend the doctrine in the House of Commons:

> Why, Sir, call it what you like—'balance of power', or any other expression—it is one which has been familiar to the minds of all mankind from the earliest ages in all parts of the globe. 'Balance of power' means only this—that a number of weaker States may unite to prevent a stronger one from acquiring a power which should be dangerous to them, and which should overthrow their independence, their liberty, and their freedom of action. It is the doctrine of self-preservation. It is the doctrine of self-defence, with the simple qualification that it is combined with sagacity and with forethought, and an endeavour to prevent imminent danger before it comes thundering at your doors.

Loss of independence, he asserted, was a calamity far worse than war.⁶ When Cobden, in the process of censuring the Government's attitude to the German war against Denmark in 1864, criticized the doctrines of intervention and balance of power, Palmerston again offered the House a definition. This time he approached the balance from the angle of international society rather than of individual states:

5. *Hansard,* 2nd ser., iv, col. 867 (21 February). If, for example, Austria took steps towards a permanent occupation of Naples she would immediately meet opposition from other states, he explained.
6. *Hansard,* 3rd ser., cxxxii, col. 279.

Why, it is a doctrine founded on the nature of man. It means that it is to the interest of the community of nations that no one nation should acquire such a preponderance as to endanger the security of the rest; and it is for the advantage of all that the smaller Powers should be respected in their independence and not swallowed up by their more powerful neighbours. That is the doctrine of the balance of power, and it is a doctrine worthy of being acted upon.[7]

For him, balance of power was the supreme principle of foreign policy.

In the Concert of Europe Palmerston saw an instrument for maintaining the balance of power. When faced with the danger of a great power subduing a weaker state he often resorted to European concert. In the early eighteen-thirties, after the July Revolution and the Belgian uprising, he met the threat of a French invasion of Belgium through a conference of the five great powers. In mediating between Holland and Belgium, he explained, the representatives assembled in London were looking after the security of their states.[8] The powers of Europe were 'bound to see that the ancient territories of Holland were not encroached upon' and entitled to interfere to protect their interests.[9] But the outstanding example was the Eastern question. At an early stage Palmerston had reached the conclusion that 'the integrity and independence of the Ottoman Empire are necessary to the maintenance of the tranquillity, the liberty, and the balance of power in the rest of Europe'.[10] Here the primary danger was of a Russian attempt to gain dominating influence through solitary intervention. Rejecting all suggestions for settling the affairs of Turkey 'by the single independent and self-regulated interference of any one Power, acting according to its own will or without concert with any other Power',[11] he repeatedly advocated a diplomatic concert between the five powers.[12] Through a common course of action he hoped

7. *Hansard,* 3rd ser., clxxvi, col. 1280 (8 July).
8. Webster: *The Foreign Policy of Palmerston, 1830–1841,* i, p. 108.
9. *Hansard,* 3rd ser., ii, col. 702 (18 February 1831).
10. Quoted in Palmerston: *Opinions and Policy . . .* , p. 246 (11 July 1833).
11. Webster: *The Foreign Policy of Palmerston,* 11, 594.
12. See, e.g., Ashley: *The Life and Correspondence of Henry John Temple Viscount Palmerston,* i, 352–3; and *The Foreign Affairs of Great Britain administered by the Right Honourable Henry John Viscount Palmerston,* pp. 241–2.

to restrain the ambitious power and maintain the peace of Europe.

The idea of balance of power through combined action of great powers reappeared in a different shape in his defence of the Crimean War. Once it had become clear that Russia intended to swallow up part of Turkey, it was 'the duty of the other countries of Europe to prevent such enormous aggrandisement of one Power as that which would result from such a change', he insisted in the House of Commons. [13] It was a question of teaching Russia that there were limits to her conquests, 'that in spite of the power which a Sovereign may be able to sway—in spite of the military resources which he is able to command—that there does exist in the Powers of Europe a respect for the principles of national independence . . .'. [14] Behind Palmerston's conception of the Concert of Europe lurked Castlereagh's idea of general security.

But their notions of the nature of the Concert and the position of its members were far from identical. Castlereagh thought of the postwar system as a standing organization which involved each of the great powers in its functions. Palmerston saw the Concert rather as a diplomatic instrument to be called into action when required. The difference was between a mechanism capable of automatic operation and a device available for deliberate application. While Castlereagh was inclined to see the system as the subject and the powers as objects, Palmerston regarded each power as a subject and the institution as an object. Of course, the difference was to a large extent a product of the change from the congress system established in the postwar years to the conference method resorted to in Palmerston's age, from a formal machinery operating continually to an informal practice resurrected occasionally. But it also reflected contrasts of temperament and philosophy between the two men. Castlereagh was a good European, Palmerston a passionate nationalist. Sharing Canning's distrust of the reactionary governments of the Eastern powers, he followed him in reducing European commitment and concentrating on British interests. Conscious of Britain's proud position in the world and her traditional role as the holder of the balance in Europe, he preferred a free hand to binding association. [15] Concert

13. *Hansard,* 3rd ser., cxxx, col. 1035 (20 February 1854).
14. Ibid., cxxxii, col. 280–1 (31 March 1854).
15. *Opinions and Policy*, p. 407; see also p. 471 ('I hold with respect to alliances, that England is a power sufficiently strong, to steer her own course, and not to tie herself as an unnecessary appendage to the policy of any other Government') and pp. 472–3.

of powers, though often enlisted, was only one among several means employed by Palmerston to maintain the balance of power. The idea of the Concert of Europe was less important in his than in Castlereagh's thought about European politics.

Both statesmen thought of the Concert of Europe as a means for maintaining balance of power. But their notions of the end differed almost as much as their conceptions of the means. Palmerston's idea of the balance of power was less static than Castlereagh's. Though Palmerston acknowledged the territorial treaties of 1815 to be 'the basis of the European system',[16] he did not consider a strict preservation of the peace settlement a prerequisite of power balance. If he believed that a proposed change in the established order would disturb the balance, he would contend for the treaties. For example, in 1851 he rejected an Austrian and Prussian suggestion for a reform of the German Confederation on the grounds that such a revision of the territorial arrangements of 1815 would upset the balance and endanger the interests of Europe.[17] And in 1863 he turned down a French proposal for a European congress to amend national boundaries with the comment that France was always trying to get rid of the Treaty of Vienna, which was England's 'main security against encroachments by France'.[18] But if he thought that a particular alteration in the old order would stabilize the balance, or would be desirable on other grounds and leave the balance undisturbed, he was prepared to bring it about or willing to accept it. In the Belgian crisis he sacrificed the boundaries of Holland to gain security against aggression by France. In 1859 he was inclined to prefer the claims of Italian nationalism to the rights of Austrian legitimacy, and thought that the British Government should not miss any opportunity that might present itself 'of doing good to Italy by means of a Conference'.[19] Palmerston saw that the idea of the balance of power transcended the reality of the established distribution of territory. When adherence to the political principle conflicted with respect for the legal fact, he put politics above law. For Castlereagh there was no such conflict. Here, too, the difference in thought was due, partly, to a change in the political

16. *Hansard,* 3rd ser., clv, col. 1241 (8 August 1859).
17. Gillessen: *Lord Palmerston und die Einigung Deutschlands,* p. 139.
18. Bell: *Lord Palmerston,* ii, 351.
19. *Hansard,* 3rd ser., clv, col. 1241 (8 August).

situation of Europe and, partly, to contrasts of character between the two men. For a chief architect of the new order, who ended his life in a Europe still dominated by the recollections of war and the experience of restoration, it was not possible to take a detached view of the territorial arrangements. But for a later statesman, who lived to see the work of the Congress lose correspondence to the condition of Europe, it was natural to view the Vienna Treaties in historical perspective. Castlereagh, lacking in feeling for the emerging nationalities and gifted with little imagination, could be content with the established territorial order. But Palmerston, inspired by sympathy with the struggling peoples and endowed with resource, could find scope for improvement in the map of Europe. While Castlereagh embedded the idea of the balance of power in the legal order, Palmerston overhauled the legal order on the principle of the balance of power. By extracting the political idea from its legal setting, Palmerston helped to liberate the balance of power tradition from the conservative way of thinking about the Concert of Europe.

John Russell, too, played an important part in the development of this tradition of thought. The essence of his conception of the balance of power was the idea of general security. The system of the balance of power, he observed in a historical survey of European affairs published in 1824, corrected the worst of the possible effects of war, namely loss of independence: 'Europe being divided into many separate states, it has been the established policy of all, that when any one, by its aggrandizement, threatened the general safety, the rest should unite to defend their independence.'[20] In the nineteenth century this system was managed by the Concert of Europe.

In Russell's view, concert between great powers was essential to the maintenance of power balance: 'I say that by alliance with those powers of Europe, so much interested in the preservation of the balance of power by continual and vigilant attention to the events which from time to time arise affecting that balance—you only can succeed in maintaining that peace and preserving that balance.'[21] When he believed that the ambitions of one of the great powers endangered the integrity of a neighbouring state and the security of Europe, he turned to a combination of the others

20. Russell: *Memoirs of the Affairs of Europe,* i, 23–4.
21. *Hansard,* 3rd ser., lvi, col. 61 (26 January 1841).

for protection and defence. In the East the danger was Russia. In 1854 he defended in the House of Commons the plan for preventing her from dominating Turkey by admitting the Sultan to the general system of Europe, and thus allowing him to 'look to the Powers of Europe, singly or united, to maintain him, as they maintain the other States of Europe in their possession'.[22] In the West it was France he feared. 'Whatever may be the mature decision of the French nation,' he wrote, even after the Franco-Prussian War, 'the other Powers of Europe are sufficiently warned; England and Italy, Germany and Prussia, Austria and Russia will do well when the Imperial Eagle flies from the towers of Notre Dame to make treaties of alliance and prepare for action.'[23] The idea of the Concert of Europe played a greater part in his than in Palmerston's thought about European politics.

Russell was more European in outlook than Palmerston, though less than Castlereagh. Palmerston, aware that the interests of Britain often coincided with those of the Continental powers, regarded the Concert of Europe as an instrument which in particular situations could be used for maintaining the balance of power. But Russell, convinced that Britain 'has duties to Europe as she has duties to her own people',[24] saw it as a system which Britain could not leave without endangering the balance of power. Whereas Palmerston manipulated the institution, Russell approached it in a spirit of participation. But he did not entertain the idea of formal commitment to a standing organization so characteristic of Castlereagh. In his earlier years he regretted that Britain, the traditional holder of the European balance, had descended from her lofty station to truckle to the Holy Alliance of the Continental powers;[25] and in later years he rejected any suggestion for the establishment of a new Areopagus of great powers.[26] Voluntary participation in an informal system was his idea of European engagement. National independence was both the aim and the condition of involvement in the affairs of the Continent.

As regards his notions of the character of the Concert and the position of Britain, Russell stood between Castlereagh and

---

22. *Hansard,* 3rd ser., cxxxv, col. 605 (24 July); see also cxxxviii, col. 1479–80.
23. Russell: *Recollections and Suggestions 1813–1873,* pp. 451–2.
24. *Hansard,* 3rd ser., clv, col. 1225 (8 August 1859).
25. *Hansard,* 2nd ser., x, col. 1234 (18 March 1824).
26. Russell: *Selections from Speeches,* ii, 345–6 (letter of 24 December 1860).

Palmerston. But in his conception of the function of the institution he surpassed Palmerston in liberating the balance of power from the settlement of Vienna. As Palmerston's foreign secretary in 1863 he declared it to be the conviction of the Government 'that the main provisions of the Treaty of 1815 are in full force; that the greater number of those provisions have not been in any way disturbed; and that on those foundations rests the balance of power in Europe'. [27] However, he was always highly critical of the order of 1815. [28] As a persistent champion of national liberty, he found it difficult to accept a distribution of territory which conflicted with the ambitions of nations. As willing as Palmerston to sacrifice the letter to preserve the spirit of the peace treaties and even more anxious than him to revise the map in the interest of the new nations, he went a stage further in divesting the political idea of its legal dress. Russell's contribution to the balance of power theory of the Concert of Europe was the idea of general security on the basis of an evolving territorial structure.

The next major statesman to contribute to this group of ideas was Gladstone. Though the term rarely appeared in his speeches and writings, the idea of the balance of power clearly had a place in his speculation about European politics. The theory of the Concert of Europe that he held between the Crimean War and the Congress of Berlin had as its base the principle of general security. In crises of European politics it was laid bare. Surveying the results of the Crimean War and the Paris Congress, he explained to the House of Commons in 1856 that the great benefit achieved was

> the great physical as well as moral demonstration which may fairly be said to have been made by all Europe, and which has impressed upon the mind of Russia the great lesson that the opinion of Europe with respect to her tendencies to aggrandisement, whether they arose from policy, or a supposed necessity, they were such as to render it a duty upon Europe to combine all the Powers for the repression of those tendencies. [29]

27. Russell: *Selections from Speeches,* ii, 424.
28. For an early example, see his speech in the House of Commons on 16 February 1830, in which he warned against 'wire-drawn refinements on the preservation of the balance of power' and spoke for the liberation of suppressed peoples (*Hansard,* 2nd ser., xxii, cols 548–9).
29. *Hansard,* 3rd ser., cxlii, col. 96 (6 May).

In an analysis of the situation created by the Franco-Prussian War, written in 1870, he said about the Germans that 'it is idle to apprehend that they have before them a career of universal conquest or absolute predominance, and that the European family is not strong enough to correct the eccentricities of its peccant and obstreperous members'.[30] In 1878 he declared himself willing to support the policy of opposing any Russian project of aggressive nature in Eastern Europe but made it a condition that 'the resistance should be conducted on the lines of European concert'.[31] In common with Castlereagh, Palmerston and Russell, he thought that in emergencies the function of the Concert of Europe was to provide collective military action.

But in Gladstone's system of general security the Concert of Europe was much more than an emergency measure for dealing with dangerous aggression. It was a lasting union for the preservation of the peace of Europe and the protection of the rights of states.

> There is but one way of maintaining permanently what I may presume to call the great international policy and law of Europe— [he declared in the House of Commons in 1855], but one way of keeping within bounds any one of the Powers possessed of such strength as France, England, or Russia, if it be bent on an aggressive policy, and that is, by maintaining not so much great fleets, or other demonstrations of physical force, which I believe to be really an insignificant part of the case, but the moral union—the effective concord of Europe.

Britain should rely on that union instead of seeking security through alliances.[32]

In his speech at West Calder in 1879 he listed as the third of six sound principles of foreign policy:

> . . . to strive to cultivate and maintain, ay, to the very uttermost, what is called the concert of Europe; to keep the Powers of Europe in union together. And why? Because by keeping all in union together you neutralize and fetter and bind up the selfish aims of each . . . common action is fatal to selfish aims.

30. Gladstone: *Gleanings of Past Years, 1843–78*, iv, 249, 'Germany, France, and England'.
31. Gladstone: *The Paths of Honour and of Shame*, pp. 26–7 (25 February).
32. *Hansard*, 3rd ser., cxxxix, cols 1810–11 (3 August).

> Common action means common objects; and the only objects for
> which you can unite together the Powers of Europe are objects
> connected with the common good of them all.[33]

The development in the attitude to European solidarity and Continental involvement had come full circle. By contending for the
idea of general security through a standing association of great
powers and in accepting the principle of British commitment,
Gladstone had returned to the position of the founder of the
balance of power tradition. But his conception of the nature of the
Concert of Europe was not the same as Castlereagh's. Whereas
Castlereagh's union was a system of states based on a formal
alliance, Gladstone's was a family of nations held together by
moral bonds. Castlereagh's idea was the germ, Gladstone's the
fruit, of the balance of power tradition of thought.

The process of releasing the balance of power tradition from
the Vienna settlement, started by Palmerston and continued by
Russell, was completed by Gladstone. His conception of general
security did not rest on the treaties of 1815. A sympathy with the
democratic and nationalist movements on the Continent which in
passion exceeded both Palmerston's and Russell's did not allow
him to subordinate just claims of peoples to the antiquated rights
of the states. Guided by the rights of natural law rather than the
titles of positive law, he was able to champion the principles of
equality and independence of states without insisting on maintenance of the territorial treaties. Concerned with the morality of
international society more than with the facts of power politics,
he could denounce acts of aggression and attempts at universal
dominion without sanctifying the established order. Natural law
and international morality provided the setting of Gladstone's
contribution to the balance of power theory of the Concert of
Europe. No sooner had the political idea of the balance tradition
finally parted company with the legal principles of territorial
conservatism than it coupled with the moral ideals of progressive
thought.

Gladstone's role in the development of British speculation
about the Concert of Europe may be compared to Castlereagh's.
Both acted as hinges. By combining two different sets of ideas,
each eased the transition from one way of thinking to another and
started a new tradition of thought. Castlereagh, while maintaining

33. Gladstone: *Political Speeches in Scotland . . . 1879*, pp. 115–16.

the principle of territorial preservation, advanced the idea of general security. Gladstone, while subscribing to the idea of general security, developed the notion of internationally organized progress. Both subordinated the former element of their contribution to the latter. Castlereagh wanted to conserve the boundaries in order to gain security; Gladstone strove for security for the sake of improving the condition of international society. Seeing general security as the supreme end, Castlereagh could be content with a system which prevented aggression. The great benefit of the peacetime alliance, he found, was that it provided counteraction to any attempt at aggrandizement.[34] But Gladstone aimed higher. The point of the union of great powers, in his view, was that it neutralized the selfish drives of each and channelled their combined energy into the pursuit of common objects. Pointing to regions where Christians suffered persecution as fields suitable for concerted action, he aimed ultimately at civilization of the world. Castlereagh, with the past on his mind, concentrated on the search for European peace and security; but Gladstone, looking far into the future, set his heart upon the advance of Christian civilization.

The same development of the balance of power tradition can be seen in other politicians. The first stage was the crisis preceding the Crimean War. When Clarendon, foreign secretary in Aberdeen's Cabinet, told the Lords in 1853 that 'not only the Porte, but Austria, Prussia, England, and France, are all acting cordially together in order to check designs which they consider inconsistent with the balance of power, or with those territorial limits which have been established by various treaties',[35] he was implying a distinction between the function of balancing power and that of maintaining boundaries. And when Aberdeen, once a supporter of conservative ideas, wrote to Gladstone the same year

34. See above, p. 119. It may be useful here to recapitulate Castlereagh's contribution to the theory of the Concert of Europe. First, he sympathized with the Continental rulers in their fear of revolutionary conspiracy; second, he insisted that the principle of the new system of politics was territorial conservation; third, he rejected the Continental doctrine of antirevolutionary intervention; and, fourth, he maintained that the function of the union of great powers was to uphold the balance of power laid down in the territorial settlement of 1815. Hence Castlereagh appears under four of the headings I have introduced to distinguish the various strands of British postwar thought about the Concert, namely dynastic conservatism, territorial conservatism, Tory criticism of dynastic conservatism, and balance of power thought.
35. *Hansard*, 3rd ser., cxxix, col. 1423 (8 August).

that, 'after all, it is the exclusion of Russia, rather than the preservation of the Turks, that we ought to have in view',[36] he was illustrating the tendency of balance thought to become divorced from the principle of territorial conservation. The second stage of the development, the approach to progressive thinking, was hastened by the Eastern crisis of the seventies and consummated during Gladstone's second government. In 1880 Odo Russell, ambassador in Berlin, wrote to Granville, his foreign secretary, that he believed that the European Concert 'compels the Powers to behave well and is a guarantee against surprizes [*sic*] in the East', and added, 'Besides which the European Concert is the only force, I believe, through which it will be possible to put a stop to bloodshed and atrocities in Turkey later on'.[37] Here he was going beyond the idea of the balance of power and entering the assumptions of progressive thought.

Some of the writings of international lawyers, too, show a tendency to depart from the principles of territorial conservatism and move towards the tenets of progressive thought. Travers Twiss, professor of international law at King's College, London, from 1852 till 1855 and then regius professor of civil law at Oxford till 1870, marked the original position. He started volume one of *The Law of Nations Considered as Independent Political Communities,* published for the first time in 1861, with the Peace of Westphalia on the grounds that it had ushered in a new era in the intercourse of commonwealths. The Treaties of Munster and Osnabruck had not only been the first practical recognition on the part of the nations of Europe of the principle of territorial sovereignty but had also supplied 'a groundwork for an European Concert to up-hold that Principle'.[38] They had laid the foundation for a balance of power amongst the greater states. To maintain this had been the object of the European Concert ever since:

> The Treaties of Utrecht in the early part of the last century were a solemn affirmation of the Right of Coalition against any Power that should seek to disturb the European Equilibrium, and the Records of the last Congress of Paris bear evidence that

36. Gordon: *The Earl of Aberdeen,* p. 240 (3 December).
37. *Letters from the Berlin Embassy, Selections from the Private Correspondence of British Representatives at Berlin and Foreign Secretary Lord Granville 1871–1874, 1880–1885.,* ed. P. Knaplund, p. 153 (10 July).
38. Preface, pp. iii–iv.

the Spirit, which dictated those Treaties, is still the governing Spirit of the European family of Nations. [39]

Since 1815 the aim of the great powers had been to uphold the European equilibrium laid down in the Vienna treaties. [40] Preventing a disturbance of the balance of power to him meant preserving the territorial stipulations of positive law. For Twiss, ultimately concerned with the principle of territorial sovereignty, as for Castlereagh, preoccupied with security, the idea of territorial conservation was an intrinsic element of the balance of power conception of the European Concert.

However, already half a dozen years earlier a lawyer rather more important than Twiss had taken steps to divorce the two sets of ideas. Robert Phillimore, between 1852 and 1857 a member of the House of Commons, where he followed his friend Gladstone and supported Aberdeen's government, and in later years a judge, wrote four volumes under the title *Commentaries upon International Law*. In the first one, which appeared in the year of the outbreak of the Crimean War, he stated that the principle of the balance of power had been, on several important occasions, 'most formally and distinctly recognised as an essential part of the system of International Law'. [41] It was a corollary of the principle of self-defence and a valid ground for intervention. Though he did not use the term 'the European Concert', he gave many examples from the period since 1815 of concerted action by the great powers for the preservation of the balance of power. [42] But in his view the function of maintaining a balance was not circumscribed by the territorial arrangements of treaties. The maintenance of the doctrine of the balance of power, he wrote,

does not require that all existing Powers should retain exactly their present territorial possessions, but rather that no single Power should be allowed to increase them in a manner which threatens the liberties of other States. The doctrine properly

39. Twiss: *The Law of Nations*, i, Preface, p. viii; see also vol. ii, 16.
40. This point was implied in his observation that the five great powers had recorded in several important international Acts, 'That the Balance of Power is a principle at the foundation of the Positive Law of Europe, and that the Powers which were Parties to the Treaties of Vienna acted upon that principle in framing the Great European Settlement of 1815'. (*Law of Nations*, i, 153).
41. Vol. i, 456.
42. Phillimore: *Commentaries,* i, 456–66.

understood does not imply a pedantic adherence to the particular system of equilibrium maintained by existing arrangements, but to such an alteration of it as the Right of Self-defence, acting by way of prevention, would authorise other Powers in opposing. [43]

Though he admitted the doctrine to the system of international law, he thought of it as a principle of European politics. For him, as for Palmerston and Russell, the political system of the balance of power transcended the legal order of the distribution of territory.

The final stage was indicated by T. E. Holland, Chichele professor of international law and diplomacy at Oxford from 1874 to 1910. In the introduction to a collection of documents, which he published in 1885 under the title *The European Concert in the Eastern Question*, he outlined the background to the tutelage of Turkey by the Concert of Europe. It was the result of both sympathy for the races subjected to Turkish rule and jealousy with Russia encroaching upon the Ottoman Empire: 'On the one hand, the Turkish Empire is placed, as it were, under the tutelage of Europe; while, on the other hand, the claim of any single power to settle the destinies of that empire without the concurrence of the rest has been repeatedly negatived.' (p. 2). Thus he presented the Concert of Europe as a means of bringing civilization to Turkey as well as an instrument for maintaining a balance of power. In his view, as in Gladstone's, international progress and European security were linked.

The development in the balance of power tradition corresponded to changes in the political situation of Europe. In the age of restoration, balance thought was intertwined with territorial conservatism. As long as the supreme concern was with the danger of French aggression, maintaining the balance of power meant preserving the territorial arrangement which the Congress of Vienna had imposed on Europe in order to contain France. Towards the middle of the century the tradition broke free and became more flexible. Once tension had shifted from the West to the East of Europe and Russia had become the potential aggressor, upholding the balance of power meant restraining Russia from encroaching upon the Ottoman Empire. Between the Congress of

43. Phillimore: *Commentaries,* i, 482–3.

Paris and the Congress of Berlin balance of power led towards progressive thought. When, through the defeat of Russia and the foundation of the German *Reich*, a new balance had been established in Europe, the way was open for going beyond the balance system in search of lasting solutions to the problems of the Ottoman Empire. The balance of power tradition, joined in the early part of its history with the ideas that presented the Concert as an instrument for preserving the Vienna settlement and in its last years with the ideas that introduced the Concert as an agent in the reformation of the regions that had been neglected by the Congress of Vienna, gave continuity to British thought about the Concert of Europe.

The balance of power theory of the Concert of Europe, in common with the territorial but contrary to the dynastic version of conservative thought, was—in the terminology adopted in my analysis of the German ideas—political in essence. It was about a system of powers, not a union of sovereigns, and had to do with tension between nations, not conflict within states. National security was the chief concern and international encroachment the supreme evil. Acts of aggression which were aimed at aggrandizement, since they tended to derange the existing balance of power and endanger vital national interests, called for intervention; and intervention, whether concerted diplomatic pressure or collective military action, was reserved primarily for dealing with such acts of aggression, whether threatened or actual. These elements of the theory—the principle of defending the territorial integrity of the members of the states system for the sake of the balance of power and the idea of limiting intervention to cases of dangerous encroachment—pointed to its roots in territorial conservatism on the one hand and Tory criticism of dynastic conservatism on the other.

The balance of power theory presented the Concert of Europe as a rudimentary system of collective security. But this idea comprised at least three distinct conceptions of the nature and function of the institution. The elementary one was of a combination of a majority of the great powers resisting an aggressor among them. Here the Concert meant a coalition in an emergency. Its function was to ward off an offence which endangered the survival of a member of the states system and indirectly threatened the security of the great powers. This conception was

L

brought to the fore by the Crimean War. A more advanced notion was of diplomatic cooperation between the great powers to restrain a potential aggressor in their circle. It made the Concert a protective arrangement, which guarded the integrity of an exposed state by involving the threatening power in common action. This notion was occasioned by the danger of a French invasion of Holland in 1830 and by the threats of Russian encroachments upon the Ottoman Empire before as well as after the Crimean War. The most developed idea was of a lasting union engaging each of the great powers. This presented the Concert as a preventive system. Its function was to maintain peace and security throughout the states system by automatically counterbalancing the expansionist tendencies of any great power and neutralizing the selfish drives of each. This idea was introduced with the restoration in 1815 and revived after the Congress of Berlin. The three conceptions of the system of security related to the situations of war, crisis and peace. They constituted a scale, ranging from temporary combination to permanent union, from physical intervention in the face of common danger to moral commitment on the basis of general agreement. Common to them all was that they presented the Concert of Europe as an instrument for maintaining the balance of power.

It was in this respect that the British balance of power theory differed from the German. The German thinkers, who understood the balance of power as a tendency governing the political relations of states, thought of the Concert of Europe as a group of principal powers involved in the operation of a sociological law. The British, who regarded the balance of power as a principle of foreign policy, saw the Concert as a means of upholding a political system. The difference was between the fatalist philosophy of a continental state and the volitional outlook of an island power. Germany, hemmed in at the centre of Europe, had acquired the sociological attitude through centuries of painful experience of the functioning of the balance of power. A more passive role in the system of the great powers allowed her to develop a theory of the Concert of Europe which practically identified it with the balance of power. Britain, in a powerful position off the shores of the Continent, had adopted the political approach consonant with a long tradition of successfully manipulating the balance of power. The practice of resorting to concerted action in the pursuit of

European balance led her to advance a theory which presented the Concert of Europe as a means to an end. It is significant that the German theory was developed by historians and the British by statesmen.

In each country it was the balance of power theory which determined the pattern of speculation about the Concert of Europe. The German historians, concentrating exclusively on power relations in their analysis of the states system, advanced a theory of strictly political quality. The contrast with the predominantly social character of the conservative and the progressive theory led to tension and rivalry between the political and the social traditions of thought. The British statesmen, going beyond narrow power considerations in their conduct of foreign policy, produced a political theory with pronounced legal or moral connotations. Their tendency to combine the notion of general security with the principle of territorial conservation or the idea of international progress caused overlapping of theories and continuity of thought. While in the earlier stages of its history the balance of power tradition rested on the basis of territorial conservatism, in the final phase it supported a superstructure of progressive thought.

2. CRITICISM

The balance of power tradition stemmed from territorial conservatism and Tory criticism of dynastic conservatism. The opposing trend sprang from the other end of the spectrum of early thought about the Concert of Europe. It had its roots in Whig criticism of dynastic and Radical criticism of territorial conservatism. To the principles of the balance of power theory it opposed the ideas of political freedom and national liberty.

The leading critics of the balance of power theory of the Concert of Europe were the Radicals Cobden and Bright. Though Cobden was not in the habit of using the term 'the Concert of Europe', he clearly recognized the existence of an informal association of the principal governments of Europe. He thought it a conspiracy against the peoples. On one occasion he accused the Austrian Government of having been a nuisance to the cause of progress and freedom in Europe ever since the fall of Napoleon, and asked what it was that sustained such a despicable rule.

> *Why, the State system of Europe which goes under the name of the Balance of Power.* This it is which alone preserves the integrity of the Austrian Empire, and deprives the nationalities of a chance of overthrowing the incubus. It is because the other Governments of Europe consider it necessary at whatever cost of internal misgovernment to keep intact a great member of the states system, rather than allow it to suffer disruption and take a new form, that these tyrannies propped up from without seem to threaten to be eternal.[44]

On the occasion of the war between Denmark and Germany in 1864 he charged the London Conference of 1852 with having settled the destinies of the people of Schleswig and Holstein without the slightest reference to its wishes and interests. 'The preamble of the treaty which was there and then agreed to stated that what those seven diplomatists were going to do was to maintain the integrity of the Danish monarchy, and to sustain the balance of power in Europe. Kings, emperors, princes were represented at that meeting, but the people had not the slightest voice or right in the matter.'[45] Cobden, in common with the men he opposed, saw the Concert of Europe as an instrument for maintaining the balance of power. It was on the end rather than the means that he concentrated his attack.

In one of his earliest literary productions, a pamphlet published in 1836 under the title *Russia*, he analysed the ideas of earlier writers on the balance of power, and contemptuously rejected them. The balance of power, he found,

> might, in the first place, be very well dismissed as a *chimera*, because no state of things, such as the 'disposition,' 'constitution', or 'union', of European powers, referred to as the basis of their system, by Vattel, Gentz, and Brougham, ever did exist;—and, secondly, the theory could, on other grounds, be discarded as *fallacious*, since it gives no definition—whether by breadth of territory, number of inhabitants, or extent of wealth —according to which, in balancing the respective powers, each state shall be estimated;—whilst, lastly, it would be altogether incomplete and inoperative, from neglecting, or refusing to

44. Hobson: *Richard Cobden: the International Man,* pp. 189–90.
45. Cobden: *Speeches on Questions of Public Policy,* ii, 341–2; see also *Hansard,* 3rd ser., clxxvi, cols 829 and 831 (5 July 1864).

provide against, the silent and peaceful aggrandizements which spring from improvement and labour.[46]

Till the end of his life he castigated in pamphlets and speeches the thought of balance of power theorists.[47]

But to Cobden the balance of power was not only an idle notion of writers. It was also a precept of foreign policy which provided statesmen with a motive for persistent diplomatic meddling and an excuse for frequent armed intervention. The desire to see England 'hold the balance' of Europe, which had inspired her foreign policy since the eighteenth century, had often led her to interfere in the affairs of other states and engage in war on the Continent, he observed.[48] In order to maintain the existing balance—a figment supposed to have grown out of 'the great unsettlement of Vienna'[49]—she was constantly employing either diplomacy or war. Such intervention he condemned on legal, political and moral grounds. Since there was no constituted authority in Europe to charge nations with the defence of any balance of power[50] and no clause in the Treaty of Vienna requiring them to use force in support of the territorial settlement,[51] Britain was neither authorized nor obliged to intervene with arms. Since she maintained large standing armaments to defend the balance but had no territorial interest on the Continent,[52] her policy was wasteful and pointless. And since the existing territorial order conflicted with the needs of nations struggling for freedom, diplomatic and military actions to uphold it were wrong. Cobden's attack on the principle of the balance of power and the practice of intervention was aimed at the foreign policy of Britain rather than the activities of the Concert of Europe. But, in so far

46. Cobden: *Political Writings,* i, 269.
47. For a late example, see his speech in the House of Commons on the Schleswig-Holstein question on 5 July 1864 (*Hansard,* 3rd ser., clxxvi, col. 838).
48. Cobden: *Political Writings,* i, pp. 5, 256–7 and 262–3; ii, 205.
49. Hansard, 3rd ser., clxxvi, col. 838 (5 July 1864).
50. Cobden: *Political Writings,* ii, 205.
51. *Hansard,* 3rd ser., clxxvi, col. 838 (5 July 1864).
52. Ibid., cxxx, col. 942: 'England has the least interest in this great European question [the Eastern question], as it is called. She is an island, invulnerable by land and impregnable by sea, so long as her commerce flourishes as it does now, and is, in fact, the only nation which has nothing to fear from the aggressions of the Czar' (20 February 1854); clxxvi, col. 838: ' . . . why do we trouble ourselves with these continental politics? We have no territorial interest on the Continent' (5 July 1864).

as British statesmen pursued the balance of power through the Concert of Europe, the attack implied a criticism of the Concert of Europe as an instrument for maintaining the balance of power. Cobden's idea was the counterpart of Palmerston's. Both thought of the Concert of Europe as one of several means for upholding the European balance of power.

Cobden's entire theory of international relations ran counter to the Concert of Europe. Throughout his life he attacked the attitudes and activities of governments and foreign offices and championed the cause of peoples and nations. Intervention in the domestic affairs of other countries was an unnecessary evil, he thought, not only when it was actuated by lust for conquest, as was normally the situation under the system of the balance of power, but also when it was motivated by the desire to grant freedom, as was sometimes the case with Palmerston's government. Diplomatizing and meddling by foreign governments never facilitated the efforts of a suppressed people. 'I believe the progress of freedom depends more upon the maintenance of peace, the spread of commerce, and the diffusion of education, than upon the labours of cabinets and foreign offices.'[53] The belief was in a natural harmony of international life, which would assert itself in the absence of artificial interference by governments. As he expected free trade to bring peace, so he assumed that unrestricted cooperation between nations would lead to freedom and progress. This laissez-faire internationalism was summed up in a maxim coined as early as 1836: 'As little intercourse as possible betwixt the *Governments,* as much connection as possible between the *nations* of the world.'[54] Such ideas were irreconcilable with any theory of the Concert of Europe. Cobden was the most thorough of opponents of this institution. While his references to the Concert contained criticisms of its practical results and his observations on the balance of power implied a condemnation of its current theory, his philosophy of international relations was entirely opposed to the very idea of a Concert of European governments.

Bright did not refer to the Concert of Europe directly. But a criticism of its balance of power theory was implied in his attack on the system of the balance of power. In condemning the theory

53. *Hansard,* 3rd ser., cxii, col. 673 (28 June 1850).
54. Cobden: *Political Writings,* i, 282–3.

and censuring the practice of this system he followed Cobden. The balance of power he described as 'a phrase to which it is difficult to attach any definite meaning',[55] and the whole notion as 'a mischievous delusion which has come down to us from past times'.[56] It was constantly leading to intervention and war. Nearly all the wars that Britain had fought since the end of the seventeenth century had been for the sake of the balance of power in Europe. While the price had been loss of life, debt and taxes, the only result had been 'a doubled peerage at one end of the social scale, and far more than a doubled pauperism at the other'.[57] Europe had been left as much in chains as before a single effort had been made by Britain to rescue her from tyranny.[58] It was with the freedom of peoples rather than the independence of states that Bright was concerned.

To the ideas on intervention associated with the balance of power he opposed the Radical doctrine of non-intervention. Britain should not interfere in the domestic affairs of other countries, he insisted, except when her interests were 'directly and obviously assailed'.[59] She should rest her policy on the eternal foundation of Christian morality rather than on the traditional principles of European politics, and seek economic prosperity instead of military glory.[60] He opposed alliances between governments and advocated unity between nations.[61] But he did not go so far as Cobden in rejecting intercourse between governments. Indeed, on several occasions in his later years he supported the idea of a diplomatic concert of the great powers to settle the future and bring order and peace to the regions of the Turkish Empire.[62] This idea belonged to the progressive set of thoughts about the Concert of Europe. His pairing an implied

55. *Hansard,* 3rd ser., cxxxii, col. 254 (31 March 1854).
56. Ibid., cxxxii, col. 258 (31 March 1854).
57. Bright: *Speeches on Questions of Public Policy,* ii, 108.
58. *Hansard,* 3rd ser., cxxxii, col. 267 (31 March 1854); *Speeches,* ii, pp. 378–9.
59. Ibid., cxxxii, col. 267 (31 March 1854).
60. Ibid., cxxxii, col. 267 (31 March 1854); *Speeches,* ii, 397: 'I believe there is no permanent greatness to a nation except it be based upon morality. I do not care for military greatness or military renown. I care for the condition of the people among whom I live' (Birmingham, 29 October 1858).
61. *Hansard,* 3rd ser., cxxxii, col. 265 (31 March 1854); see also Bright: *Public Addresses,* p. 308, where he argued that the Suez Canal might become a bond of union between the nations of Europe.
62. Ibid., clx, cols 650–1 (3 August 1860); Bright: *Public Addresses,* p. 396 (1877).

criticism of the balance of power theory with a suggestion of support for the progressive views pointed to a connection between the Manchester School and the progressive tradition.

Among the international lawyers contemporary with Cobden and Bright there was one who helped to undermine faith in the balance of power. In the eighteen-sixties Montague Bernard, the first Chichele Professor of international law and diplomacy at Oxford, delivered four lectures on subjects connected with diplomacy. In the second of these he referred to the Concert of Europe and discussed the balance of power. His references to the new system of European politics were critical of dynastic and territorial conservatism. 'The plan of general concert', introduced at Vienna and developed by Metternich, had sometimes succeeded and sometimes failed, he observed; of late years its failures had been more conspicuous than its successes: 'forces too strong to be overcome have fought—and happily, as I believe, will always fight—against any system tending to control artificially the action of those causes by which Europe is gradually transformed, and to stereotype either existing forms of government or existing territorial arrangements'.[63]

He started his discussion of the balance of power by correcting those writers who had been led to speak of it as embodying a rule or principle of positive international law. They had committed an inaccuracy. 'At the utmost, it is no more than a practical security, of recognized importance, for the observance of International Law—which is a very different thing.' Following its best interpreters, he defined the balance of power as 'a short expression of the political maxim that no single State ought to be suffered to become strong enough to overbear the aggregate strength of the rest, or some considerable but undefinable proportion of their aggregate strength'. As a result of the impossibility of fixing precisely the point at which such excessive preponderance was reached, and of making sure how many lesser powers would actually throw their weight into the opposite scale, the term had come to mean more than this, he went on to explain: 'every aggrandizement likely to jeopardise the actual state of possession has been treated as a displacement *pro tanto* of the equilibrium; and the equilibrium itself meant such a distribution of force among the different countries of Europe as offered a security for the

63. Bernard: *Four Lectures on Subjects connected with Diplomacy*, pp. 95–6.

existing state of possession.'[64] Here he was pointing to the element of territorial conservatism in the idea of the balance of power.

To protect or redress the European balance, he observed, had been among the nominal objects of almost every political treaty concluded and declaration of war issued during the eighteenth and nineteenth centuries; 'and there is no doubt that it has sometimes served as the pretext for a quarrel, and repeatedly made hostilities general which would otherwise have been shut up within a comparatively small area'.[65] But he did not attack the balance of power. Declarations for and against the doctrine were in his view alike unprofitable. It had its origin in the instinct of self-preservation and would remain a guide for statesmanship as long as nations felt threatened by the strength of rivals.

> Yet recent experience seems to show that time has much allayed that uneasy sensitiveness which trembled at every slight disturbance of subsisting arrangements, took umbrage at every accession of power which might fall to the lot of a neighbour, weighed out in nice scales souls by the thousand and territories by the square mile, and attached extravagant importance to remote possibilities of loss or gain.

He believed that the tendencies of modern society were such as to diminish the necessity for precautions of this kind. A growing sense of justice and an increase in generosity were encouraging the novel practice of referring disputes of secondary importance to arbitration. 'But if history has any lesson for us on this subject, it is this, that less is to be hoped from any direct endeavours to abolish wars or diminish their frequency than from the silent growth of interest, habits of life, modes of government, and a public opinion, favourable to peace.' Turning to the factors of progress, he set out to discuss the spread of commerce, the multiplication of considerable states, and the advance of free institutions and popular government.[66] Though he made his points with the caution of a scholar instead of the passion of a Radical politician, Bernard joined Cobden and Bright in taking leave of the old system of European politics and greeting a new order of international society.

In his inclination to favour political isolationism, too, Bernard

64. Ibid., pp. 97–8.   65. Ibid., pp. 98–9.   66. Ibid., pp. 99–101.

resembled the leaders of the Manchester School. When he criticized the record of the conservative Concert of Europe he reminded his listeners of Bolingbroke's opinion that the true wisdom of an English statesman was to use the advantage of a situation which made his country, though a neighbour to the Continent, not a part of it. Comparing with envy the Channel to the Atlantic, he quoted with approval Washington's advice to his countrymen to avoid all foreign alliances whatever.[67] That sentiment precluded support for any theory of the Concert of Europe.

This group of thinkers opposed both of the leading ideas of the balance of power theory of the Concert of Europe. Against the principle of territorial integrity they set the idea of national freedom. The balance of power theorists, preoccupied with security, concentrated on power relations between states. Their opponents, concerned with the advance of civilization, turned to intercourse between nations. The balance of power theorists thought of the Concert of Europe as a protection against aggression. Their opponents saw it as an obstacle to the rise of nations and the advance of democracy. The difference was between men guided by rules of prudence and men inspired by faith in progress.

Against the established principle of non-intervention, which owed its name to its contrast with the Continental doctrine of antirevolutionary intervention, the Manchester School set the Radical dogma of non-intervention. The balance of power theorists, conscious that national security depended on European equilibrium, insisted on the right to intervene to prevent a rival power from gaining dangerous aggrandizement. Their opponents, convinced that the welfare of the people had nothing to do with the balance of power, allowed intervention only when national interests were threatened directly. The balance of power theorists rested their case on the traditions of European politics. Their opponents took their stand on the rules of Christian morality. Here the conflict was between those who liked to control the existing political system and those who wanted to develop a new international order.

In one of the most famous passages of his speeches Bright drew attention to the connection between social class and attitude to the balance of power: 'The more you examine this matter the more you will come to the conclusion which I have arrived at, that this

67. Bernard: *Four Lectures on Subjects connected with Diplomacy*, p. 96.

foreign policy, this regard for "the liberties of Europe", this care at one time for "the Protestant interests", this excessive love for "the balance of power", is neither more nor less than a gigantic system of out-door relief for the aristocracy of Great Britain.'[68] It was aristocratic statesmen in the habit of playing a part in European politics who developed the balance of power theory of the Concert, and middleclass Radicals representing the industry and trade of the country who criticized it. In the last resort, the ideas on both sides of the argument were conditioned by the situation of Britain. Those which championed the Concert of Europe as an instrument for maintaining the balance of power reflected her geographical position. Placed off the shores of the Continent, she had become the traditional holder of the European balance. Those ideas which demanded a break with the states system and a strengthening of the non-political bonds of international society reflected her economic situation. Endowed with coal and a genius for invention, she had become the first industrial nation and the leader of world trade. These sets of ideas could not have arisen in Germany.

Neither the balance of power tradition nor its opponent survived the Eastern crisis of the late eighteen-seventies. But the central idea of each reappeared between the Congress of Berlin and the First World War. The principle of security of states through balance of power was taken over by the nationalists and imperialists, the notion of international order through national freedom carried on by progressive thinkers.

68. Bright: *Speeches,* ii, 382.

Chapter Three

THE PROGRESSIVE THEORY

1. DEVELOPMENT

The view of the Concert of Europe that had fewest supporters in Germany became dominant in Britain. In the late eighteen-seventies British progressive thought was still a superstructure of the balance of power tradition. But, as the balance tradition earlier in the century had liberated itself from the hold of conservative ideas, so progressive thought soon cut the ties with balance of power principles and took an independent course. Between the Berlin Congress and the First World War it established itself as the leading British tradition of thought about the Concert of Europe.

Inspired by the ideas of freedom and progress, which had guided also the opponents of conservative and balance of power thought, the progressive thinkers presented the Concert of Europe as an agent in the reform and organization of international society. While at first the emphasis was on collective action to improve the situation of oppressed peoples, in the later stages it was on international organization to secure peace and order in Europe. The ideas characteristic of the former period are here called humanitarian, those of the latter organizational. Both types of progressive thought found supporters among statesmen as well as scholars.

Humanitarian ideas

The progressive thinkers introduced a new doctrine of intervention. According to the conservative view, the purpose of concerted interference in the domestic affairs of a sovereign state had been to preserve the legal order of 1815; according to the balance of power idea, to maintain the European balance of power. But the earlier progressive writers and statesmen advocated intervention for humanitarian ends. Deeply disturbed by the suffering of suppressed peoples, they saw in the Concert of

Europe a means either of reforming the oppressor or of liberating the oppressed. The former view, which went with a more practical and moderate approach to politics, found its first formulation in the official correspondence of Stratford de Redcliffe. The latter one, which was a product of a more ideological and radical attitude, originated in the writings of John Stuart Mill.

Stratford de Redcliffe developed his idea of intervention in the course of his dealings with the Ottoman Empire. One of the earliest hints of his Turkish policy appeared in a despatch to Palmerston of 1832: 'The Turkish Empire is evidently hastening to its dissolution, and an approach to the civilization of Christendom affords the only chance of keeping it together for any length of time.'[1] To civilize Turkey became the preoccupation of his public life. On many occasions, stretching over a period which began a decade or two before the Crimean War and ended in the Eastern crisis of the seventies, he advocated joint intervention by the great powers to reduce abuse and bring about reform in the administration of the Empire.[2] His concern was not only to preserve the balance of power, which he thought would be upset if a rival power was allowed to gain special influence through unilateral intervention, and to prevent a European war, which he believed would be the outcome of a collapse of the Ottoman Empire, but also to benefit those subjects of Turkey who were suffering persecution. The chief powers of Christendom were justified in interfering in the affairs of Turkey, he argued in a letter to *The Times* in 1876: 'Their objects would be the maintenance of peace, the correction of pernicious abuses, the rescue of millions from injustice and degradation, the retention by Turkey of as much sovereign and national individuality as circumstances originating from itself allow it to enjoy.'[3] The idea of joint intervention by the great powers to extend Christian civilization became an important element in progressive thought.

It was the struggle of the Italian subjects of the Austrian Emperor, rather than the suffering of the Christian subjects of

1. Lane-Poole: *The Life of the Right Honourable Stratford Canning Viscount Stratford de Redcliffe*, ii, 78.
2. See, e.g., ibid., ii, 86 (1844); Hansard, 3rd ser., clx, cols 607 and 625–6 (3 August); Hansard, 3rd ser., clxi, col. 872 1860 (25 February 1861); and Stratford de Redcliffe: *The Eastern Question, Being a Selection from his Writings during the Last Five Years of his Life*, p. 7 (1875), pp. 23–8, and p. 29 (1876).
3. Stratford de Redcliffe: *The Eastern Question*, p. 18.

Turkey, which inspired Mill to formulate his doctrine of intervention. The February Revolution of 1848 in Paris had revived the old debate on the right to interfere. Brougham, who in his later years had veered towards territorial conservatism and become a determined supporter of the Vienna settlement, had reacted sharply to what he understood to be an appeal by the new French government to revolutionaries everywhere to rise against their oppressors. Dreading the possibility that Britain might side with France in encouraging and assisting the efforts of the Italians to gain freedom, he had denounced in speeches and writings the idea of prorevolutionary interference and the principle of nationality. [4]

Mill answered him in an article which he published in 1849 under the title 'Vindication of the French Revolution of February 1848'. He based his case on precedents. An entirely new principle of international law had been established within the last thirty years, he observed. It was, that whenever two countries, or two parts of the same country, were engaged in war, and the war either continued long undecided or threatened to be decided in a way involving consequences repugnant to humanity or to the general interest, other countries had a right to step in and, if necessary, impose what they considered reasonable terms of accommodation. A combination of the great powers had acted on this doctrine when they interfered between Greece and Turkey at Navarino, between Holland and Belgium at Antwerp, and between Turkey and Egypt at St Jean d'Acre. After these precedents it was too late in the day, he insisted, 'to tell us that nations may not forcibly interfere with one another for the sole purpose of stopping mischief and benefiting humanity'. No motive to such interference could be of a more binding character than that of preventing the liberty of a nation which had risen in arms against its foreign conquerors from being crushed by tyrannical oppressors. Every liberal government or people, he declared, 'has a right to assist struggling liberalism, by mediation, by money, or by arms, wherever it can prudently do so; as every despotic government, when its aid is needed or asked for, never scruples to aid despotic governments'. [5] Here Mill went

4. See Brougham: *Speech . . . in the House of Lords, on Italian and French Affairs. April 11, 1848; Speech . . . in the House of Lords, August 18, 1848, on the Affairs of Austria and Italy*; and *Letter to the Marquess of Lansdowne . . . on the Late Revolution in France*.
5. Mill: *Dissertations and Discussions, Political, Philosophical, and Historical*, ii, 379–81. In 1859, when the fate of Italy was being decided, he again took up the subject of

a step further than the Whigs of the previous generation. Whereas they merely had inverted the conservative doctrine of revolutionary conspiracy, he inverted the conservative doctrine of anti-revolutionary intervention.

Stratford de Redcliffe's idea of intervention, which was inspired by his determination to preserve the Ottoman Empire as well as a desire to relieve her Christian subjects, linked progressive thought to the balance of power tradition. But Mill's bond was with Whig and Radical criticism of the conservative ideas. He was closer to the Radicals than to the Whigs. The Whigs who had concentrated their criticism on the dynastic version of conservatism, had been concerned with political and not with national freedom. But the Radicals, who directed their attack against the territorial version, were interested as much in national as in political liberty. Mill, too, wanted both. He believed that free institutions for suppressed peoples, his ultimate aim, presupposed national freedom. 'Nationality is desirable, as a means to the attainment of liberty . . .'[6] This pairing of constitutionalism with nationalism became one of the characteristics of the earlier phase of the progressive tradition of thought. Both the idea of intervention to bring about reform, which Stratford de Redcliffe urged on the great powers, and the idea of intervention to liberate peoples, which Mill deduced from the past practice of the Concert and recommended to the liberal powers, influenced Gladstone's theory of the Concert of Europe.

The European sense manifested in Gladstone's contribution to the balance of power theory, where he presented the Concert as an institution of European politics rather than as an instrument of British foreign policy, conditioned his entire political thought. The moral condition of the Christian part of the world interested him more than the material interests of his country. On the stage of Europe he saw the forces of violence clashing continually with those of justice. In this drama he involved himself as the champion of morality. Guided by the principles of Christianity and inspired by the ideas of classical literature,[7] he challenged

intervention. Repeating the argument set forth in 1849, he added a new rule: 'Intervention to enforce non-intervention is always rightful, always moral, if not always prudent' (ibid., iii, 172 and 176–7).
6. Ibid., ii, 383.
7. The fundamental principles of Gladstone's political thought are analysed in J. L. Hammond: *Gladstone and the Irish Nation,* ch. v.

and opposed the enemies of religion, reason, justice and humanity.

History, he believed, was on his side in the great struggle: ' . . . there is going on a profound mysterious movement, that, whether we will or not, is bringing the nations of the civilised world, as well as the uncivilised, morally as well as physically nearer to one another, and making them more and more respons- ible before God for one another's welfare.'[8] This development in international morality was reflected in the law of nations. 'Certain it is,' he wrote during the Franco-Prussian War, 'that a new law of nations is gradually taking hold of the mind, and coming to sway the practice, of the world; a law which recognises independ- ence, which frowns upon aggression, which favours the pacific, not the bloody settlement of disputes, which aims at permanent and not temporary adjustments; above all, which recognises, as a tribunal of paramount authority, the general judgment of civilised mankind.'[9]

The supreme manifestation of the influence of the new morality and law was the Concert of Europe. During the three decades after the Crimean War Gladstone repeatedly presented the Con- cert as a product of the advancing civilization. The system that had grown up of late, under which the powers of Europe had formed themselves into a sort of police for the purpose of main- taining peace and putting down wrongdoers, was evidence of a gradual recognition of the community of interest in nations, he implied in a speech in the House of Commons in 1864 about the Schleswig-Holstein question.[10] The concerted action and collective guarantee of the European powers which in the Crimean War had replaced the individual action and sole interference of one of them had been an expression of a European conscience, he asserted in 1876.[11] The powers of Europe were 'the highest and most authentic organ of modern Christian civilisation', he said in 1884.[12]

8. Morley: *The Life of William Ewart Gladstone*, ii, 596 (speech of 1879). See also Gladstone's admission in a letter to Granville of 8 October 1870: 'In moral forces, and in their growing effect upon European politics, I have a great faith: possibly on that very account, I am free to confess, sometimes a misleading one' (*The Political Correspondence of Mr Gladstone and Lord Granville 1868–1876*, i, 140).

9. Gladstone: *Gleanings,* iv, 256.

10. *Hansard,* 3rd ser., clxxvi, col. 768 (4 July).

11. Ibid., ccxxxi, col. 184 (31 July).

12. Gladstone: *Egypt and the Soudan,* p. 14; and *Third Midlothian Campaign, Political Speeches delivered in August and September 1884,* p. 45.

But the Concert of Europe itself, according to Gladstone's view, was an important factor in the advance of civilization. Its functions in this respect were to enforce international law, to preserve European peace and to relieve oppressed peoples. While the first two carried the emphasis in his thought during the eighteen-fifties and sixties, the last one gained predominance in the late seventies. The Anglo-French Alliance, he insisted in 1855 and repeated in later years, was not an arbitrary combination, but 'a representation of the great European combination of Powers, acting against Russia, to vindicate and enforce against her the public law of Europe'.[13] On several occasions during the decades following the Crimean War he congratulated the Concert of Europe on its record of settling local differences and averting war.[14]

During the great crisis in the Eastern question Gladstone's faith in the institution reached its climax. When the suffering of the Christian subjects of the Ottoman Empire roused his passion, he turned to the Concert of Europe for action. In speeches and writings he demanded collective measures to put an end to atrocities. These measures included the traditional one of exacting reform from the Porte in the government of Turkey.[15] But Gladstone went a step further. During the two years that preceded the Congress of Berlin he developed the idea of self-government for the disturbed provinces. This he did by separating the two elements of the policy that Britain had pursued in the Crimean War and since maintained, that of upholding the integrity and the independence of Turkey. By territorial integrity, which he characterized as negative, he meant titular sovereignty, absence of sovereign rights of other powers. Independence, the positive element, he understood as a state of affairs in which the Porte was left in the actual, daily, and free administration of all its provinces.[16] The former he wanted to retain in order to avoid a scramble for

13. *Hansard,* 3rd ser., cxxxviii, col. 1071 (24 May). Also Gladstone: *Gleanings,* i, 'Life of the Prince Consort' (1877), 103–4.
14. Ibid., cxxxviii, col. 1070 (24 May 1855); clxxvi, col. 768 (4 July 1864); and cxciv, col. 76–7 (16 February 1869).
15. Ibid., ccxxxiv, col. 101–2, where he called upon the Government to exert its influence 'to promoting the concert of the European Powers in exacting from the Ottoman Porte, by their united authority, such changes in the Government of Turkey as they may deem to be necessary for the purposes of humanity and justice, for effectual defence against intrigue, and for the peace of the world' (30 April 1877).
16. Gladstone: *Bulgarian Horrors and the Question of the East,* pp. 50–1.

M

territory among the great powers interested in the lands of the Ottoman Empire. The latter he was against. A withdrawal of Turkish authorities in the oppressed provinces and a development of 'local liberty and practical self-government', he thought, would put an end to atrocities.[17] This was the policy that he urged on the Concert of Europe. 'I argue that we ought to use our influence in the great Council of Europe for the effectual deliverance of these Provinces from oppression, but not for their transfer to any foreign dominion.'[18] By combining in his scheme for concerted intervention in Turkey the idea of reform and the principle of liberation Gladstone produced a synthesis of Stratford de Redcliffe's and Mill's doctrines.

In Gladstone's conception of the Concert of Europe as an instrument for advancing civilization can be seen the first indications of the tendency of progressive thought to divorce itself from the balance of power tradition. They are apparent in the shift of emphasis from the ideas of upholding the law and preserving the peace of Europe to that of relieving the provinces of Turkey. To the extent that the former notions sprang from a concern to prevent dangerous acts of aggression and aggrandizement, his earlier progressivism was a function of his balance of power thought. The humanitarian ideas of the later period were not. By demanding reform in Turkey for the sake of the Christian subjects and by insisting on a reconstruction of the Empire on the basis of self-government, he prepared the ground for an independent progressive tradition. But he went no further. In retaining the element of territorial integrity, the cornerstone of the balance of power policy, he let his progressive thought be supported by balance of power ideas. It was left to his successors to separate the two.

The year 1880 was a turning-point in Gladstone's attitude to the Concert of Europe. In the autumn of that year the development of the Eastern question moved him once more to confess his faith in the Concert. Reviewing the progress achieved in the settlement of the difficulty over the Montenegrin frontier, he wrote to his wife, 'It is the working of the European Concert for purposes of justice, peace and liberty, with efficiency and success,

17. *Hansard*, 3rd ser., ccxxxiv, col. 101 (30 April 1877); ccxxxi, col. 198 (31 July 1876); and Gladstone: *A Speech delivered at Blackheath on . . . September 9th, 1876 . . .* pp. 22–3.
18. *Hansard*, 3rd ser., ccxxxiv, col. 426 (7 May 1877); see also Gladstone: *A Speech del. at Blackheath*, pp. 24–5, and *The Paths*, p. 17.

which is the great matter at issue. That has always been the ideal of my life in Foreign Policy: and if this goes forward rightly to the end it will be the most conspicuous instance yet recorded, the best case of success achieved.'[19] But his optimism turned out to be unjustified. A few days later, when the course of events had shattered his hopes, he referred to the institution in a letter to the Foreign Secretary as 'the old jade concert'.[20] During his second ministry, when he faced Bismarck in European politics, it became clear to him that it was no longer possible to establish a diplomatic concert of the principal powers. Though he always hoped one day to see the great powers brought together for humanitarian ends, in those years he rarely advocated his idea of the European Concert.[21]

In the second half of the eighteen-nineties he reached the last position in his attitude towards the Concert of Europe. Lord Salisbury, in order to strengthen his hand in the current issues of the Eastern question, had called up the Concert of Europe. Gladstone, aware that the institution no longer was serving the goals he had in mind, criticized it. In a speech of 1896 on the Armenian atrocities he described the Concert as 'a powerful, an august, and in many cases a most useful instrument of good', but pointed out that its success had not been uniform. In the Eastern question it had usually failed in its objects and brought disgrace upon the great powers.[22] Six months later he delivered his most trenchant attack on the new Concert of Europe. In an open letter to the Duke of Westminster he repeated that the Concert was an immensely valuable instrument when it could be made subservient to the purposes of honour, duty, liberty and humanity, but a source of mischief when it was not in working order. In the latter case it came to mean 'the concealment of dissents, the lapse into generalities, and the settling down upon negations at junctures when duty loudly calls for positive action'.[23] To this he added a more fundamental point of criticism. This pretended and ineffectual cooperation of the governments shut out the peoples, he

19. *Gladstone to his Wife,* pp. 232–3 (10 October).
20. Knaplund: *Gladstone's Foreign Policy,* p. 13 (14 October).
21. See Medlicott: *Bismarck, Gladstone, and the Concert of Europe*; the last chapter deals with Gladstone's attitude to the Concert after its breakdown.
22. Gladstone: *Verbatim Report of the ... Speech on the Armenian Atrocities, ... 1896,* pp. 7–8.
23. Gladstone: *The Eastern Crisis. A Letter to the Duke of Westminster, K.C.,* pp. 4–6.

complained. 'It is difficult enough for a people to use *ad hoc* a sufficient influence over its Government standing single, but what is our case when we find ourselves standing in the face of our Government with five other Governments behind it, which we cannot call to account, and over which we cannot reasonably expect to exercise the smallest influence?'[24] In the present case only a small and determined people had been able to assume enterprise. While none of the principal governments, all paralysed by dissension, nor any of the great peoples, all shut out by the Concert, was able to liberate Crete in 1897, the Greeks were attempting it. Greece, challenging the Concert of Europe, was 'a David facing six Goliaths'.[25] Gladstone had almost returned to the position of the Whig and Radical opponents of the conservative ideas. In describing the Concert as an institution shutting out the peoples he came close to the Whig critics of dynastic conservatism, in presenting it as the opponent of a people striving for a national solution close to the Radical critics of territorial conservatism. That the principal champion of a progressive should end up as a critic of a conservative Concert of Europe indicates the nature of the logical connection between humanitarian and conservative thought. The theory that presented the Concert of Europe as a body of nations engaged in reforming governments and liberating peoples was the reverse of the theory in which it appeared as an association of governments bent on preserving the established political and territorial order.

The two tendencies in Gladstone's thought, to depart from the basis of balance of power ideas and to return to the position of the enemies of conservatism, were characteristic of humanitarian progressivism in general. Three positions marked the development of this type of thought about the Concert of Europe. The starting-point was where it still rested on the balance of power tradition, the intermediate one where it had branched off, and the final one where it had succumbed to its anticonservative complement. The originators of the humanitarian ideas staked out the route. Stratford de Redcliffe marked the first position, Gladstone in the seventies a point somewhere between the first and the second, Mill the second, and Gladstone in the nineties a point close to the final one. The lesser contributors to this set of ideas followed the same course.

24. Ibid., p. 6; also p. 16.   25. Ibid., p. 12.

The initial position was taken both by Gladstone's foreign secretary and by his ambassador in Berlin. Earl Granville, who advocated European concert during the great crisis in the Eastern question, demanded collective diplomatic action to protect the Christian subjects of Turkey and to preserve the peace of Europe.[26] But, in calling for internal reform of the Turkish Empire, he did not sacrifice the traditional doctrine of her territorial integrity. Odo Russell, who strongly supported the foreign policy of the Liberal government in 1880, saw in the European Concert the only possible means of ending atrocities in Turkey. But he thought of it also as a protection against aggression and a guarantee for peace, order and concord in Europe.[27] In both Granville's and Russell's conception of the ends of the European Concert humanitarian ideas were linked to balance of power notions. The new idea of reform for the sake of the oppressed subjects of Turkey had not yet separated itself from the older principle of reform for the sake of the European balance of power.

The chief defenders of the second position were Canon Malcolm MacColl, friend of Gladstone, and Sir William Harcourt, a Liberal member of Parliament. During the Eastern crisis MacColl wrote a couple of highly polemical pamphlets, in which he defended the conduct of Russia and attacked the policy of Disraeli's government.[28] His aim was to prove that the Turkish government had been deteriorating steadily since the Crimean War and was now on the verge of dissolution—'a catastrophe from which the enforcement, by the Great Powers, of a scheme of real reform giving practical autonomy to the disturbed provinces, offers the only escape'.[29] He denied that the integrity and independence of the Turkish Empire were necessary to the interests of England and, in any case, refused to allow respect for the material interests of the nation to override the claims of humanity and natural justice.[30] Harcourt hated the Ottoman power. In 1877 he declared in the House of Commons that he rejoiced to hear the passing bell of Turkey and to see the day approaching

26. *Hansard,* 3rd ser., ccxxxi, col. 93 (31 July 1876); ccxxxii, col. 31 (8 February 1877); and ccxxxiii, col. 1191 (16 April 1877).
27. *Letters from the Berlin Embassy,* pp. 143 and 153.
28. The 'Bulgarian atrocities agitation' has been studied from inside by R. T. Shannon: see his *Gladstone and the Bulgarian Agitation 1876.*
29. MacColl: *The Eastern Question: Its Facts and Fallacies,* Preface, p. vi.
30. Ibid., pp. 1–2.

when better hopes would dawn for her oppressed inhabitants. Once the war was over and Turkey was destroyed, England would have to settle the affairs of Eastern Europe in concert with the five great powers. Then she 'could not disregard those great principles of nationality which for the last 10 or 20 years had been re-constituting Europe'.[31] In both MacColl's and Harcourt's thoughts on the function of the Concert of Europe in the Eastern question the idea of liberating oppressed peoples and establishing new nations was divorced from the doctrine of preserving the territorial integrity of Turkey and maintaining the European balance of power.

In later years MacColl and Harcourt moved to the final position. 'The Concert of Europe has been the parent of all the mischief both in Greece and in Armenia', MacColl wrote in a private letter of 1897.[32] In two books on the issue arising from the Armenian atrocities, published the previous year, he accused the great powers of selfishness and folly in their attitude to the suffering subjects of Turkey and attacked the European Concert for its impotence in dealing with the Sultan.[33] To revert to the state of affairs that had existed before the Crimean War, and allow Russia, France and Britain to resume the right to protect separate sections of the Christian population of Turkey was now the policy he favoured in the Eastern question.[34] In 1897 Harcourt, who in that year assumed the leadership of the Liberal party, delivered a number of speeches in which he attacked the new Concert of Europe. Rejecting the idea of a federated legislature for Europe, which Salisbury recently had defended, he described the Concert as 'the hierophants who minister to the shrine of the integrity of the Ottoman Empire'. The human sacrifices were the Armenian massacres. The cause of humanity and the claims of freedom were sacrificed to the jealousies and selfish interests of the great powers.[35] The foremost principles of this institution, he observed, were the same as those of the Holy Alliance—'to maintain peace

31. *Hansard,* 3rd ser., ccxxxiv, cols 883 and 885 (14 May).
32. MacColl: *Memoirs and Correspondence,* p. 208 (3 September). His letters of those years contain numerous references to the Concert of Europe and the need to coerce Turkey (see especially chapter viii: Armenia).
33. MacColl: *England's Responsibility towards Armenia,* and *The Sultan and the Powers.* From the latter book: 'It seems plain that the Concert of Europe can, as a rule, be depended on for nothing except the negation of its name' (p. 290).
34. MacColl: *The Sultan,* pp. 289–90.
35. *Hansard,* 4th ser., xlviii, cols 980 and 989 (12 April).

in Europe and the integrity of all the despotic thrones'.[36] In their attack on the European Concert of the late eighteen-nineties MacColl and Harcourt combined the two principal strands of the earlier criticism of conservative thought. Opposition to dynastic conservatism, more pronounced in their support for the Armenians, and opposition to territorial conservatism, more prominent in their approval of the efforts to liberate Crete,[37] joined in a general condemnation of the policy of maintaining the Empire that stood in the way of political liberty and national freedom in the East. The observations of less important critics provide further evidence that the attack on the European Concert's way of dealing with the Armenian and Cretan questions was a late synthesis of the two elements of traditional anticonservative thought.[38]

The attitude to the European Concert of what later came to be known as the left in British politics had come full circle. These Liberals, who twenty years earlier had championed the progressive Concert, were successors of the Radical opponents of the balance of power and of the Whig and Radical critics of the conservative Concert of Europe. The ideas of political and national freedom, which had inspired, in turn, opposition to the conservative, criticism of the balance of power and support for the progressive theory of the Concert of Europe, had led back to opposition to conservative thought.

Though within twenty years of freeing itself from the balance of power tradition the humanitarian trend of progressive thought had given way to anticonservative criticism, it had not reached the end. The idea of reforming the government of uncivilized states through concerted efforts of the great powers survived the crisis of the late nineties. It retained a place in the thought of a number of leading Liberals who refused to reject the Concert of Europe.

36. Harcourt: *The Home and Foreign Policy of the Government, Speech delivered . . . on March 17th, 1897*, p. 13.
37. Harcourt wanted Crete to be annexed to Greece: see his speech of 13 April 1897 printed in *The 'Eighty' Club (1898)*. 'On the Concert of Europe', pp. 22–4.
38. See, e.g., the debate on Crete in the House of Commons in 1897. Sir Charles Dilke and John Ellis presented the Concert of Europe as a new 'Holy Alliance', bent on repression (*Hansard*, 4th ser., xlviii, col. 963 (12 April) and xlix, col. 26–7 (7 May), respectively). W. S. Robson and F. S. Stevenson criticized it for oppressing the smaller but rising nations and excluding them from the councils that decided the affairs of the East (Ibid., xlix, col. 19 (7 May) and xlviii, col. 1007 (12 April), respectively).

In 1896 Lord Rosebery admitted that he, politically bred and suckled on the Concert of Europe as he was, could not so readily give it up. Discussing the Armenian massacres, he demanded improvement in Turkish affairs and declared: 'I venture to say that a question of the magnitude of the Eastern Question can only be settled by that august tribunal which is called the Concert of European Powers.'[39] Joseph Chamberlain, who twenty years earlier had shared Gladstone's faith in the Concert of Europe,[40] welcomed its reestablishment in 1897. He hoped that it would be effective 'to prevent the recurrence of anything like those outrages which have shocked the conscience of the civilised world'.[41] But that this conception of the European Concert survived till well into the twentieth century was due mainly to Sir Edward Grey.

Despite its successive failures, Grey retained his faith in the Concert as an instrument for reform almost till the eve of the World War. In 1897 and 1898 he advocated action through the Concert of Europe to save the Christians of Armenia and Crete. His reaction to the miserable record of the institution was to urge Salisbury to spur it on.[42] In 1908 he wished to see the Concert maintained as 'an instrument of Macedonian reform'.[43] Aware of its record of comparative failure in this capacity and afraid that it might perish for lack of vitality, he called for union and determination, demanding that the work of the Concert be directed to substantial and effective improvement instead of trivial things and paper reform.[44] As late as 1913 he invoked the Concert of Europe for the purpose of reform in Turkey. The European powers, he then thought, should consult with the Turkish government and draw up a comprehensive scheme of reform for her Asiatic provinces.[45]

39. Coates: *Lord Rosebery. His Life and Speeches,* ii, 877.
40. On 7 May 1877 he had supported the resolutions on the Concert of Europe and the Eastern question that Gladstone had proposed (*Hansard,* 3rd ser., ccxxxiv, col. 455).
41. Chamberlain: *Foreign and Colonial Speeches,* p. 231.
42. Trevelyan: *Grey of Fallodon,* p. 65.
43. Grey: *Speeches on Foreign Affairs, 1904–1914,* p. 85.
44. Ibid., pp. 89–90.
45. *Hansard,* 5th ser., liii, col. 397 (29 May) and lvi, col. 2290 (12 August). In 1900 Grey believed in using the Concert of Europe for reforming the administration of China. But here his primary motivation was not, as in the case of Turkey, sympathy with oppressed subjects, but concern for the integrity of China. He favoured concerted pressure for internal reform in the hope of averting a partition. The doctrine that he adopted in this case was closer to that of the balance of power

The weakness of the Concert of Europe provoked a few Radical writers to call on the great powers to take a more active part in the administration of Turkey. In a book about Macedonia, published in 1906, H. N. Brailsford delivered a bitter attack on the record of the Concert. Its weak but irritating intervention in Turkey had caused more suffering to the native Christians than it had prevented, he maintained. [46] For Macedonia he proposed a withdrawal of the actual government from Constantinople and the establishment of a board of delegates from the five protecting powers, who should reside in the province and enjoy the authority of ministers in a constitutional country. [47] The following year Noel Buxton published *Europe and the Turks,* which was a plea for the Concert of Europe to assume control, as distinct from mere supervision, of the execution of reform in the Christian provinces of Turkey. Without European control of the administration, he concluded from history, interference was positively harmful. [48] Between the Macedonian crisis of 1906 and the outbreak of the World War his hope that the Concert of Europe would coerce Turkey was gradually overcome by disappointment at its lack of achievement. History shows, he wrote in 1914, that the Concert 'can seldom move at all, and never with effect, except in regard to frontiers'. It lacked both common aims and a recognized leader. [49] In search of an effective alternative to concerted control, he proposed that Russia be given a mandate to impose reform in the administration of Armenia. [50]

During the great crisis in the Eastern question and in the

theorists, who preferred collective measures to individual action for the reform of Turkey because they wanted to preserve her territorial integrity, than to that of the supporters of Gladstonian progressivism, who championed the Concert of Europe because they thought it the most effective instrument for relieving the Christian subjects of Turkey. (Grey's ideas on the role of the Concert in China may be studied in his speeches in the House of Commons in 1900: see especially *Hansard,* 4th ser., lxxxi, cols 893–4 (30 March); lxxxv, col. 434 (3 July); and lxxxvii, cols 479–80 (2 August). The more critical and sceptical view of the Concert which he held in the later stage of the Chinese issue is explained in two speeches of 1901, in the House of Commons on 26 July (Hansard, 4th ser., xcviii, cols 278–81) and at Hotel Cecil on 20 February (*The 'Eighty Club' (1901). 'The War and After',* pp. 14–15).
46. Brailsford: *Macedonia. Its Races and their Future,* p. 18.
47. Ibid., p. 322.
48. Buxton: *Europe and the Turks,* v and vi; see also Buxton and Buxton: *Travel and Politics in Armenia,* p. 138.
49. Buxton and Buxton: *Travel and Politics,* p. 137; see also Buxton: *With the Bulgarian Staff,* in ch. vi of which he expressed contempt for the Concert of Europe.
50. Buxton and Buxton: *Travel and Politics,* p. 145.

following years the stronger element in the humanitarian strand of progressive thought had been the doctrine of national liberation of oppressed peoples. Between the crisis over Armenia and Crete and the outbreak of the World War it was the idea of administrative reform of the oppressing government. The dominant influence was no longer John Stuart Mill's but Stratford de Redcliffe's. While the Liberal statesmen urged the Concert of Europe to apply diplomatic pressure, the Radical writers demanded coercion. When the Concert persistently failed to reform Turkey they began to look for alternative means. Some of them also turned the Concert to other ends. During the last half dozen years before 1914, when it became increasingly clear that the greater danger to civilization was not Turkish misgovernment but European war, most of the progressive thinkers looked to the Concert of Europe for preservation of peace.

Organizational ideas

Though the earlier phase of humanitarian thought had been transformed and the later one diverted, the progressive tradition survived. While the strand that had been inspired by sympathy for oppressed peoples and a determination to extend Christian civilization was losing strength, another one was gaining support. In the last decades before the First World War a set of ideas which sprang from fear of European war and a desire for international order became ascendant in British thought about the Concert of Europe. Its central notion, that the Concert marked a stage in a progress from complete anarchy to a formal organization of the states system, found supporters among statesmen and publicists as well as international lawyers and historians.

Statesmen and publicists. The most prominent contributor to this set of ideas was Lord Salisbury. His views of the Concert of Europe were very different from Gladstone's, his opposite number in the other strand of the progressive tradition. Gladstone's progressive thought rested on balance of power principles and pointed towards humanitarian ends. Salisbury's had another basis and took a different direction.

On two important occasions, the crises in the Eastern question of 1878[51] and 1896,[52] Salisbury advocated the policy of using the

51. See the circular to the powers of 1 April 1878, in which Salisbury insisted that the whole of the San Stefano treaty should be submitted to discussion by the powers at

Concert of Europe for maintaining the balance of power. Yet at other times he spoke strongly against the idea of relying on the Concert to perform this function, arguing that it had been tried out in the Eastern question and had proved unsuccessful. The statesmen of 1856, he said in the House of Lords in 1877, had attempted the impossible when they endeavoured through the Concert of Europe to prevent Russia from reducing Turkey to a state of dependence by means of assumed claims over a certain portion of her subjects. Certainly, the pretension of Russia was injurious to the interests of other powers, and contrary to the policy of Europe.

But that six European Powers should undertake the tutelage of the subject population of Turkey and exercise that tutelage, not only by remonstrances, but in case of need by united naval and military action, was a chimera which it is difficult to understand how any one who has studied the history of the world could entertain. The thing was impossible. It was a matter of absolute certainty that when it came to the test, and the six Powers had to carry out that policy, some of them for good reasons or bad, others from circumstances arising out of the state of affairs, would decline the task, and then the united tutelage of the six Powers would be at an end.

Influence over Turkey would then again belong to Russia, the power prepared to fight for the subject people there.[53] The following year, when the Government was criticized for having

the coming congress (Temperley and Penson, *Foundations* . . . , pp. 372–80). As to the balance of power, see his letter to Disraeli of 21 March 1878, where he wrote, '. . . I think we should put in the forefront of our objections: (1) Those articles which menace the balance of power in the Egean' (ibid., p. 366), and the circular of 1 April, where he referred to 'the balance of maritime power' (ibid., p. 379).

52. See the circular of 20 October 1896, in which Salisbury demanded that the crisis in the East should be dealt with by united action and not settled according to the policy of any one of the great powers alone (Grenville: *Lord Salisbury and Foreign Policy*, p. 83). In September 1885 Salisbury had taken a similar line in the Eastern Question: see his telegram to Constantinople of 22 September, in which he emphasized that his policy was 'to act with the other Powers in upholding [the] Treaty of Berlin . . . our interests are not sufficient to justify our acting alone' (Temperley and Penson, *Foundations* . . . , p. 429).

53. *Hansard*, 3rd ser., ccxxxii, col. 690 (20 February). However, it might be noted that in one of the essays he had written in his younger years he had accepted the method of concerted tutelage of a state which was in danger of losing its independence (Salisbury: *Essays: Foreign Politics*, 'Poland' (1863), pp. 41–2).

concluded the Anglo-Turkish Convention, he declared that he was not alarmed by the condemnation that Britain had departed from the Concert of Europe.

> What will the future historian think of the 'European concert' when he comes to record what that concert has promised and what it performed? The 'European concert' in 1856 was to preserve the integrity and independence of the Turkish Empire; and certainly a more imposing machinery could not be devised. But 20 years have passed, and not one member of the 'European concert' has lifted its hand in defence of the integrity of the Turkish Empire.

A bilateral engagement, which left no doubt as to the pledges being fulfilled, was better than the misty and shadowy guarantees of the great powers.[54]

The progressive side of Gladstone's view of the Concert he found even more difficult to accept. Intervention for ideological and humanitarian ends had no place in his philosophy of foreign politics. This was made clear already in some of the biographical essays that he wrote in the early sixties. Pitt, he here noted with approval, had not gone to war for an idea. The war with France had not been a crusade against Jacobinism, but a war of self-defence. After the fashion of all wars, it had aimed simply at damaging an enemy, 'not at protecting "religion and humanity" '.[55] Especially the idea of establishing new nations by liberating oppressed peoples left him cold. The principle of nationality, from which it was derived, even provoked his sarcasm. 'The modern theory of nationality,' he wrote in his study of Castlereagh, 'is safe from refutation. The blows of argument fall harmlessly upon its unsubstantial forms. Controversy is waste labour in a domain of thought where no term is defined, no principle laid down, and no question propounded for investigation.'[56] The moral debate touched off by the Eastern crisis gave him an occasion to set forth his own conception of foreign policy. In the year when Gladstone's moral feeling against the Turkish misgovernment and passionate sympathy for the suffering

54. *Hansard,* 3rd ser., ccxlii, cols 509–10 (29 July).
55. Salisbury: *Essays: Biographical,* pp. 184–5.
56. Ibid., p. 39.

Christians led him to champion the Concert of Europe as an instrument for civilizing Turkey, Salisbury explained that politics was a matter of business.

> At any risk, therefore, of being called selfish and egotistical, at any risk of being accused of denying all Christian duty, I must still maintain that the first business of the English Government is, as honest trustees, to consider English interests, and that if they swerve out of their own personal feelings or wishes one iota from the straight line, they are guilty of breaking a trust which is reposed in them.

His point was that the cause in the Eastern war did not concern Britain.[57]

Both before and after the Congress of Berlin Salisbury attacked the Concert of Europe. But twenty years later, when separate alliances governed the political structure of the Continent and rising tension threatened the peace of Europe, he turned to the Concert for order and peace. In defence of the position he had taken in the issues over Armenia and Crete, he advanced an idea of the Concert of Europe which up till then had been the property of international lawyers. Its basic principle was conservative. In a debate on the Eastern question in the House of Lords in 1897, in which the Earl of Kimberley had argued that British policy should not be based on the integrity of Turkey, Salisbury upheld the doctrine of maintaining the territorial arrangement that was contained in the treaties concluded by the great powers. The integrity of the Ottoman Empire, he pointed out, had been established by 'the only authority competent to create law for Europe'. This authority had suffered from the somewhat absurd name which had been given to it—the Concert of Europe; and its intense importance had been buried under the bad jokes to which the word had given rise.

> But the federated action of Europe—if we can maintain it, if we can maintain this Legislature—is our sole hope of escaping from the constant terror and the calamity of war, the constant pressure of the burdens of an armed peace which weigh down the spirits and darken the prospects of every nation in this part of the world. The federation of Europe is the only hope we have; but that federation is only to be maintained by observing the

57. Salisbury: *A Speech delivered at Bradford*. . . p. 7.

conditions on which every Legislature must depend, on which every judicial system must be based—the engagements into which it enters must be respected.

In the interest of peace, the great powers appeared as the defenders of international law.[58] Salisbury based his contribution to progressive thought on the old principle of territorial conservation. That was the reason why adherents of the humanitarian view of the Concert opposed his ideas of 1897. By reviving one of the doctrines of the conservative theory, he helped to transform the earlier progressivism into anti-conservatism.

The rest of Salisbury's progressive idea of the Concert was set forth in his speech at the Guildhall banquet the same year. Estimating the recent achievements of the institution of the great powers, he admitted its limitations but emphasized its advantages. The inchoate federation of Europe, as he preferred to call it, had failed to prevent Greece from going to war but, with that exception, had succeeded in preserving the peace of Europe. It was like a steam-roller, very slow but very powerful. Though it had achieved more in the past year than any single power could have done, its greatest importance lay in its potentialities. This institution was 'the embryo of the only possible structure of Europe which can save civilization from the desolating effects of a disastrous war'. The competition in armaments, which involved each nation, was increasing from year to year.

> The one hope that we have to prevent this competition from ending in a terrible effort of mutual destruction which will be fatal to Christian civilization—the one hope we have is that the Powers may gradually be brought together, to act together in a friendly spirit on all questions of difference which may arise, until at last they shall be welded in some international constitution which shall give to the world, as a result of their great strength, a long spell of unfettered and prosperous trade and continued peace.[59]

This was Salisbury's contribution to progressive thought: the great powers acting together, whether as a body creating law for Europe or collectively defending their legislative work, were agents in the ordering of the states system; the Concert of Europe,

58. *Hansard,* 4th ser., xlvii, cols 1012–14 (19 March).
59. *The Times,* 10 November 1897, p. 6.

averting war in the immediate situation and organizing peace in the future, could be a step towards international government.

In a number of important respects Salisbury's contribution resembled Castlereagh's conservatism more than Gladstone's progressivism. The ideas of both the Tory and the Conservative sprang from preoccupation with the political situation of Europe, whereas those of the Liberal were a product of concern about the moral condition of the world. Castlereagh, who had experienced European war, and Salisbury, who saw it coming, were more interested in peace than in justice. But Gladstone, moved by the suffering of oppressed peoples and inspired by the ideas of nationality and self-government, strove for justice. Castlereagh, who sometimes expressed what might be called an organic conception of the congress system, and Salisbury, who in 1897 hoped that the European Concert would lead to some sort of international constitution, countenanced organization of the society of states. But Gladstone, advocating reform and reorganization in Turkey, concentrated on civilization of barbaric governments. Castlereagh, who identified himself with the territorial arrangement of the Vienna Congress, and Salisbury, who defended the work of the Berlin Congress, based their views on a positive law of treaties. But Gladstone rested his ideas on a natural law of rights. However, while Castlereagh's conception of the congress system was essentially conservative, the picture that Salisbury presented of the Concert of Europe in 1897 was progressive. Castlereagh, with the past on his mind, maintained the principle of European Concert for the sake of conserving the territorial order. But Salisbury, fearing the future, upheld the doctrine of territorial conservation in the hope of developing the Concert of Europe. He liked to see the Concert not only as a guarantee system for the established European order but also as an embryonic organ of a new international society. So, despite the contrasts with Gladstone, Salisbury too had a place among those who advanced progressive views of the Concert. As Gladstone in the seventies had linked balance of power thought and humanitarian notions, so Salisbury twenty years later combined conservatism with organizational ideas.

In the remaining years before 1914, when rising tension between the powers made it seem more important to organize peace than to reform Turkey, it was Salisbury's views of the Concert, rather than Gladstone's, which characterized progressive thought. The supporters of this tradition, whether politicians or scholars, tended to look to the Concert of Europe to save civilization. Arthur James Balfour, nephew and successor of Salisbury, adhered faithfully to his uncle's changing views. In 1879 he found that experience proved the Concert of Europe to be 'a perfectly worthless instrument' and that common sense pointed to the same conclusion. Turning round Gladstone's dictum, he then observed that the selfish views of the great powers were fatal to common action. 'The European Concert is, in fact, an instrument for doing as little as possible with the greatest possible amount of friction.'[60] In 1897 he defended the Concert of Europe and described it as a 'powerful, useful, and effective instrument'. During the previous few years this institution, though slow and, sometimes, imperfect in action, had rendered services to mankind and to civilization which, whether regarded in relation to the particular places in Eastern Europe or regarded in relation to the peace of Europe as a whole, had been incalculable.[61] Ten years later Noel Buxton saw in the concerted efforts of the great powers in connection with the Macedonian question the beginning of a revival of the comity of nations. 'In spite of all the rivalries aroused, Macedonia compels the Powers to work together, and to peoples whose officers cooperate in the same police force the thought of war seems increasingly absurd; the very perplexities of the task may be but the birth throes of a new unity.'[62]

But it was in the internationalism of Sir Edward Grey that this type of progressivism found its most prominent expression after 1900. In 1908 Grey went beyond the humanitarian tradition when he explained that the Concert was not only an instrument for Macedonian reform but also a guarantee for European peace. It kept the great powers in touch and prevented dangerous misunderstandings from creeping in between them.[63] In later years it was generally on this function that he placed the emphasis. 'The first business of the Concert of Europe, after all,' he declared

60. A. J. Balfour: *Mr Gladstone's Scotch Speeches,* pp. 6–7.
61. *Hansard,* 4th ser., xlvi, cols. 1518–20 (2 March).
62. Buxton: *Europe and the Turks,* pp. 120–1. In the second edition of the book, published in 1912 this passage had been rewritten. The tone had become more pessimistic, the emphasis now falling on the fact of dissension as much as on the ideal of unity (p. 84).
63. Grey: *Speeches,* p. 85 (House of Commons, 25 February).

in the House of Commons during the Second Balkan War, 'is to preserve peace and harmony between the component parts. If that were not secured the consequences to Europe would be far more disastrous than anything which has yet occurred.'[64] The decision of the Concert of Europe to limit itself to the object of localizing this war was on the whole wise: 'To attempt more might have been to endanger the whole Concert.'[65]

In those years Grey did not follow Salisbury in suggesting that the European Concert might be the germ of a formal institution. It was to the immediate political situation rather than to a future international order that he related the Concert, as may be seen from his attitude to conference diplomacy. The *ad hoc* conferences of the prewar period were then to him an 'emergency expedient'.[66] It was only much later, when he was writing his autobiography, that he expressed regret that some permanent machinery of ambassadorial conferences had not been set up between the Second Balkan War and the First World War.[67] After 1914, how-ever, he turned his mind to the future. His dreams in 1915 of a new and much improved substitute for the prewar Concert,[68] his pamphlet of 1918 on a League of Nations, and his acceptance of the institution inaugurated in January 1920 show that he came to associate the Concert of Europe with the idea of an advancing organization of the international society.

To Grey the Concert of Europe was a means of bringing the great powers together in a time of approaching war, rather than an instrument for maintaining the balance of power. Inclined to view the Concert of Europe as an alternative to the balance of power, he sometimes ignored the latter in the pursuit of the former.[69] Some of his Radical contemporaries drew an even clearer line

64. Hansard, 5th ser., lv, col. 1032 (14 July 1913). See also the retrospective view of the Concert of 1912–13 presented in Grey's autobiography *Twenty-Five Years 1892–1916*: 'We [the London Conference] had been something to which point after point could be referred; we had been a means of keeping all the six Powers in direct and friendly touch. The mere fact that we were in existence, and that we should have to be broken up before peace was broken, was in itself an appreciable barrier against war' (i, 272).
65. *Hansard,* 5th ser., lvi, col. 2294 (12 August 1913).
66. Ibid., lvi col. 2288 (12 August 1913).
67. Grey: *Twenty-Five Years,* i, 275–7.
68. Trevelyan, *Grey of Fallodon,* pp. 107–8.
69. Grey: *Twenty-Five Years,* i, 5: 'I have never, so far as I recollect, used the phrase "Balance of Power". I have of tendeliberately avoided the use of it, and I have never consciously set it before me as something to be pursued, attained, and preserved.'

between the two. Arthur Ponsonby, a pacifist member of Parliament and a founder of the Union of Democratic Control, saw the balance of power as a source of war and the Concert of Europe as a protector of peace. The policy of the balance of power, he wrote in 1912, divided Europe into two opposite camps and entailed a constant adjustment of the scales of the balance. It meant perpetual interference and the arrangement of ententes, alliances and secret agreements, and led to jealousy, suspicion, the general strain and tension of diplomatic relations and, worst of all, the ruinous and devastating rivalry in armaments. The final result of this policy might be a war in which Britain was likely to be fighting for the material interests of some other nation. 'The alternative policy of the Concert of Europe may be a slow and perhaps negative policy, but it kept us from embarrassing engagements and allowed us freedom of action.'[70] The following year he welcomed the establishment of the Concert of Europe and praised its success in preventing war, at the same time taking the opportunity to call for concerted action to limit expenditure on arms.[71] When, finally, the balance of power had resulted in European war, he suggested the formation of a European Council of representatives, to whom matters of dispute should be submitted and the conduct of negotiations entrusted. Such a solution, he emphasized, would be possible only if in the future the powers would act in concert and not in groups.[72] To Ponsonby the Concert of Europe was a step towards international organization. This institution, which to the Radicals of the nineteenth century had represented all that they disliked in foreign politics, was to some Radicals of this century the welcome alternative to the hated balance of power.

More farreaching plans for international organization were advanced by Brailsford in 1914. In *The War of Steel and Gold. A Study of the Armed Peace* he argued that the traditional principle of preserving in Europe a balance of power, though still receiving lip service, had become obsolete. In earlier times, when national liberty could be endangered by conquest, it had had a point. Now, when war and aggression no longer were aimed at territorial

70. Ponsonby: *Democracy and the Control of Foreign Affairs*, pp. 16–17. See also his speech in the House of Commons on the outbreak of the First World War (*Hansard*, 5th ser., lxv, col. 1841 (3 August)).
71. *Hansard*, 5th ser., liii, cols 373–6 (29 May 1913).
72. Ponsonby: *Democracy and Diplomacy*, p. 62.

conquest but at economic exploitation, it had lost it.[73] To renounce the principle of the balance and to drop the phrase—'a metaphor of venerable hypocrisy which serves only to disguise the perennial struggle for power and predominance'[74]—was his advice. Instead he pointed to the ideal of international government. To supersede the existing system of rigid and hostile groups, which Britain had joined in the name of the balance of power, he desired a council of all the great powers. 'Such a concert or Council of Powers is comparable not to a Court of Law or to a private mediator, but to a Federal Government or Council, which is expected to take broad decisions of policy in the name of the common good.'[75] The nucleus of the proposed institution existed already. Despite the failures and blunders which constituted so large a part of the century-old history of the Concert of Europe, destiny still pointed to its function as the germ of international government. The London Conference of 1912–13, generally believed to have prevented an outbreak of war between the great powers, was a model for the future. Factors moulding a Europe which would learn to act as a unity were at work. They included not only various strands of public opinion but also non-moral forces. In particular, the rise of world powers, to whom every political event was of interest, produced new perils and confusions and accentuated the need for an authoritative Concert to settle world politics. Brailsford clearly expected the Concert of Europe to develop into a government of the world.[76]

Though he did not attempt to draw up a constitution, Brailsford did outline the basic principles of the future system of politics. Firstly, there should be no change in the international *status quo* without the sanction of the institution representing the general body of civilized opinion. 'It is obvious that this principle, and this principle alone, can set a check upon lawless aggression, appease the rivalries of predatory Powers, and create a tribunal to which the weak may appeal.'[77] Secondly, alliances of the old-world, dynastic type, which would stand in the way of any decision based on the merits of the case, should not be allowed. To the latter rule there was one exception. In a situation where any

73. Brailsford: *The War of Steel and Gold,* p. 36.
74. Ibid., p. 28.   75. Ibid., p. 284.   76. Ibid., pp. 284–90.   77. Ibid., p. 290.

power or group of powers tried to evade the control of the Concert by refusing to submit common European affairs to its judgment or by defying its decisions, a temporary alliance of the others would be required.[78] Brailsford not only anticipated the establishment of the League of Nations but also sketched two of the principal ideas of its theory, those of peaceful change and collective security.

It is now possible to see the two strands of progressive thought in relation to the rest of British speculation about the Concert of Europe. Humanitarian thought was a digression. When Gladstone and his disciples departed from the balance of power tradition in pursuit of humanitarian ends they were going off at a tangent, in the sense that they were looking beyond the political relations of the states and focusing on the moral issues of civilization. Organizational thought, on the other hand, represented a return towards traditional ways of thinking. When Salisbury and the other members of this group speculated about the pacification and organization of the states system they were addressing themselves to the central problems of European politics. They were concentrating on the rivalry among the great powers and the threat of European war, and searching for security and peace.

International lawyers and historians. When Lord Salisbury in the late nineties gave currency to the organizational notion of the Concert this idea had already reached an advanced stage of development in the writings of certain international lawyers. Here it may be traced back to the middle of the century. In the year of the outbreak of the Crimean War William Whewell—the Master of Trinity who founded the professorship of international law at Cambridge in the belief that it was possible to realize even 'the most equitable and moral codes of International Law which Jurists have ever promulgated'[79]—saw in the congresses and alliances of his times an approximation to the idea of an international tribunal and a step towards the goal of perpetual peace.[80] But it was during the last three decades before 1914 that the argument reached its most developed form.

78. Brailsford: *The War of Steel and Gold*, pp. 292–3.
79. Whewell: *The Elements of Morality, Including Polity,* 1845, ii, 401.
80. Whewell: *The Elements . . .* 3rd edn, 1854, ii, Supplement, 337–8. This Supplement did not appear in the two earlier editions.

The earliest of the more substantial contributions came from James Lorimer, who in 1865 had been appointed to the chair of the law of nature and of nations at Edinburgh. His way of thinking resembled Bluntschli's.[81] In *The Institutes of the Law of Nations. A Treatise of the Jural Relations of Separate Political Communities,* published in 1883 and 1884, he stated that the ultimate problem of international jurisprudence was to find international equivalents for the factors known to national law as legislation, jurisdiction, and execution.[82] So far they did not exist. Neither the system of the balance of power nor that of voluntary arbitration had proved adequate. And attempts at solving the problems of international organization along either economical or religious and educational lines as well as schemes for a direct solution had all failed. In an irregular form the European Concert, for the present, charged itself with the functions of framing, applying and enforcing the positive laws that defined the mutual relations of states.[83] But it was a most imperfect institution. As an international legislative assembly the Concert, operating through occasional congresses, was destitute of organization and lacking in principle.[84] As a sort of international executive it suffered from an inability to give any permanent direction to its own activity. 'It does not contain the element of self-control, on which even its external action is dependent; it never can be either wiser or stronger than the particular treaty which it professes to execute.'[85] Held together by no permanent bond of union, it acted, if at all, only after the event.[86] Aiming at a more perfect solution, he put forward a detailed scheme of his own. To organize international society it was necessary, he thought, to determine the relative value of each state and assign to it its international position. He discarded the traditional principle of the equality and independence of states, which in his view had been repudiated by history and reason alike,[87] and substituted the doctrine of interdependence. In rejecting the existing institution in favour of his utopian plan, Lorimer recognized the European Concert as an attempt at

81. See above pp. 66–8.
82. Lorimer: *The Institutes of the Law of Nations,* ii, 186.
83. Ibid., i, 447.
84. Ibid., i, 175–7.
85. Ibid., i, 57.
86. Ibid., ii, 275.
87. Ibid., i, 44.

international organization but saw no possibility of its evolving.

T. E. Holland was less critical of the Concert of Europe. In a lecture delivered in 1886 he praised it for having prevented Balkan events from giving rise to a European war. A more or less perfectly harmonious action of the six great western powers had taken the place of the shifting combinations for the preservation of the balance of power, which had been so fruitful of great wars. Uniform pressure had been brought to bear on those Balkan peoples whose national ambitions had endangered the peace of Europe. 'I venture to assert that we have been witnesses of a triumph of right reason—not of unjustifiable dictation by strong to weak Powers, but of a desirable prevalence of great interests over small.' The moral sanction of the authority of the great powers, he continued, 'is derived from that general acquiescence on the part of all civilized States which is the very breath of life of International Law'.[88] Holland tried to reconcile the political fact of the authority of the Concert of Europe with the legal principle of the equality and independence of states. In one of his later lectures he welcomed the assumption by the great powers of a sort of oligarchical superintendence over the rest of Europe as a practical step towards international unity, pointing out that progress in this direction took place through treaties—by contract and not by law-making—and thus, in theory, did not interfere with the independence of states.[89]

John Westlake, Professor of international law at Cambridge between 1888 and 1908, rejected Lorimer's approach to international organization and was closer to Holland. In his opinion, an ordered commonwealth of nations would come about not by constitution-mongering but through evolution. In the history of the Concert of Europe he saw clear evidence that tendencies which in a remote future might crystallize into some form of international government were operating.[90] For a time after 1815, he observed, 'the pentarchy' had been worked in the interest of the principle of legitimacy. Later it had been used to settle the separation of Holland and Belgium and to deal with several phases of the Eastern question. From 1848 it had ceased to exist. But, as the Congress of Berlin had shown, the controlling autho-

88. Holland: *Studies in International Law*, p. 268.
89. Holland: *Lectures on International Law*, p. 32.
90. Westlake: *International Law*, 2nd edn, pt i, pp. 352-3 (article of 1896).

rity of the great powers in congress had sunk so far into European habits as still to carry both moral and material weight. In this political inequality of the members of the European system lay the hope for the future. 'It may prove to be a step towards the establishment of a European government, and in no society can peace and order be permanently enjoyed without a government.'[91] In his *International Law* he took up the question whether the existence in Europe of the great powers as a separate and recognized class could be reconciled with the equality and independence which international law deemed to belong to the smaller powers. He started his answer with an extract from Lord Salisbury's speech in the House of Lords in 1897 in defence of the Concert of Europe,[92] adding the comment that it would be impossible to put better the argument in favour of the position assumed by the great powers. If each of their proceedings be considered separately, he went on, the ratification subsequently conceded to it by the states affected saved it from being a substantial breach of their equality and independence, leaving it open only to the charge of a want of courtesy in manner. It stood as an example of political action, not to be condemned if just. But when such proceedings were habitual they presented another character.

> They then carry the connotation of right which by virtue of human nature accretes to settled custom, and the acquiescence of the smaller powers in them loses the last semblance of independent ratification. We are in presence of the first stages of a process which in the course of ages may lead to organised government among states, as the indispensable condition of their peace, just as organised national government has been the indispensable condition of peace between private individuals. The world in which the largest intercourse of civilised men has been from time to time carried on has not always been distributed into equal and independent states, and we are reminded by what we see that it may not always continue to be so distributed.[93]

On these grounds he accepted the erosion of the principle of legal equality.

91. Westlake: *Collected Papers . . . on Public International Law*, pt i, pp. 99–101.
92. See above pp. 179–80.
93. Westlake: *International Law*, 2nd edn, pt i, pp. 321–3 (reprinted from the first edition of 1904).

T. J. Lawrence, reader in international law at Bristol, went a step further. His attitude to the principle of equality was indicated already in the title of an essay which he published in 1884, 'The Primacy of the Great Powers'. The Concert of Europe, which he defined as the agreement of the great powers,[94] existed as a kind of International Court of Appeal, he wrote there. But, since its procedure was not settled and the nature and extent of its jurisdiction not determined, it did not yet amount to a formal European Areopagus. 'All we have at present is a very real superiority before the law on the part of the Great Powers.'[95] This rudimentary institution was slow in deliberation and uncertain in action. And often its decisions fell short of the demands of justice. But, with all its faults, it had done great good by settling disputes which could have led to war. However, it was not so much on the achievements of the European Concert as on its potentialities that he put the emphasis. Since it was a natural and healthy growth, it possessed a chance of permanence. 'It is probably destined to become more and more effective as the desire for a peaceful settlement of their quarrels increases among the nations; and it may in some far distant time develop into that Supreme Court of International Appeal, for which statesmen, philosophers, and divines have longed throughout the last three centuries.'[96] This expectation led him to relinquish the traditional principle of the legal equality of states. In *The Principles of International Law*, of which the first edition appeared in 1895, he argued that it was time to alter the principle in deference to the established practice of nations. The role of the powers of the Concert of Europe, who during the greater part of the nineteenth century had exercised a kind of superintendence over certain European questions, as well as of the United States, who in the same period had risen to the position of unofficial leader and protector of the other independent republics of America, gave them certain rights. Though individually they had no greater rights in ordinary matters than any other member of the family of nations, collectively the great powers of Europe acted in the questions over which they had gained control pretty much as the committee of a club. 'That is to say, they possess a regulative authority and are

94. Lawrence: *Essays on Some Disputed Questions in Modern International Law*, p. 193.
95. Ibid., pp. 210–12.
96. Ibid., p. 213.

deemed to speak for the whole body of European states.' Their authority rested not, as in the case of a club, on definite rules but on the tacit consent of the other states.[97] The old doctrine, which he attributed to Grotius, was becoming obsolete and must be superseded by the principle of the primacy of the foremost powers of the civilized world.[98] 'There is no moral or jural necessity about the doctrine of equality', he insisted in a later edition.[99]

In the fourth edition of this work, published in 1910, Lawrence took his conception of a Concert of great powers beyond the boundaries of Europe. The end of isolation for the United States and the rise of nations in the Far East, especially Japan, had extended the circle of great powers, he saw. The recent history of international conferences had shown that for some purposes these non-European powers, too, could act as members of the body of great powers. Just as the six European great powers played the part of leaders when important matters concerning the states of Europe came up for settlement, so the eight great powers of the world took the lead when all the states of the civilized world came together to settle questions connected with the preservation of peace and the humanizing of war.[100] From this he concluded that a Concert of the World might be developing. However, there were also powerful influences working against it. To the idea that anything which militated against the absolute equality of all independent states in all matters was to be reprobated as an attack on international justice he added, probably with Germany in his mind, the attitude that objected to any organization of international society because it would mean a limitation on the power of a strong and masterful state to dictate such rules as it deemed to act in its own favour. Whether the rudimentary Concert of the World would triumph over the combined opposition of these two extremes and develop into 'a regular organ of international life' depended in the last resort on the opinion of the rulers and peoples of civilized mankind, he thought.[101]

Of these international lawyers, only Lorimer attempted a direct solution of the problem of international organization. The

97. Lawrence: *Principles,* 1895, pp. 65–6.
98. Ibid., pp. 242 and 245–7.
99. Lawrence: *Principles,* 4th edn, 1910, p. 277.
100. Ibid., pp. 274–5.
101. Ibid., pp. 278–9.

others hoped for an evolution from the Concert of Europe. While Lorimer immediately rejected the doctrine of legal equality of all states, the others departed from it in stages. Holland tried to reconcile it with the state of political inequality between great powers and other states. Westlake accepted its erosion in the interest of future international government. Lawrence, acting in response to signs that a formal organ of international society was emerging, replaced it with the doctrine of legal primacy of the great powers. The more each of the three believed in the potentialities of the existing institution for developing into a permanent system of international order, the readier he was to abandon the principle of legal equality.

However, not all the international lawyers followed this trend. The great positivist W. E. Hall, whose *International Law,* first published in 1880, attained greater authority than any of the writings of the Concert-minded lawyers, showed little interest either in the European Concert or in the great powers. And the even more influential Lassa Oppenheim, who taught first at the London School of Economics and then at Cambridge, where he succeeded Westlake in the chair of international law, went against the tendency of his predecessors. Writing in 1905, he insisted on maintaining the distinction between political and legal equality. However important the position and influence of the great powers in the family of nations, they were by no means derived from a legal basis or rule, he asserted. 'It is nothing else than powerful example which makes the smaller States agree to arrangements of the Great Powers.' Nor had a state the character of a great power by law. 'It is nothing else than its actual size and strength which makes a State a Great Power.'[102]

Towards the end of the period a few historians tackled the problem of international organization from a different angle. Conceiving of the European Concert as an experiment, they set out to analyse its history in order to extract its lessons for future attempts to bring order to the relations between states. A. W. Ward, for many years professor of history and English language and literature at Manchester, and later Master of Peterhouse, Cambridge, was interested especially in the earlier history of the Concert. In the system that the four victorious powers had inaugurated in 1815, and which France later had joined, he saw a

102. Oppenheim: *International Law,* i, 163.

machinery for peaceful change and general security. It was the very opposite of a hard and fast system, he wrote in 1873. 'Instead of the Great Powers swearing, as it were, to maintain for ever the existing condition of things in Europe, a tribunal was, on the contrary, established designed expressly to provide, not of course for rash changes, but for the sanction of such modifications as might from time to time become necessary.'[103]

He did not assert that the system had been as adequately administered in the interests of national development as in those of the maintenance of peace, but pointed out that a number of changes consonant with the progress of national life and the right of self-determination had been accomplished with the sanction of this alliance. The best examples were the recognition of the independence of Greece and of Belgium. Furthermore, the system had provided security against aggression. Though the will had not been wanting, not one of the great powers had been able to pursue its designs of self-aggrandizement uncontrolled by the authority of the tribunal. He regretted that this 'common system of a guaranteed security', though still nominally in force, had been signally impaired in its efficiency, and ascribed the fact mainly to a growing tendency of the great powers to act independently.[104] The remedy, in his view, lay in an enlargement and elevation of the principle of joint action and in the progress of enlightenment.[105] In a lecture given almost thirty years later he again reviewed the early history of the European Concert. Comparing the political situation of the first decade of the twentieth century with that of the congressional period, he pointed out that any system of separate alliances between particular powers was far more likely to lead to the policy of an armed peace, by which he meant near-war, than was the system of an alliance of all the great powers.[106] In search of an alternative to the tense international relations of his own times Ward looked to the early Concert of Europe for example.

In 1913 Alison Phillips, later professor of modern history at Dublin, delivered six lectures at Oxford, which he published the following year under the title *The Confederation of Europe: A Study of the European Alliance, 1813–1823 as an Experiment in the*

---

103. Ward: *Collected Papers,* i, 26.
104. Ibid., i, 27–8.   105. Ibid., i, 53.   106. Ibid., ii, 273.

International Organization of Peace. Their main purpose, he explained at the outset, was 'to study the history of the European Coalition which succeeded to Napoleon's dictatorship in Europe, from the point of view of an experiment in the international organization of peace, in order to see what light it throws on those modern peace projects to the promulgation of which so great an impulse was given by the Hague Conferences of 1899 and 1907 and the magnificent prize founded by the late M. Nobel'.[107] At the end of the Napoleonic Wars, he recalled, the great powers, by invoking the legend of a prerevolutionary European juridical system, had consecrated the principle of an international law and, 'by committing themselves to the task of acting in concert for the maintenance of the sanctity of treaties', had given to it a wholly new sanction. They had attempted to solve the problem of reconciling central and general control by a 'European Confederation' with the maintenance of the liberties of its constituent states.[108] This attempt to establish a juridical system had failed. Within eight years of the signature of the Treaty of Chaumont the coalition of the great powers had foundered after collision with the revolutionary movements. While Britain's attitude to intervention as practised in the early eighteen-twenties had made the harmonious cohesion of the European system impossible, the French Revolution of 1830 had led to a division of the five powers into two hostile groups. The later history of Europe had been a struggle between the revolutionary forces of nationalism and constitutional liberty, encouraged by the two western liberal powers, and the conservative forces of the Holy Alliance, the league of the three eastern members of the original coalition. The outcome had been defeat of the conservative forces and collapse of the Holy Alliance.[109]

From his analysis of the congress system Phillips concluded that any attempt at international organization would come up against the difficulty that had caused the failure of the experiment of 1815: the authority of the international institution would clash with the sovereignty of its constituent states. The institution would have to follow the principle of preserving the *status quo,* in his view the only practical basis of international organization,

107. Phillips: *The Confederation,* pp. 9–10.
108. Ibid., p. 9.
109. Ibid., pp. 292–3.

and hence would have to meet the challenge of revolutionary forces. On the one hand, it would be led to interfere in the domestic relations of individual states: 'The important thing is that for any international organization . . . a certain uniformity of political system is essential, and that, sooner or later, this uniformity would be enforced by armed intervention.' On the other hand, the international institution would have no choice but to oppose attempts to overthrow the established territorial order. Revisionist efforts by discontented peoples, the inevitable product of the strong spirit of nationalism, would be suppressed with arms. In either case there would be neither harmony nor peace but conflict between principles and struggle between the international confederation and its constituent parts.[110]

Though the experiment of 1815 had failed, the effort had not been wasted. By revealing the difficulties of international organization, it had provided a lesson for future attempts. Furthermore, not all had been lost, he pointed out. Though the system established at Vienna had been shattered, a feeling of common interests among nations and a respect for international law, both strong factors making for peace, had remained. And the Concert of Europe, to which the world owed so much, had survived.[111] The European coalition was not merely a warning against attempts at a direct solution of the problem of international organization but also the origin of traditions which tended to bring mankind closer to the ideals of order and peace.

Phillips's views on the Concert of Europe contained both conservative and progressive ideas. On the one hand, his thoughts about international organization rested on principles of territorial and dynastic conservation. He not only believed, like Salisbury, that any attempt to organize the society of states must be based on the principle of maintaining the order laid down by treaty, but went further than Castlereagh in sympathy with the ideas of the Holy Alliance and Alexander I. On the other hand,

110. Ibid., pp. 293–8; the quotation is on p. 296.
111. Ibid., pp. 298–9. In an earlier work he had noted the extension of the idea of the Concert of Europe that had taken place during the last decades of the nineteenth century. Referring to the participation of the United States in the Berlin Conference of 1884–85, he wrote, 'The process had already begun which was accentuated by the Conference at The Hague. The idea of the Concert of Europe was expanding into that of the Concert of the World' (Phillips: *Modern Europe 1815–1899*, 2nd edn, 1902, p. 542).

his analysis of the problem of the organization of peace was a contribution to the progressive tradition. Though he adopted a critical approach and reached pessimistic conclusions, his speculations about the possibility of overcoming the difficulties of international organization resembled those of more progressive thinkers.

The debate on international organization continued after the outbreak of the war. In 1916 Ramsay Muir, professor of modern history first at Liverpool and then at Manchester and an active member of the Liberal party, published *Nationalism and Internationalism: The Culmination of Modern History*. The section on internationalism contained an answer to the thesis advanced in *The Confederation of Europe*. Muir argued that Phillips had failed to realize the importance of having a territorial order based on national feelings and had erred in thinking that intervention was inherent in any form of international organization, and rejected his pessimistic conclusions. The experiment of 1815 had failed, he explained, because it had been founded on a territorial settlement which took no account of nationality, because it had lacked a machinery for revising treaties, because it had been a league of sovereigns instead of a league of peoples, and—a corollary of the previous reason—because it had led to intervention in the domestic affairs of states. The failure could not fairly be regarded as having proved the bankruptcy of the international idea. On the contrary, it might rather be said to have contributed to a clearer understanding of the problem. To correct the four faults of the Vienna system and to find a more satisfactory way of regulating common European affairs might not be impossible.[112] The way to go about it was to establish a better organized Concert. The Concert of Europe, initiated in 1815, had survived the collapse of the postwar union of great powers and had succeeded in preserving peace during two long periods of the century. Lately it had been murdered by Germany—'a power with which reasonable relations are all but impossible', he wrote in 1914, 'a power which simply declines to play a straightforward part in the Concert of Europe . . . '.[113] If it were recreated on the basis of boundaries drawn in accordance with the desires of the peoples, it could secure a permanent peace for the world and provide an effective protection

112. Muir: *Nationalism and Internationalism*.
113. Ibid., *Britain's Case Against Germany: An Examination of the Historical Background of the German Action in 1914*, p. 157; see also p. 172.

for the smaller nations: 'A Concert of Europe can only become a fully effective organ when the lines of division between states, and the modes of organization within the states, are such as in the main to reflect the real wishes and feelings of the peoples concerned.'[114] According to Muir, nationalism and internationalism went hand in hand. Phillips believed it important to preserve the established order against all challenges, and found conflict between the international institution and its constituent members inevitable; Muir, hoping for a more perfect territorial and political order, believed harmony to be possible.

Ideas of this kind, seen in different degrees in some of Salisbury's later speeches and in the writings of the publicists, lawyers and historians, mentioned, might be regarded as the bridge from the Concert of Europe to the League Covenant. To view the Concert as the germ of a formal organization of sovereign states was to anticipate the League of Nations and the United Nations. But the organizational set of ideas contained also elements which seemed to point towards a more ambitious goal. When Salisbury spoke about an 'international constitution', Brailsford about a 'Federal Government or Council' and Westlake about a 'European government' they may have had in mind something more than a development and consolidation of the existing type of international society. To judge by the words they used, they were looking beyond the traditional European order of independent states in the direction of world government. If so, they were departing from previous ways of thinking about the European Concert and international politics. The conservatives, who had sought order through maintaining the territorial settlement of 1815, the balance of power thinkers, who had looked for security through regulating the power relations between states, and the humanitarians, who had tended to neglect the political relations of states for the moral condition of Europe, all had accepted the anarchical character of European society.[115] So did most of the present group

114. Ibid., p. 170; see also the 2nd edition of Muir: *Nationalism and Internationalism*, published 1919, p. 193: The record of the Concert of Europe 'encourages the hope that a better organized Concert of civilised states might avail to secure a permanent peace for the world'.

115. In their tendency to go beyond the anarchical state of international society in the direction of European or world government, these isolated British thinkers had some affinity with the central European advocates of dynastic conservatism in the restoration period. When Gentz and Metternich, and those who thought like them, advanced the notion of a union of sovereigns to protect the society of Europe and

of thinkers. By international organization they generally meant merely extending and formalizing the oligarchical tendencies of the nineteenth-century society of states. Before 1914, those who showed that they might be prepared to exchange state sovereignty for some form of European or world government were only a small minority. What is more, neither of them provided evidence that they had thought out, or even were fully aware of, the problem of the conflict between national interests and supranational authority. Yet it is possible to see in the organizational trend of thought not only the germ of the international institutions of 1920 and 1945 but also hints of the modern dream of a world state.

2. CRITICISM

Though the progressive superseded the balance of power tradition and retained its position till the First World War, it never enjoyed unchallenged supremacy. In both its earlier and its later phase it encountered opposition from nationalist and imperialist quarters. The chief enemy was Disraeli. In the years when Gladstone went beyond the balance of power principle and advocated using the Concert of Europe to relieve the subjects of Turkey, Disraeli insisted that humanitarian must be subordinated to political considerations. The cause of the Christian subjects struggling to liberate themselves from the Ottoman Empire did not appeal to him. He had little sympathy for the Balkan peoples and did not understand the true nature of the national movements in the East. In common with Metternich, whom he admired, he was inclined to see Continental politics as a conflict between the secret societies of the revolutionary movement, 'ever prepared to ravage Europe', and the governments.[116] When Servia declared war upon Turkey in 1876 he maintained that it was really the secret societies of Europe which were declaring war.[117] But it was not merely a lack in sympathy and understanding which led him to oppose the humanitarian version of progressive thought. It was also a conviction that the Eastern question presented political elements which were of decisive importance to the great powers.

defended the principle of intervention to suppress revolution, they came close to advocating a new kind of European order and to denying the traditional principle of state sovereignty (see above, ch. 1).

116. Disraeli: *Lord George Bentinck*, 8th edn, ch. xxvii, especially p. 397.

117. Disraeli: *The Eastern Question. Speeches by the Earl of Beaconsfield and Lord Derby*, pt i: Lord Beaconsfield's Speech at Aylesbury, p. 11.

Surely some of the elements of the distribution of power in the world are involved in it. It is a question in which is involved the existence of Empires; and really it does appear to me we shall never come to its solution . . . if we are to discard from it every political consideration, and to believe that the only element with which we have to deal is the amelioration of the condition of the Christian subjects of the Porte.[118]

He was in the Palmerstonian tradition. Fearing Russian designs, he subscribed to the old balance of power doctrine of maintaining the territorial integrity and independence of the Ottoman Empire.[119]

But Disraeli did not have the European spirit which characterized some of the other leading adherents of the balance of power principle of foreign policy. Though he recognized that united action by the great powers was sometimes more calculated to lead to success than isolated intervention by Britain,[120] he shared Salisbury's critical opinion of the Concert of Europe as an instrument for maintaining the balance of power. Inclined, with Canning, for Europe to read England, he went beyond Palmerston in his concern for British interests. He upheld the power and prestige of the Empire, and looked to the world beyond Europe. On several occasions he appealed to England to set aside the cosmopolitan principles of liberalism, which he thought would tie her to the Continent and restrict her expansion, and to embrace the national ideas, which he was convinced would lead her to a great future as an imperial country.[121] 'It has been said,' he remarked at the end of a speech in the House of Lords in 1877 on the Eastern question, 'that the people of this country are deeply interested in the humanitarian and philanthropic considerations involved in it. All must appreciate such feelings. But I am mistaken if there be not a yet deeper sentiment on the part of the people of this country, one with which I cannot doubt your Lordships will ever sympathise, and that is—the determination to maintain the Empire of England.'[122] A nationalism which

118. *Hansard,* 3rd ser., ccxxxii, cols 51–2 (8 February 1877).
119. Ibid., ccxxxii, cols 710–11: the territorial integrity and independence of the Turkish Empire 'embodies a principle which always has been accepted by statesmen' (20 February 1877).
120. See, e.g., *Hansard,* 3rd ser., ccxxxi, col. 206 (31 July 1876).
121. See, e.g., *Speech of the Right Hon. B. Disraeli, M.P., . . . Crystal Palace, June 24, 1872,* p. 11.
122. *Hansard,* 3rd ser., ccxxxii, col. 726 (20 February).

o

enjoined Britain to keep a 'proud reserve' from Europe and pursue her interests in the world was not only opposed to the idea of joint intervention for humanitarian ends but also irreconcilable with the notion of international organization for peace. As his insistence on putting politics before morality had made Disraeli the principal opponent of humanitarianism, so his nationalism and imperialism made him the chief influence against the organizational version of progressive thought.

Though most imperialists were inclined simply to ignore the Concert of Europe, a number of Disraeli's disciples criticized both the earlier and the later type of progressivism. One of them was H. A. M. Butler-Johnstone, a member of Parliament and a writer with Turcophil passions. In a speech in the House of Commons in 1877, protesting against the policy of pressing reforms upon Turkey in the name of the Concert of Europe, he ridiculed the Concert and, in the manner of Bismarck, doubted the existence of Europe. Arguing that the government could not divorce religion from politics, he championed the integrity and independence of the Ottoman Empire against humanitarian intervention.[123] In some articles written in 1896 for a Belgian journal he attacked the policy of pursuing peace through the Concert of Europe. The European Concert, not founded on homogeneity of sentiment or identity of interests, was no real Concert at all but 'at best a temporary makeshift, and in all probability a conspiracy of intrigue'.[124] Historically speaking, it was merely a high-sounding term which Gladstone had invented and used as a stick with which to beat the Disraeli cabinet. To persist in this policy of peace and to adhere to the Concert of Europe, he warned, might lead to stultification of English policy and destruction of the British Empire.[125] He followed with some sarcastic references to Salisbury's use of the expression 'the Federation of Europe' as an alias for the Concert. If the Concert of Europe had broken down from lack of common elements among the parties, what were the chances of the same parties associating into the closer and more intimate partnership connoted by the term federation, he asked. The Europe Bismarck had plunged back into the chaotic conditions of international relations that had existed before the

123. *Hansard*, 3rd ser., ccxxxiii, cols 1154, 1157 and 1159 (13 April).
124. Butler-Johnstone: *Imperialism, Federation, and Policy* (repr. from *The Belgian Times and News*, 1896), p. 147.
125. Ibid., pp. 149–50.

Peace of Westphalia was very far from the goal of a federation of nations. ' . . . a Federation of Europe in the present condition of Europe for purposes of peace and progress is sheer nonsense and contradiction.'[126] Britain should federate with her colonies and ally herself with America instead. Like Disraeli, he turned his back on the Concert and looked to the Empire. While his views of 1877 clashed with humanitarianism, those of 1896 conflicted with organizational thought.

Sir Ellis Ashmead-Bartlett, a Conservative member of Parliament and author of a number of pamphlets on imperial issues, was an even more outspoken critic of Gladstone's and Salisbury's Concert of Europe. In a speech in the House of Commons in 1881 he referred to 'this preposterous theory of "the Concert of Europe" ' which had been invented to take the place, in the popular imagination, of 'the old manly and British policy in the East—the policy of Pitt and Wellington, of Palmerston and Beaconsfield'. Though eminently calculated to tickle the fancy of the uninformed and the sentimental, the term was completely misleading as a description of the actual relationship between the great powers.[127] Almost twenty years later, when the Concert of Europe had been invoked to deal with China, he used even stronger language. In speeches in the House of Commons he described the Concert variously as a 'chimera', a 'farce', a 'will-o'-the-wisp', a 'mischievous fiction', a 'cheap fallacy', and a 'cuckoo cry'.[128] As practised in China, it had been 'the most wicked, cruel, and disastrous failure that any Government has put before the country'. It had reduced the prestige and weakened the power of Britain as well as raised international tension.[129] As in 1881 he had urged the government to return to Disraeli's policy of stable alliances and defence of the balance of power, so he now encouraged Britain to cut adrift from the Concert of Europe and pursue her own policy in alliance with those states whose interests and views coincided with hers. Ashmead-Bartlett, an open admirer of Disraeli's self-centred nationalism, shared the anti-European attitude of the imperialists.

The balance of power ideas that Disraeli and his disciples set against Gladstonian humanitarianism were different from earlier

126. Ibid., pp. 154–6.
127. *Hansard,* 3rd ser., cclxv, cols 781–2 (23 August).
128. *Hansard,* 4th ser., lxxxv, cols 424 and 426; lxxxvii, cols 466, 467 and 982; and xcii, cols 166 and 167 (3 July, 2 August and 8 August 1900 and 28 March 1901).
129. *Hansard,* xcii, col. 166 (28 March 1901).

balance of power thought. In the first place, they were completely divorced from the territorial order of 1815. While the conservatives had combined the principle of power balance with that of territorial conservation, the balance of power thinkers had taken steps to separate the two. But Disraeli denied any connection between them: ' . . . I never will confound the maintenance of the balance of power', he said in the House of Commons in 1854, 'with the maintenance of the present territorial distribution of Europe. They have nothing to do with each other; and if we confound them, this country may be involved in great dangers and difficulties . . . it is not true that the distribution of territory sanctioned by the treaties of Vienna has necessarily anything to do with the balance of power.'[130] Secondly, these ideas took account of extra-European powers. The conservatives and the balance of power thinkers had tended to include only the states of Europe in the balance of power; but Disraeli repeatedly pointed to the importance of the non-European elements.[131] Thirdly, they had pronounced isolationist tendencies. Both the conservatives and the balance of power thinkers, though with a varying degree of commitment, had accepted the Concert of Europe as a means for maintaining the balance of power; but Disraeli and his followers were inclined to ignore the Concert and to rely on separate and *ad hoc* alliances. Yet in general their views resembled those of the earlier thinkers. The nationalists and imperialists, too, sought security through balance of power and subscribed to the principles of territorial integrity and non-intervention. Against those who advocated collective intervention to bring about national liberation and political reform, they asserted that it was more important to prevent encroachments by rival great powers and that measures of intervention should be confined to cases of direct threat to the interests of Britain or to the balance of Europe.[132]

The history of British thought about the Concert of Europe

130. *Hansard,* 3rd ser., cxxx, col. 1027 (20 February).
131. See, e.g., *Hansard,* 3rd ser., clxxvi, col. 731 (4 July 1864); and Disraeli: *A Voice from the Grave, Speech by the late Earl of Beaconsfield . . . April 3, 1872,* p. 28.
132. See, e.g., Disraeli's speech in the House of Commons on 24 January, 1860, in which he declared himself to be in favour of 'that policy which is popularly known by the name of the policy of non-interference': 'There are conditions under which it may be our imperative duty to interfere. We may clearly interfere in the affairs of foreign countries when the interests or the honour of England are at stake, or when, in our opinion, the independence of Europe is menaced.' But Britain ought not to interfere unless there was a clear necessity (*Hansard,* 3rd ser., clvi, col. 95).

might be described as a relay race with two sets of ideas. On the one side, the notions of political freedom and national liberty, which first had inspired Whigs to oppose dynastic and Radicals to criticize territorial conservatism and then had guided Radicals into opposition to balance of power thought, were carried on by the humanitarian progressives. On the other side, the principles of territorial integrity and non-intervention, which had been developed by the supporters of territorial and the Tory opponents of dynastic conservatism and had been upheld by the balance of power thinkers, were taken over by the nationalists and imperialists. This continuity of thought might be expressed diagrammatically:

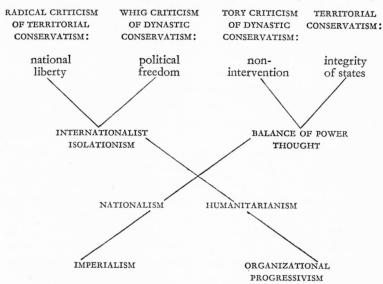

RADICAL CRITICISM OF TERRITORIAL CONSERVATISM:

WHIG CRITICISM OF DYNASTIC CONSERVATISM:

TORY CRITICISM OF DYNASTIC CONSERVATISM:

TERRITORIAL CONSERVATISM:

national liberty

political freedom

non-intervention

integrity of states

INTERNATIONALIST ISOLATIONISM

BALANCE OF POWER THOUGHT

NATIONALISM

HUMANITARIANISM

IMPERIALISM

ORGANIZATIONAL PROGRESSIVISM

The intersection of the lines in the diagram illustrates the intermixture of balance of power thought and internationalist isolationism which appears to have taken place in the late eighteen-seventies. Signs of such a meeting of opposed traditions might be seen in Gladstone's as well as in Salisbury's and Disraeli's reactions to the Eastern crisis. Gladstone allowed his liberal internationalist policy of reform and liberation to be limited by balance of power considerations. The two Conservatives managed, on the one hand, to advocate a European congress to restore the balance after San Stefano and, on the other, to attack the Concert of Europe in the name of a nationalism which contained strong hints of isolationism. An interaction between the two traditions could explain the novel combinations of attitudes and the new trends of thought that became apparent after the Eastern crisis. On the one hand, a European outlook, till then a mark of balance of power thought, and liberal views, characteristic of the internationalist isolationism of the Manchester School, joined each other in the humanitarian trend; on the other hand, the principle developed by the balance of power thinkers, that of preventing the aggrandizement of rival powers, and the doctrine advocated by their opponents, that of keeping aloof from Europe, met in the nationalist trend. The humanitarians set aside balance of power considerations and devoted their efforts to moral ends; the nationalists turned their back on Europe and concentrated on the interests of Britain in the world. While Gladstone's disciples saw the Concert of Europe as the means to their end, Disraeli's regarded it as a distraction from their pursuits.

This is the paradox in the pattern of British thought about European politics. Those who carried on the ideas of political freedom and national liberty, which stemmed from the left side of the spectrum of the earliest ideas about the Concert and which traditionally had been associated with isolationism, became interventionists; those who took over the idea of security through balance of power, which emanated from the right side of the spectrum and which previously had implied some degree of European involvement, moved towards isolationism. The left, till then against the Concert, came to its defence; the right, so far for the Concert, went against it. The cross-fertilization between different traditions of thought was the chief feature of British speculation about the Concert of Europe.

The diagram indicates also the later development of the humanitarian and the nationalist trend. The former became dominated by anticonservatism, its negative complement, and was superseded by organizational thought, the other element of the progressive tradition. The latter, extending the idea of the balance of power to the world beyond Europe, turned into imperialism. By the end of the century the conflict was already, as it was in the interwar years, between the internationalist doctrine of European organization and the imperialist principle of extra-European responsibilities. By 1914 the latter had not yet prevailed: the progressive tradition survived to inspire the League of Nations.

CONCLUSION

The idea of the Concert of Europe as an instrument of territorial and dynastic conservation, which dominated its early days, was in fact a comparatively novel notion in European international thought—a response to and counterpart of international Jacobinism. The ideas linking the Concert to the system of the balance of power, though they did not gain ascendancy until the second generation of the nineteenth century, belonged to a tradition of European thought nearly as old as the states system itself. And what I have called the progressive ideas of the Concert, which flowered in the later part of the century, may be seen as a revival of a still older tradition, namely that of natural law, with its Christian and rationalist elements.

The conservative theory belonged primarily to Austria and Prussia. It mirrored the interests that the governments of those powers had in upholding the existing European order against the forces of movement and change. The German version of the balance of power theory arose in the northern states and developed in the *Reich*. It was an expression of the Prussian experience of European politics, projecting first Prussia's ambition to strengthen her position in Germany and Europe and then the Empire's determination to increase its power in the world. The English version of this theory reflected, from one point of view, Britain's need to prevent the rise of a dangerous rival on the Continent and, from another, her interest in securing immunity from competing powers in the world beyond Europe. The progressive theory was largely a product of British thought. In its humanitarian form it expressed the concern of Englishmen with the moral condition of European life and Christian civilization, in its organizational form the advantage that Britain in particular stood to gain from an orderly states system and a peaceful Europe. The German contribution to the theory of the Concert of Europe was that of a continental power with limitations to overcome and ambitions to fulfil, the British contribution that of a maritime power with a position to defend and competitors to check.

Speculation about the Concert of Europe took different courses in the two countries. In Germany, balance of power thought eclipsed dynastic conservatism but became dominated by anti-European views. In England, balance of power thought liberated itself from territorial conservatism but was superseded by progressive notions. In both cases there was a movement away from the original balance of power ideas, but in opposite directions. While German thought was tending to extreme nationalism, British thought moved towards internationalism. The former development prepared the way for an attempt to overthrow the European system; the latter led to new experiments in international organization. The ideas of the nineteenth foreshadowed the events of the twentieth century.

BIBLIOGRAPHY

PART ONE, German ideas, p. 211; PART TWO, British ideas, p. 232

Introductory and general

ALBRECHT-CARRIE, R. *The Concert of Europe,* in the series *Documentary History of Western Civilization,* New York, Harper Torchbooks, 1968.

—— *A Diplomatic History of Europe Since the Congress of Vienna,* London, Methuen, 1958.

—— *The Unity of Europe. An Historical Survey,* London, Secker & Warburg, 1966.

ANDERSON, M. S. *The Eastern Question, 1774–1923,* London, Macmillan, 1966.

BARRACLOUGH, G. *European Unity in Thought and Action,* Oxford, Blackwell, 1963.

—— *History in a Changing World,* Oxford, Blackwell, 1957.

BEALES, A. C. F. *The History of Peace. A Short Account of the Organised Movements for International Peace,* London, Bell, 1931.

BINKLEY, R. C. *Realism and Nationalism 1852–1871,* New York, Harper, 1935.

BOURQUIN, M. *Histoire de la Sainte Alliance,* Geneva, Georg & Cie, 1954.

BUTLER, G. G. G. and MACCOBY, S. *The Development of International Law,* London, Longmans, 1928.

BUTTERFIELD, H. and WIGHT, M., ed. *Diplomatic Investigations. Essays in the Theory of International Politics,* London, Allen & Unwin, 1966.

The Cambridge History of British Foreign Policy 1783–1919, ed. A. W. Ward and G. P. Gooch, vol. ii, Cambridge U. P., 1923.

The Cambridge Modern History, ed. A. W. Ward, G. W. Prothero and S. Leathes, Cambridge U.P., 1902–11; See also *The New Cambridge Modern History.*

CARROLL, E. M. *Germany and the Great Powers 1866–1914. A Study in Public Opinion and Foreign Policy,* Hamden, Conn., Archon Books, 1966.

CRAIG, G. A. *Europe Since 1815,* 2nd edn, New York, Holt, Rinehart & Winston, 1966.

CRESSON, W. P. *The Holy Alliance. The European Background of the Monroe Doctrine,* New York, Oxford U.P., 1922.

DEHIO, L. *The Precarious Balance. The Politics of Power in Europe*

1494–1945, trans. C. Fullman, London, Chatto & Windus, 1963.

DUPUIS, C. *Le droit des gens et les rapports des grandes puissances avec les autres états avant le pacte de la Société des Nations,* Paris, Plon-Nourrit, 1921.

—— *Le principe d'équilibre et le Concert Européen de la paix de Westphalie à l'acte d'Algeciras,* Paris, Perrin, 1909.

FAY, S. B. 'Concert of Powers', in *Encyclopaedia of the Social Sciences,* ed. E. R. A. Seligman and A. Johnson, New York, Macmillan, 1935, vol. iv.

GOETZ, W., ed. *Propyläen-Weltgeschichte,* vol. viii, *Liberalismus und Nationalismus 1848–1890,* Berlin, 1930. F. Luckwaldt: 'Das europäische Staatensystem 1850–1890'.

GOOCH, G. P. *History and Historians in the Nineteenth Century,* London, Longmans, 2nd edn, 1952.

GULICK, E. V. *Europe's Classical Balance of Power. A case history of the theory and practice of one of the great concepts of European state-craft,* Ithaca, N.Y., Cornell U.P., 1955.

HALECKI, O. *The Limits and Divisions of European History,* London, Sheed & Ward, 1950.

HINSLEY, F. H. Introduction to vol. xi of *The New Cambridge Modern History (q.v.).*

—— *Power and the Pursuit of Peace. Theory and Practice in the History of Relations between States,* Cambridge U.P., 1963.

HOFFMANN, S. *Organisations internationales et pouvoirs politiques des Etats,* Cahiers de la Fondation Nationale des Sciences Politiques, No. 52, Paris, Armand Colin, 1954.

—— *The State of War. Essays on the Theory and Practice of International Politics,* New York, Praeger, 1965.

HOLBORN, H. *The Political Collapse of Europe,* New York, Knopf, 1951.

KAEBER, E. *Die Idee des europäischen Gleichgewichts in der publizistischen Literatur vom 16. bis zur Mitte des 18. Jahrhunderts,* Berlin, Duncker, 1907.

KISSINGER, H. A. *A World Restored. Metternich, Castlereagh and the Problems of Peace 1812–22,* London, Weidenfeld & Nicolson, 1957.

KJELLEN, R. *Stormakterna. Konturer kring Samtidens Storpolitik,* Stockholm, Gebers, 2nd edn, 1911–13.

LISKA, G. *Europe Ascendant. The International Politics of Unification,* Baltimore, Johns Hopkins Press, 1964.

—— *International Equilibrium. A Theoretical Essay on the Politics and Organization of Security,* Cambridge, Mass., Harvard U.P., 1957.

LUCKWALOT, F. 'Das europaische Staatensystem 1850–1890', in *Propyläen Weltgeschichte,* ed. W. Goetz, vol. viii, *Liberalismus und Nationalismus 1848–1890,* Berlin, 1930.

MARRIOTT, J. A. R. *The European Commonwealth. Problems Historical and Diplomatic,* Oxford, Clarendon Press, 1918.

MEDLICOTT, W. N. *Bismarck, Gladstone, and the Concert of Europe,* London, Althone Press, 1956.

—— *The Congress of Berlin and After. A Diplomatic History of the Near Eastern Settlement 1878–1880,* London, Methuen, 1938.

MEINECKE, F. 'Liberalism and Nationality in Germany and Austria (1840–48)', in *The Cambridge Modern History (q.v.)* vol. xi.

MEISNER, H. O. 'Vom europäischen Gleichgewicht', *Preussische Jahrbücher,* clxxvi (1919).

MORGENTHAU, H. J. *Politics among Nations. The Struggle for Power and Peace,* 4th edn, New York, Knopf, 1967.

MOSSE, W. E. *The European Powers and the German Question, 1848–71.* With special reference to England and Russia, Cambridge U.P., 1958.

MOWAT, R. B. *The Concert of Europe,* London, Macmillan, 1930.

—— *The European States System. A Study of International Relations,* London, Oxford U.P., 1923.

The New Cambridge Modern History, vol. xi, ed. F. H. Hinsley, Cambridge U.P., 1962, F. H. Hinsley, 'Introduction'.

NICOLSON, H. *The Congress of Vienna. A study in Allied Unity: 1812–1822,* London, Constable, 1946.

NYS, E. 'Le Concert Européen et la notion du droit international', *Revue de droit international et de législation comparée,* 2nd ser., vol. i (1899).

PHILLIPS, W. A. 'Great Britain and the Continental Alliance 1816–1822' in *The Cambridge History of British Foreign Policy 1783–1919 (q.v.),* vol. ii.

—— 'The Congresses, 1815–22', in *The Cambridge Modern History (q.v.),* vol. x.

PIRENNE, J.–H. *La Sainte-Alliance. Organisation européenne de la paix mondiale,* 2 vols, Neuchatel, La Baconnière, 1946–49.

POTTER, P. B. *An Introduction to the Study of International Organization*, New York, Appleton-Century-Crofts, 5th edn, 1948.

PRIBRAM, A. F. *England and the International Policy of the European Great Powers. 1871–1914*, Oxford, Clarendon Press, 1931.

RAMSAY, A. A. W. *Idealism and Foreign Policy. A Study of the Relations of Great Britain with Germany and France, 1860–1878*, London, Murray, 1925.

REIN, A. 'Über die Bedeutung der überseeischen Ausdehnung für das europäische Staaten-System', *Historische Zeitschrift*, cxxxvii (1928).

RENOUVIN, P. *Le XIXe siècle* (1815–1871 and 1871–1914), vols v and vi of *Histoire des relations internationales*, ed. P. Renouvin, Paris, Hachette, 1954–55.

—— *L'Idée de fédération Européenne dans la pensée politique du XIXe siècle*, Oxford, Clarendon, 1949.

ROSECRANCE, R. N. *Action and Reaction in World Politics. International Systems in Perspective*, Boston, Little, Brown & Co., 1963.

RUSSELL, B. *Freedom and Organization, 1814–1914*, London, Allen & Unwin, 1934.

SATOW, E. M. *A Guide to Diplomatic Practice*, London, Longmans, 2nd edn, 1922, vol. ii.

—— *International Congresses*, Foreign Office Handbooks, no. 151, London, 1920.

SCHENK, H. G. *The Aftermath of the Napoleonic Wars. The Concert of Europe—an Experiment*, London, Kegan Paul, 1947.

SCHIFFER, W. *The Legal Community of Mankind. A Critical Analysis of the Modern Concept of World Organization*, New York, Columbia U.P., 1954.

SOREL, A. *L'Europe et la Révolution Française*, Paris, Plon, 1887.

STIEGLITZ, A. de. *De l'équilibre politique du légitimisme et du principe des nationalités*, Paris, Pedone-Lauriel, 1893–97, vol. i.

STRAUS, H. A. *The Attitude of the Congress of Vienna toward Nationalism in Germany, Italy, and Poland*, New York, Columbia U.P., 1949.

STREIT, G. 'Les grandes puissances dans le droit international', *Revue de droit international et de législation comparée*, 2nd ser., ii (1900).

STRUPP, K., ed., *Wörterbuch des Völkerrechts und der Diplomatie*,

Berlin, Gruyter, 1924–29; ed. H.-J. Schlochauer, Berlin, Gruyter, 1960–62.

TAYLOR, A. J. P. *The Struggle for Mastery in Europe, 1848–1918*, Oxford, Clarendon Press, 1954.

TRAZ, R. DE. *De l'alliance des rois à la ligue des peuples,* Paris, Grasset, 1936.

VIETSCH, E. VON. *Das europäische Gleichgewicht, politische Idee und Staatsmännisches Handeln,* Leipzig, Koehler & Amelang, 1942.

—— *Die Tradition der grossen Mächte,* Stuttgart, Union Deutsche Verlagsgesellschaft, 1950.

WEBSTER, C. *The Art and Practice of Diplomacy,* London, Chatto & Windus, 1961, especially 'The Council of Europe in the Nineteenth Century'.

—— *The Congress of Vienna 1814–1815*, London, Bell, 1950.

WINDELBAND, W. *Die auswärtige Politik der Grossmächte in der Neuzeit, von 1494 bis zur Gegenwart,* 3rd edn, Essen, Essener Verlagsanstalt, 1936.

WOODWARD, E. L. *War and Peace in Europe, 1815–1870. And other essays,* London, Constable, 1931, first essay.

ZIMMERN, A. *The League of Nations and the Rule of Law, 1918–1935*, London, Macmillan, 2nd edn, 1939, ch. vi.

German Ideas

ALBRECHT, C. *Die Triaspolitik des Frhr. K. Aug. v. Wangenheim,* vol. xiv of *Darstellungen aus der Württembergischen Geschichte,* Stuttgart, Kohlhammer, 1914.

ANCILLON, F. *Tableau des Révolutions du système politique de l'Europe, depuis la fin du quinzième siècle,* Berlin, 1803–05; Brussels, Meline, 1839.

—— *Ueber den Geist der Staatsverfassungen und dessen Einfluss auf die Gesetzgebung,* Berlin, Duncker, 1825.

ARNDT, E. M. *Versuch in vergleichender Völkergeschichte,* Leipzig, Weidmannsche, 1844.

BERNHARDI, F. VON. *Deutschland und der nächste Krieg,* Stuttgart, Cotta, 1912.

—— *Unsere Zukunft. Ein Mahnwort an das deutsche Volk,* Stuttgart, Cotta, 1912.

BERTIER DE SAUVIGNY, G. DE. *Metternich and his Times,* trans. P. Ryde, London, Darton, Longman & Todd, 1962.

BISMARCK. O. VON *Deutscher Staat,* selected documents, ed. H. Rothfels, *Der deutsche Staatsgedanke,* 1st ser., xxi, Munich, Drei Masken, 1925.

—— *Gedanken und Erinnerungen,* Stuttgart, Cotta, 1898–1919.

—— *Die gesammelten Werke,* vols. i–vi (b), ed. H. v. Petersdorff and F. Thimme, Berlin, Deutsche Verlags-Gesellschaft, 2nd impr., 1924–31.

—— *Die politischen Reden des Fürsten Bismarck. Historisch-kritische Gesammtausgabe,* ed. H. Kohl, Stuttgart, Cotta, 1892; Stuttgart and Berlin, 1905.

BLUNTSCHLI, J. C. 'Le Congrès de Berlin et sa portée au point de vue du droit international', *Revue de Droit international et de Législation comparée,* vol. xii (1880).

—— *Denkwürdiges aus meinem Leben,* Nördlingen, Beck, 1884.

—— *Deutsche Statslehre und die heutige Statenwelt. Ein Grundriss mit vorzüglicher Rücksicht auf die Verfassung von Deutschland und Oesterreich-Ungarn,* Nördlingen, Beck, 1880.

—— *Gesammelte kleine Schriften,* Nördlingen, Beck, 1879–81.

—— *Lehre vom Modernen Stat,* vol. i: *Allgemeine Statslehre,* Stuttgart, Cotta, 1875; vol. iii: *Politik als Wissenschaft,* Stuttgart, Cotta, 1876.

—— *Das moderne Völkerrecht der civilisirten Staten, als Rechtsbuch dargestellt,* Nördlingen, Beck, 1868.

—— *Das moderne Völkerrecht in dem französisch-deutschen Kriege von 1870,* Heidelberg, Bassermann, 1871.

—— 'Völkerrechtliche Briefe', *Die Gegenwart,* Nos. 50 (9 December 1876) and 52 (23 December 1876).

BLUNTSCHLI, J. C. and BRATER, K. ed. *Deutsches Staats-Wörterbuch,* Stuttgart and Leipzig, 1856–70, vols iii, iv, v and xi.

BRAUER, A. VON. 'Bismarcks Staatskunst auf dem Gebiete der auswärtigen Politik', in *Neues Bismarck-Jahrbuch,* ed. Poschinger (*q.v.*), vol. i.

BROCKHAUS, F. *Das Legitimitätsprincip. Eine staatsrechtliche Abhandlung,* Leipzig, Brockhaus, 1868.

BÜLOW, FÜRST VON. *Deutsche Politik,* Berlin, Hobbing, 1916.

—— *Reden, nebst urkundlichen Beiträgen zu seiner Politik,* vols i and ii, ed. J. Penzler, Berlin, Reimer, 1907 and vol. iii, ed. O. Hötzsch, Berlin, Reimer, 1909.

BUNSEN, C. C. J. VON. *Christianity and Mankind, their Beginnings and Prospects,* London, Longmans, 1854.

BUNSEN, C. C. J. VON. *Christian Carl Josias Freiherr von Bunsen. Aus seinen Briefen und nach eigener Erinnerung geschildert von seiner Witwe,* ed. F. Nippold, Leipzig, Brockhaus, 1868–71.

CAEMMERER, H. VON. 'Rankes "Grosse Mächte" und die Geschichtschreibung des 18. Jahrhunderts', in *Studien und Versuchen zur neueren Geschichte (q.v.).*

CAPRIVI, GRAF VON. *Die Reden des Grafen von Caprivi im Deutschen Reichstage, Preussischen Landtage und bei besonderen Anlässen, 1883–1893,* ed. R. Arndt, Berlin, Hofmann, 1894.

CECIL, A. *Metternich, 1773–1859. A Study of his Period and Personality,* London, Eyre and Spottiswoode, 1933.

CLARK, C. W. *Franz Joseph and Bismarck. The Diplomacy of Austria before the War of 1866,* Harvard Historical Studies, vol. xxxvi, Harvard U.P., 1934.

CLAUSEWITZ, C. VON. *Politische Schriften und Briefe,* ed. H. Rothfels, Munich, Drei Masken, 1922.

DALBERG-ACTON, J. E. E. *Historical Essays and Studies,* ed. J. N. Figgis and R. V. Laurence, London, Macmillan, 1907, 'German Schools of History' (1886).

DEHIO, L. *Deutschland und die Weltpolitik im 20. Jahrhundert,* Munich, Oldenbourg, 1955; English trans. D. Pevsner: *Germany and World Politics in the Twentieth Century,* London, Chatto & Windus, 1959.

DELBRÜCK, H. *Erinnerungen Aufsätze und Reden,* Berlin, Stilke, 1902.

—— *Vor und nach dem Weltkrieg. Politische und historische Aufsätze 1902–1925,* Berlin, Stollberg, 1926.

DIETHER, O. *Leopold von Ranke als Politiker. Historisch-psychologische Studie über das Verhältniss des reinen Historikers zur praktischen Politik,* Leipzig, Duncker, 1911.

DROYSEN, J. G. *Abhandlungen. Zur neueren Geschichte,* Leipzig, Veit, 1876, 'Ein historischer Beitrag zur Lehre von den Congressen'.

—— *Politische Schriften,* ed. F. Gilbert, Munich, Oldenbourg, 1933.

—— *Vorlesungen über die Freiheitskriege,* Kiel, Universitäts-Buchh., 1846.

ENGELS, F. and MARX, K. *On Colonialism,* London (Moscow), Lawrence & Wishart, 1960.

—— —— *The Russian Menace to Europe,* A Collection of Articles, Speeches, Letters and News Despatches selected and edited by

P. W. Blackstock and B. F. Hoselitz, London, Allen & Unwin, 1953.

FALLATI, J. B. 'Die Genesis der Völkergesellschaft. Ein Beitrag zur Revision der Völkerrechtswissenschaft', *Zeitschrift für die gesammte Staatswissenschaft*, vol. i, Tübingen, Laupp, 1844.

FRANTZ, C. *Deutsche Antwort auf die orientalische Frage*, Leipzig, Bidder, 1877.

—— *Der Föderalismus, als das leitende Princip für die sociale, staatliche, und internationale Organisation, unter besonderer Bezugnahme auf Deutschland*, Mainz, Kirchheim, 1879.

—— *Das neue Deutschland. Beleuchtet in Briefen an einen preussischen Staatsmann*, Leipzig, Rossberg, 1871.

—— *Die Religion des Nationalliberalismus*, Leipzig, Rossberg, 1872.

—— *Untersuchungen über das Europäische Gleichgewicht*, Berlin, Schneider, 1859. (Published anonymously.)

—— *Die Weltpolitik unter besonderer Bezugnahme auf Deutschland*, Chemnitz, Schmeitzner, 1882–83.

—— *Die Wiederherstellung Deutschlands*, Berlin, Schneider, 1865.

FRANTZ, C. and SCHUCHARDT, O. *Die deutsche Politik der Zukunft*, Celle, Schulbuchh., 1899.

FREDERICK WILLIAM III. *Briefwechsel König Friedrich Wilhelm's III und der Königin Luise mit Kaiser Alexander I*, ed. P. Bailleu, Publicationen aus den K. Preussischen Staatsarchiven, vol. lxxv, Leipzig, Hirzel, 1900.

FREDERICK WILLIAM IV. *Vollständige Sammlung der Reden Seiner Majestät des Königs Friedrich Wilhelm des Vierten*, ed. J. Killisch, Berlin, Kühn, 1861.

FRÖBEL, J. *Amerika, Europa und die politischen Gesichtspunkte der Gegenwart*, Berlin, Springer, 1859.

—— *Kleine Politische Schriften*, Stuttgart, Cotta, 1866.

—— *Theorie der Politik, als Ergebniss einer erneuerten Prüfung demokratischer Lehrmeinungen*, vol. ii, Vienna, Gerold, 1864.

GAGERN, H. C. VON. *Critik des Völkerrechts. Mit practischer Anwendung auf unsre Zeit*, Leipzig, Brockhaus, 1840.

—— *Der Einsiedler oder Fragmente über Sittenlehre, Staatsrecht und Politik*, Stuttgart, Cotta, 1822–23.

—— *Mein Antheil an der Politik*, vol. v, *Der zweite Pariser Frieden*, Leipzig, Brockhaus, 1845.

—— *Deutscher Liberalismus im Vormärz. Heinrich von Gagern.*

Briefe und Reden 1815–1848, ed. P. Wentzcke and W. Klötzer, Göttingen, Musterschmidt, 1959.

GENTZ, F. *Fragments upon the Balance of Power in Europe*, trans., London, Peltier, 1806.

—— *Ueber den Ursprung und Charakter des Krieges gegen die Französische Revoluzion*, Berlin, Frölich, 1801.

—— *Von dem Politischen Zustande von Europa vor und nach der Französischen Revoluzion. Eine Prüfung des Buches: De l'état de la France à la fin de l'an VIII*, Berlin, Frölich, 1801.

—— *Briefe von Friedrich von Gentz an Pilat: Ein Beitrag zur Geschichte Deutschlands im XIX Jahrhundert*, ed. K. Mendelssohn-Bartholdy, Leipzig, Vogel, 1868.

—— *Briefe von und an Friedrich von Gentz*, ed. F. C. Wittichen and E. Salzer, Munich and Berlin, Oldenbourg, 1909–13, vol. iii, 'Schriftwechsel mit Metternich'.

—— *Briefwechsel zwischen Friedrich Gentz und Adam Heinrich Müller, 1800–1829*, Stuttgart, Cotta, 1857.

—— *Dépêches inédites du Chevalier de Gentz aux Hospodars de Valachie, pour servir à l'histoire de la politique européenne (1813 à 1828)*, ed. A. Prokesch-Osten, Paris, Plon, 1876–77.

—— *Friedrich von Gentz. Staatsschriften und Briefe*, vol. ii, 'Friedrich von Gentz und die deutsche Freiheit, Schriften und Briefe aus den Jahren 1815–1832', ed. H. v. Eckardt, Munich, Drei Masken, 1921.

—— *Schriften von Friedrich von Gentz. Ein Denkmal*, ed. G. Schlesier, Mannheim, Hoff, 1839–40.

GERLACH, LEOPOLD VON. *Briefe des Generals Leopold von Gerlach an Otto von Bismarck*, ed. H. Kohl, Stuttgart and Berlin, Cotta, 1912.

—— *Denkwürdigkeiten aus dem Leben Leopold von Gerlachs*, ed. his daughter, Berlin, Hertz, 1891–92.

GERVINUS, G. G. *Einleitung in die Geschichte des neunzehnten Jahrhunderts*, Leipzig, Engelmann, 1853.

—— *Geschichte des neunzehnten Jahrhunderts seit den Wiener Verträgen*, Leipzig, Engelmann, 1855–66.

—— *Hinterlassene Schriften*, ed. V. Gervinus, Vienna, Braumüller, 1872, 'Denkschrift zum Frieden. An das Preussische Königshaus' (1870).

GIESE, G. *Hegels Staatsidee und der Begriff der Staatserziehung*, Halle/Saale, Niemeyer, 1926.

[GOLDMANN]. *Die europäische Pentarchie*, Leipzig, Wigand, 1839.

P

GOLLWITZER, H. *Europabild und Europagedanke. Beiträge zur deutschen Geistesgeschichte des 18. und 19. Jahrhunderts,* Munich, Beck, 2nd edn, 1964.

GOOCH, G. P. *Studies in German History,* London, Longmans, 1948.

GÖRRES, J. VON *Gesammelte Schriften,* ed. M. Görres, vols iv and v, Munich, lit.-art Anstalt, 1856–59.

—— *Die heilige Allianz und die Völker auf dem Congresse von Verona,* Stuttgart, Metzler, 1822.

GUILLAND, A. *Modern Germany and her Historians,* London, Jarrold, 1915.

HAAKE, P. *Johann Peter Friedrich Ancillon und Kronprinz Friedrich Wilhelm IV. von Preussen,* Historische Bibliothek, vol. xlii, Munich and Berlin, Oldenbourg, 1920.

HEEREN, A. H. L. *Historische Werke,* Göttingen, Röwer, 4th edn, 1821–26, vol. ii: 'Der Deutsche Bund in seinen Verhältnissen zu dem Europäischen Staatensystem'; and vols viii and ix: *Handbuch der Geschichte des Europäischen Staatensystems und seiner Colonien, von seiner Bildung seit der Entdeckung beider Indien bis zu seiner Wiederherstellung nach dem Fall des Französischen Kaiserthrons, und der Freiwerdung von Amerika.*

HEGEL, G. W. F. *Sämtliche Werke,* ed. H. Glockner, Stuttgart, Frommann, 1927–39, vol. vi: *Enzyklopädie der philosophischen Wissenschaften im Grundrisse;* vol. vii: *Grundlinien der Philosophie des Rechts; oder Naturrecht und Staatswissenschaft im Grundrisse;* and vol. xi: *Vorlesungen über die Philosophie der Geschichte.*

—— *Die Verfassung des Deutschen Reichs. Eine politische Flugschrift,* ed. G. Mollat, Stuttgart, Frommann, 1935.

HELLER, H. *Hegel und der nationale Machtstaatsgedanke in Deutschland,* Leipzig and Berlin, Teubner, 1921; reprint Aalen, Zeller, 1963.

HINTZE, O. 'Deutschland und das Weltstaatensystem', in Hintze et al., ed. *Deutschland und der Weltkrieg (q.v.).*

—— *Staat und Verfassung. Gesammelte Abhandlungen zur allgemeinen Verfassungsgeschichte,* ed. F. Hartung, Leipzig, Koehler, 1941.

HINTZE, O. *et al. Deutschland und der Weltkrieg,* ed. O. Hintze, F. Meinecke, H. Oncken and H. Schumacher, Leipzig and Berlin, Teubner, 1915.

HOLBORN, H. *A History of Modern Germany,* 2 vols, 1648–1840 and 1840–1945, London, Eyre & Spottiswoode, 1965–

KLEISINGER. E. *Bismarck und der Gedanke der europäischen Ordnung.*

Eine völkerrechtliche Untersuchung, Würzburg-Aumühle, Triltsch, 1939.

KLÜBER, J. L. *Pragmatische Geschichte der nationalen und politischen Wiedergeburt Griechenlands, bis zu dem Regierungsantritt des Königs Otto,* Frankfurt am Main, Varrentrapp, 1835.

KNESEBECK, K. F. VON. *Denkschrift, betreffend die Gleichgewichts-Lage Europa's, beim Zusammentritte des Wiener Congresses,* Berlin, Reimer, 1854.

KOHN, H. *The Mind of Germany. The Education of a Nation,* London, Macmillan, 1961.

KRUG, W. T. *Krug's gesammelte Schriften,* Politische und juridische Schriften, Braunschweig, Bieweg, 1830–41.

LASSALLE, FERDINAND. *Gesamtwerke,* ed. E. Blum, Leipzig, Pfau, 1899–1909, vol. ii, 'Der italienische Krieg und die Aufgabe Preussens' (1859).

LASSON, A. *Das Culturideal und der Krieg,* Berlin, Moeser, 1868.

VON LAUE, T. H. *Leopold Ranke: the Formative Years,* Princeton U.P., 1950.

LENZ, M. *Die grossen Mächte. Ein Rückblick auf unser Jahrhundert,* Berlin, Paetel, 1900.

—— *Kleine Historische Schriften,* Munich and Berlin, Oldenbourg, 2nd edn, 1913.

LEPSIUS, J. *et al,* ed. *Die Grosse Politik der Europäischen Kabinette, 1871–1914,* ed. J. Lepsius, A. Mendelssohn-Bartholdy and F. Thimme, Berlin, D.V.f.P.u.G., 1921–27.

LESUR, C.-L. *Annuaire historique universel pour 1823,* Paris, Desplaces, 1824.

LINDNER. F. L. *Europa und der Orient. Verschiedene Auffassung der türkischen Frage,* Stuttgart, Metzler, 1839.

—— *Geheime Papiere,* Stuttgart, Franckh., 1824.

[LINDNER, F. L.] *Manuscript aus Süd-Deutschland,* publ. George Erichson (pseud.), London, Griphi, 1820.

LÖWENSTEIN, J. *Hegels Staatsidee: ihr Doppelgesicht und ihr Einfluss im 19. Jahrhundert,* Berlin, Springer, 1927.

MANN, G. *Secretary of Europe: the Life of Friedrich Gentz, Enemy of Napoleon,* trans. W. H. Woglom, New Haven, Yale U.P., 1946.

MANTEUFFEL, O. VON. See Poschinger, H. von, ed.

MARCKS, E. *Männer und Zeiten: Aufsätze und Reden zur neueren Geschichte,* Leipzig, Quelle & Meyer, 1911, vol. ii, 'Die imperialistische Idee in der Gegenwart' (1903).

MARX, KARL. *The Eastern Question. A Reprint of Letters written 1853–1856 dealing with the events of the Crimean War,* ed. E. Marx Aveling and E. Aveling, London, Sonnenschein, 1897.

MARX, KARL and ENGELS, F. *Selected Works,* London (Moscow), Lawrence & Wishart, 1950.

—— —— *Karl Marx Friedrich Engels, Historisch-kritische Gesamt-ausgabe: Werke/Schriften/Briefe,* ed. D. Rjazanov and V. Adoratskij, Frankfurt/M., Berlin, Moscow, Leningrad, Marx-Engels-Institut (Moscow), 1927–36(?).

—— *On Colonialism,* London (Moscow), Lawrence & Wishart, 1960.

—— *The Russian Menace to Europe,* A Collection of Articles, Speeches, Letters and News Despatches selected and edited by P. W. Blackstock and B. F. Hoselitz, London, Allen & Unwin, 1953.

MEINECKE, F. *Aphorismen und Skizzen zur Geschichte,* Leipzig, Koehler, 1942.

—— 'Kultur, Machtpolitik und Militarismus', in Hintze *et al,* ed. *Deutschland und der Weltkriege (q.v.).*

—— *Machiavellism: the Doctrine of Raison d'Etat and its Place in Modern History,* trans. D. Scott, London, Routledge, 1957.

—— *Radowitz und die deutsche Revolution,* Berlin, Mittler, 1913.

—— *Weltbürgertum und Nationalstaat,* Munich and Berlin, Olden-bourg, 3rd edn, 1915; *Friedrich Meinecke Werke,* ed. H. Herzfeld, C. Hinrichs and W. Hofer, vol. v, Munich, Oldenbourg, 1962.

—— 'Zur Beurteilung Rankes', *Historische Zeitschrift,* vol. cxi (1913).

MENZEL. W. *Die letzten 120 Jahre der Weltgeschichte (1740–1860),* vol. iv, Stuttgart, Krabbe, 1860.

METTERNICH, PRINCE DE. *Mémoires, documents et écrits divers laissés par le prince de Metternich,* publ. R. de Metternich, ed. M. A. de Klinkowstroem, Paris, Plon, 1880–84.

MEYER, H. C. *Mitteleuropa in German Thought and Action 1815–1945,* The Hague, Martinus Nijhoff, 1955.

MOLTIKE, H. VON. *Gesammelte Schriften und Denkwürdigkeiten des General-Feldmarschalls Grafen Helmuth von Moltke,* Berlin, Mittler, 1891–93.

MOMMSEN. T. 'A German's Appeal to the English. Ein Deutscher an die Engländer', *The Independent Review,* vol. i (1903).

—— *Reden und Aufsätze,* Berlin, Weidmannsche, 1905.

MOMMSEN, T. STRAUSS, D. F. MÜLLER F. MAX and CARLYLE, T. *Letters on the War between Germany and France,* London, Trübner, 1871.

NAUMANN, F. *Demokratie und Kaisertum. Ein Handbuch für innere Politik,* Berlin-Schöneberg, 'Hilfe', 1905.

ONCKEN, H. *Historisch-politische Aufsätze und Reden,* Munich and Berlin, Oldenbourg, 1914, vol. i, 'Amerika und die Grossen Mächte' (1910, 1914), 'Deutschland und England' (1912) and 'Über die Nationalität hinaus' (1913).

OPPENHEIM, H. B. *Friedensglossen zum Kriegsjahr,* Leipzig, Duncker, 1871.

PERTZ, G. H. *Das Leben des Ministers Freiherrn vom Stein,* Berlin, Reimer, 1849–55.

PFLANZE, O. *Bismarck and the Development of Germany. The Period of Unification, 1815–1871,* Princeton U.P., 1963.

PFLEIDERER, O. *Die Idee des ewigen Friedens,* Berlin, Becker, 1895.

PÖLITZ, K. H. L. *Die Staatensysteme Europa's und Amerika's seit dem Jahre 1783, geschichtlich-politisch dargestellt,* Leipzig, Hinrichsche, 1826, pt. iii.

—— *Die Staatswissenschaften im Lichte unsrer Zeit,* Leipzig, Hinrichsche, 1827–28.

POSCHINGER, H. VON, ed. *Neues Bismarck-Jahrbuch,* Vienna, Konegen, 1911.

—— *Preussens auswärtige Politik 1850 bis 1858. Unveröffentliche Dokumente aus dem Nachlasse des Ministerpräsidenten Otto Frhrn. v. Manteuffel,* Berlin, Mittler, 1902.

RADOWITZ, J. VON. *Gesammelte Schriften,* Berlin, Reimer, 1852–53.

RANKE, L. VON. *Das Briefwerk,* ed. W. P. Fuchs, Hamburg, Hoffmann, 1949.

—— *Sämmtliche Werke,* Leipzig, Duncker, 1867–1890, vol. xxiv, 'Die grossen Mächte'; vol. xliii–xliv, *Serbien und die Türkei im 19. Jahrh.*; vol. xlviii, *Hardenberg und die Geschichte des preussischen Staates von 1793–1813*; vol. xlix–l *Zur Geschichte Deutschlands und Frankreichs im neunzehnten Jahrhundert*; and vol. liii–iv, *Zur eigenen Lebensgeschichte.*

—— *Ueber die Epochen der neueren Geschichte,* ed. A. Dove, Leipzig, Duncker, 1888.

—— *Weltgeschichte,* Leipzig, Duncker, 1881–86, vol. i.

RATHENAU. W. *Gesammelte Schriften,* vol. i, Berlin, Fischer, 1918, 'England und wir. Eine Philippika' (1912).

REDLICH, J. *Emperor Francis Joseph of Austria,* London, Macmillan, 1929.

RICH, N. *Friedrich von Holstein. Politics and Diplomacy in the Era of Bismarck and Wilhelm II,* 2 vols., Cambridge U.P., 1965.

RIEBEN, H. *Prinzipiengrundlage und Diplomatie in Metternichs Europapolitik 1815–1848,* Aarau, Sauerländer, 1942.

RITTER, G. *Europa und die deutsche Frage. Betrachtungen über die geschichtliche Eigenart des deutschen Staatsdenkens,* Munich, Münchner, 1948.

ROHRBACH, P. *Der deutsche Gedanke in der Welt,* Düsseldorf and Leipzig, Langewiesche, 1912.

—— *Deutschland unter den Weltvölkern, Materialen zur auswärtigen Politik,* Berlin-Schöneberg, 'Hilfe', 1908.

ROSENZWEIG, F. *Hegel und der Staat,* Munich and Berlin, Oldenbourg, 1920.

RÖSSLER, C. *System der Staatslehre,* Leipzig, Falcke & Roessler, 1857.

ROTHFELS, H. *Carl von Clausewitz. Politik und Krieg. Eine ideengeschichtliche Studie,* Berlin, Dümmlers, 1920.

ROTTECK, H. VON. *Das Recht der Einmischung in die inneren Angelegenheiten eines fremden Staates vom vernunftrechtlichen, historischen und politischen Standpunkte erörtert,* Freiburg im Breisgau, Emmerling, 1845.

ROTTECK, K. VON. *Allgemeine Weltgeschichte für alle Stände, von den frühesten Zeiten bis zum Jahr 1840,* Stuttgart, Scheible, 1846.

—— *Dr. Carl von Rotteck's gesammelte und nachgelassene Schriften mit Biographie und Briefwechsel,* ed. Hermann v. Rotteck, Pforzheim, Finck, 1841–43.

ROTTECK, C. VON. and WELCKER, C., ed. *Staats-Lexikon, oder Encyklopädie der Staatswissenschaften,* Altona, Hammerich, 1843.

RUGE, A. *Geschichte unsrer Zeit von den Freiheitskriegen bis zum Ausbruche des deutsch-französischen Krieges,* Leipzig, Winter, 1881.

SCHAUMANN, A. F. H. *Geschichte des Congresses von Verona,* in *Historisches Taschenbuch,* ed. Fr. V. Raumer, dritte Folge, sechster Jahrgang, Leipzig, Brockhaus, 1855.

—— *Geschichte des zweiten Pariser Friedens für Deutschland,* Göttingen, Vandenhoeck, 1844.

SCHIEDER, T. *Begegnungen mit der Geschichte,* Göttingen, Vandenhoeck & Ruprecht, 1962; 'Bismarck und Europa'.

SCHNABEL. F. *Deutsche Geschichte im Neunzehnten Jahrhundert,* vol. ii, Freiburg, Herder, 1949.

SCHUCHARDT, O. *Der mitteleuropäische Bund,* Dresden, Zahn, 1913.
—— *Umrisse einer Staatsverfassung für das mittlere Europa. Eine Ergänzung zur Politik der Zukunft,* Dresden, Zahn, 1905.

SCHÜCKING, W. 'Die Organisation der Welt', in *Staatsrechtliche Abhandlungen: Festgabe für Paul Laband,* vol. i, Tübingen, Mohr, 1908.

SCHWEITZER, J. B. VON. *Widerlegung von Carl Vogt's Studien zur gegenwärtigen Lage Europa's,* Frankfurt am Main, Auffarth, 1859.
—— [anon]; *Oesterreichs Sache ist Deutschlands Sache. Ein Beitrag zur Befestigung der öffentlichen Meinung in Deutschland,* Frankfurt am Main, Auffarth, 1859.
—— *Politische Aufsätze und Reden von J. B. von Schweitzer,* ed. F. Mehring, Berlin, Singer, 1912.

SEPP, J. N. *Görres,* Berlin, Hofmann, 1896.

SRBIK. H. R. VON. 'Franz Joseph I. Charakter und Regierungs-grundsätze', *Historische Zeitschrift,* cxliv (1931).
—— *Metternich der Staatsmann und der Mensch,* vols i and ii, Munich, Bruckmann, 1925–26.

STAHL, FR. J. *Parlamentarische Reden,* ed. J. P. M. Treuherz, Berlin, Hollstein, undated.
—— *Siebzehn parlamentarische Reden und drei Vorträge,* Berlin, Hertz, 1862.

STEIN, FREIHERR VOM. *Briefwechsel, Denkschriften und Aufzeich-nungen,* ed. E. Botzenhart, Berlin, Heymann, 1931–37.

STRAUCH, H. *Zur Interventions-Lehre. Eine völkerrechtliche Studie,* Heidelberg, Winter, 1879.

Studien und Versuche zur neueren Geschichte, Max Lenz Festschrift, Berlin, Paetel, 1910.

TAYLOR, A. J. P. *The Course of German History. A Survey of the Development of German History since 1815,* London, Methuen, 1961.
—— *The Habsburg Monarchy 1809–1918. A History of the Austrian Empire and Austria-Hungary,* London, Hamish Hamilton, new ed., 1957.

TREITSCHKE, H. VON. *Deutsche Geschichte im Neunzehnten Jahrhundert,* 2 vols, Leipzig, Hirzel, 1897.
—— *Deutsche Kämpfe, Neue Folge, Schriften zur Tagespolitik,* Leipzig, Hirzel, 1896.

TREITSCHKE, H. VON. *Historische und Politische Aufsätze*, vol. ii, Leipzig, Hirzel 5th edn, 1886.

—— *History of Germany in the Nineteenth Century*, London, Jarrolds, 1915–19.

—— *Politik*, ed. M. Cornicelius, Leipzig, Hirzel, 1897–98; English trans. B. Dugdale and T. de Bille: *Politics*, London, Constable, 1916.

—— *Rede, gehalten zur Feier der fünfundzwanzig iährigen Regierung Seiner Majestät des Kaisers und Königs Wilhelm I*, Berlin, Vogt, 1886.

—— *Zehn Jahre Deutscher Kämpfe. Schriften zur Tagespolitik*, Berlin, Reimer, 2nd edn, 1879.

—— *Reden von Heinrich von Treitschke im Deutschen Reichstage 1871– 1884*, ed. O. Mittelstädt, Leipzig, Hirzel, 1896.

TÜRCKHEIM, J. VON. *Betrachtungen auf dem Gebiet der Verfassungs- und Staatenpolitik*, Karlsruhe and Freiburg, Herder, 1842–45.

VIRCHOW, R. L. C. *Krieg und Frieden*, Berlin, Rosenthal, 1877.

VITZTHUM VON ECKSTÄDT, GRAFEN K. F. *Berlin und Wien in den Jahren 1845–1852. Politische Privatbriefe*, Stuttgart, Cotta, 1886.

VOGT, C. *Andeutungen zur gegenwärtigen Lage*, Franfurt am Main, Baist, 1864.

—*Carl Vogt's Politische Briefe an Friedrich Kolb*, Biel, Kuhn, 1870.

VON LAUE, T. H. *Leopold Ranke: the Formative Years*, Princeton U.P., 1950.

WAGNER, A. *Vom Territorialstaat zur Weltmacht*, Berlin, Schade, 1900.

WANGENHEIM, K. A. VON. *Österreich, Preussen und das reine Deutschland auf der Grundlage des deutschen Staatenbundes organisch zum deutschen Bundesstaate vereinigt* ('Ein Verfassungsvorschlag hervorgegangen aus redlicher Forschung und reicher Erfahrung'), Weimar, Landes-Industrie-Comptoirs, 1849.

—— *Die Wahl des Freiherrn von Wangenheim, K. Würtembergischen Staatsministers ausser Dienst, zum Abgeordneten in die Würtembergische Ständeversammlung*, Tübingen, Laupp, 1832.

WESTPHAL, O. *Welt-und Staatsauffassung des deutschen Liberalismus. Eine Untersuchung über die Preussischen Jahrbücher und den konstitutionellen Liberalismus in Deutschland von 1858 bis 1863*, Historische Bibliothek, vol. xli, Munich and Berlin, Oldenbourg, 1919.

WILLIAM I. *Briefe Kaiser Wilhelms des Ersten. Nebst Denkschriften und anderen Aufzeichnungen im Auswahl,* ed. E. Brandenburg, Leipzig, Insel, 1911.

WILLIAM II. *Briefe Wilhelms II. an den Zaren 1894–1914,* ed. W. Goetz, trans. M. T. Behrmann, Berlin, Ullstein, Preface dd. 1920.

—— *Die Randbemerkungen Wilhelms II. in den Akten der auswärtigen Politik als historische und psychologische Quelle,* ed. L. Franke, Sammlung Heitz, Akademische Abhandlungen zur Kultur-geschichte, ser. v, vol. i, Strassburg, Heitz, 1934.

WOODWARD, E. L. *Three Studies in European Conservatism,* London, Constable, 1929.

WÜNSCH, H. *Die politische Ideenwelt des Generaladjutanten Karl Friedrich von dem Knesebeck,* doctoral thesis, Berlin, Funk, 1935.

ZACHARIÄ, KARL SALOMO. *Vierzig Bücher vom Staate,* vol. v, Heidelberg, Akademische Verlagsbuchhandel, Winter, 1841.

British Ideas

ARGYLL, DUKE OF. *Speech of the Duke of Argyll: What the Turks are, and how we have been helping them;* City Hall, Glasgow, Sept. 19, 1876, Glasgow, Maclehose, 2nd edn, 1876.

ASHLEY, E. *The Life and Correspondence of Henry John Temple Viscount Palmerston,* London, Bentley, 1879.

BALFOUR, A. J. *Mr Gladstone's Scotch Speeches. Being an Address delivered at Edinburgh, Dec. 12, 1879, to the Conservative Working Men's Association,* Edinburgh, Blackwood, 1880.

BALFOUR, F. *The Life of George Fourth Earl of Aberdeen,* London, Hodder, 1923.

BARTLETT, C. J. *Castlereagh,* London, Macmillan, 1966.

BEACONSFIELD, EARL OF. See Disraeli.

BELL, H. C. F. *Lord Palmerston,* Longmans, 1936.

BERNARD, M. *Four Lectures on Subjects connected with Diplomacy,* London, Macmillan, 1868.

BLAKE, R. *Disraeli,* London, Eyre & Spottiswoode, 1966.

BRAILSFORD, H. N. *Macedonia. Its Races and Their Future,* London, Methuen, 1906.

—— *The War of Steel and Gold. A Study of the Armed Peace,* London, Bell, 1914.

BRIGHT, JOHN. *Public Addresses by John Bright, M.P.,* ed. J. E. Thorold Rogers, London, Macmillan, 1879.

BRIGHT, JOHN. *The Public Letters of the Right Hon. John Bright, M.P.*, ed. H. J. Leech, London, Sampson Low, 1885.

—— *Speeches on Questions of Public Policy by John Bright, M.P.*, ed. J. E. Thorold Rogers, London, Macmillan, 1868.

BROUGHAM, LORD. *Letter to the Marquess of Lansdowne . . . on the Late Revolution in France*, London, Ridgway, 1848.

—— *Speech of Lord Brougham in the House of Lords, on Italian and French Affairs. April 11, 1848*, London, Ridgway, 1848.

—— *Speech of Lord Brougham in the House of Lords, August 18, 1848, on the Affairs of Austria and Italy*, London, Ridgway, 1848.

BUTLER-JOHNSTONE, H. M. *Imperialism, Federation, and Policy*, repr. from *The Belgian Times and News*, 1896, London, Allen, 1902.

BUXTON, H. and BUXTON, N. *Travel and Politics in Armenia*, London, Smith, Elder, 1914.

BUXTON, N. *Europe and the Turks*, London, 1st edn, Murray, 1907; 2nd edn, Methuen, 1912.

—— *With the Bulgarian Staff*, London, Smith, Elder, 1913.

CANNING, GEORGE. *The Speeches of the Right Honourable George Canning*. With a Memoir of his Life by R. Therry, London, Ridgway, 1828.

CASTLEREAGH, VISCOUNT. *Memoirs and Correspondence of Viscount Castlereagh, Second Marquess of Londonderry*, ed. C. Vane, London, Murray, 1848–53.

CECIL, A. *British Foreign Secretaries, 1807–1916. Studies in personality and policy*, London, Bell, 1927.

CECIL, G. *Life of Robert, Marquis of Salisbury*, London, Hodder & Stoughton, 1921–32.

CHAMBERLAIN, J. *Foreign and Colonial Speeches*, London, Routledge, 1897.

COATES, T. F. G. *Lord Rosebery. His Life and Speeches*, London, Hutchinson, 1900.

COBDEN, RICHARD. *The Political Writings of Richard Cobden*, London, Ridgway, 1867.

—— *Speeches on Questions of Public Policy by Richard Cobden, M.P.*, ed. J. Bright and J. E. Thorold Rogers, London, Macmillan, 1870.

DAWSON, W. H. *Richard Cobden and Foreign Policy. A Critical Exposition, with special reference to our day and its problems*, London, Allen & Unwin, 1926.

DILKE, C. W. *The Eastern Question,* London, Bush, 1878.

DISRAELI, BENJAMIN. *Lord George Bentinck: A Political Biography,* London, Longmans, 8th edn, 1872.

—— *Speech of the Right Hon. B. Disraeli, M.P., at the Banquet of the National Union of Conservative and Constitutional Associations. At the Crystal Palace, June 24, 1872,* Publications of the National Union, No. xvi, London, Mitchell, 1872.

—— *The Eastern Question. Speeches by the Earl of Beaconsfield and Lord Derby,* part i: Lord Beaconsfield's Speech at Aylesbury, London, Holmes, 1876.

—— *A Voice from the Grave. Speech by the late Earl of Beaconsfield, K.G., at the Free Trade Hall, Manchester, April 3, 1872,* Publications of the National Union, No. xiv, May 1885.

The 'Eighty' Club (1898). 'On the Concert of Europe.', London, 1898.

The 'Eighty' Club' (1901). 'The War and After.', London, 1901.

FREEMAN, E. A. *Four Oxford Lectures, 1887: Fifty Years of European History and Teutonic Conquest in Gaul and Britain,* London, Macmillan, 1888.

—— *The Ottoman Power in Europe, its Nature, its Growth, and its Decline,* London, Macmillan, 1877.

GAMBIER, J. W. 'England and the European Concert', *The Fortnightly Review,* lxii, July 1897.

GEORGE IV. *The Letters of King George IV 1812–1830,* ed. A. Aspinall, Cambridge U.P., 1938.

GILLESSEN, G. *Lord Palmerston und die Einigung Deutschlands. Die englische Politik von der Paulskirche bis zu den Dresdener Konferenzen (1848–1851);* Historische Studien, No. 384, Lübeck & Hamburg, Matthiesen, 1961.

GLADSTONE, W. E. *Bulgarian Horrors and the Question of the East,* London, Murray, 1876.

—— *Gleanings of Past Years, 1843–78,* London, Murray, 1879.

—— *The Paths of Honour and of Shame,* London, Tinsley, 1878.

—— *Political Speeches in Scotland, November and December 1879,* ed. J. J. R., Edinburgh, Elliot, 1880.

—— *A Speech delivered at Blackheath on . . . September 9th, 1876; together with Letters on the Question of the East,* London, Murray, 1876.

—— *The Eastern Crisis. A Letter to the Duke of Westminster, K.G., from the Right Honourable W. E. Gladstone,* London, Murray, 1897.

GLADSTONE, W. E. *Egypt and the Soudan. Speech delivered by the Right Hon. W. E. Gladstone, M.P., in the House of Commons . . . on 12th February, 1884*, London, National Press Agency, 1884.

—— *Gladstone to his Wife,* ed. A. Tilney Bassett, London, Methuen, 1936.

—— *The Political Correspondence of Mr. Gladstone and Lord Granville 1868–1876*, ed. A. Ramm, Camden Third Series vols lxxxi and lxxxii, London, Royal Historical Society, 1952.

—— *Third Midlothian Campaign. Political Speeches delivered in August and September 1884, by the Right Hon. W. E. Gladstone, M.P.,* Edinburgh, Elliot.

—— *Verbatim Report of the Rt. Hon. W. E. Gladstone's Great Speech on the Armenian Atrocities, delivered at Liverpool, September 24th, 1896*, London, Sears.

GOOCH, G. P. and TEMPERLEY, H., ed. *British Documents on the Origins of the War, 1898–1914*, London, 1926–38.

GORDON, A. *The Earl of Aberdeen*, London, Sampson Low, 1893; in the series *The Prime Ministers of Queen Victoria,* ed. S. J. Reid.

GRENVILLE, J. A. S. *Lord Salisbury and Foreign Policy, the Close of the Nineteenth Century,* London, Athlone Press, 1964.

GREY, SIR EDWARD. *Speeches on Foreign Affairs, 1904–1914,* ed. P. Knaplund, London, Allen & Unwin, 1931.

—— *Twenty-Five Years 1892–1916,* London, Hodder & Stoughton, 1925.

HALL, W. E. *International Law,* Oxford, Clarendon Press, 1880.

HAMMOND, J. L. *Gladstone and the Irish Nation,* London, Longmans, 1938.

Hansard's Parliamentary Debates, House of Lords and House of Commons, 1814–1914.

HARCOURT, SIR WILLIAM. *The Home and Foreign Policy of the Government. Speech delivered by the Right Hon. Sir William Harcourt, M.P., at Norwich, on March 17th, 1897,* London, The Liberal Publication Department, 1897.

HARRIS, JAMES, 1ST EARL OF MALMESBURY. *Diaries and Correspondence of James Harris, First Earl of Malmesbury,* ed. the Third Earl, London, Bentley, 2nd edn, 1845.

HENDERSON, G. B. *Crimean War Diplomacy and Other Historical Essays,* Glasgow University Publications, No. 68, Glasgow, Jackson, 1947, 'The Foreign Policy of Lord Palmerston'.

HOBSON, J. A. *Richard Cobden: the International Man,* London, Fisher Unwin, 1918.

HOLLAND, T. E. *The European Concert in the Eastern Question,* Oxford, Clarendon Press, 1885.

—— *Lectures on International Law,* ed. T. A. Walker and W. L. Walker, London, Sweet & Maxwell, 1933.

—— *Studies in International Law,* Oxford, Clarendon Press, 1898.

HORNER, FRANCIS. *Memoirs and Correspondence of Francis Horner, M.P.,* ed. L. Horner, Boston and London, Little & Murray, 2nd edn, 1853.

KNAPLUND, P. *Gladstone's Foreign Policy,* New York, Harper, 1935.

—— ed. *Letters from the Berlin Embassy. Selections from the Private Correspondence of British Representatives at Berlin and Foreign Secretary Lord Granville 1871–1874, 1880–1885.* Annual Report of the American Historical Association for the Year 1942, vol. ii, Washington, 1944.

LANE-POOLE, S. *The Life of the Right Honourable Stratford Canning Viscount Stratford de Redcliffe. From his Memoirs and Private and Official Papers,* London, Longmans, 1888.

LAWRENCE, T. J. *Essays on Some Disputed Questions in Modern International Law,* Cambridge, Deighton, 1884.

—— *International Problems and Hague Conferences,* London, Dent, 1908.

—— *The Principles of International Law,* London, Macmillan, 1st edn, 1895, 4th edn, 1910.

LORIMER, J. *The Institutes of the Law of Nations. A Treatise of the Jural Relations of Separate Political Communities,* Edinburgh and London, Blackwood, 1883–84.

—— *Studies National and International. Being occasional lectures delivered in the University of Edinburgh 1864–1889,* Edinburgh, Green, 1890.

MACCOLL, M. *The Eastern Question: Its Facts and Fallacies,* London, Longmans, 1877.

—— *England's Responsibility towards Armenia,* London, Longmans, 1895.

—— *The Sultan and the Powers,* London, Longmans, 1896.

—— *Memoirs and Correspondence,* ed. G. W. E. Russell, London, Smith, Elder, 1914.

MAGNUS, P. *Gladstone. A Biography,* London, Murray, 1954.

MILL, J. S. *Dissertations and Discussions, Political, Philosophical, and*

Historical, vol. ii, London, Parker, 1859; vol. iii, London, Longmans, 1867.

MORLEY, J. *The Life of William Ewart Gladstone,* London, Macmillan, 1903.

MUIR, R. *Britain's Case Against Germany: An Examination of the Historical Background of the German Action in 1914,* Manchester U.P., 1914.

—— *Nationalism and Internationalism: The Culmination of Modern History,* London, Constable, 1st edn, 1916: 2nd edn, 1919.

OPPENHEIM, L. *International Law: A Treatise,* London, Longmans, 1905–6.

PALMERSTON, VISCOUNT. *Opinions and Policy of the Right Honourable Viscount Palmerston, as Minister, Diplomatist, and Statesman, during more than forty years of public life.* With a Memoir by G. H. Francis, London, Colburn, 1852.

[PALMERSTON VISCOUNT]. *The Foreign Affairs of Great Britain administered by the Right Honourable Henry John Viscount Palmerston,* privately printed, London, Reid, 1841.

PENSON, L. *Foreign Affairs under the Third Marquis of Salisbury.* The Creighton Lecture in History, 1960, University of London, 1962.

PETRIE, C. *George Canning,* London, Eyre & Spottiswoode, 2nd edn, 1946.

PHILLIMORE, R. *Commentaries upon International Law,* vol. i, London, Benning, 1854.

PHILLIPS, W. A. *The Confederation of Europe, a Study of the European Alliance, 1813–1823 as an Experiment in the International Organization of Peace,* London, Longmans, 1914.

—— *Modern Europe 1815–1899,* London, Rivingtons, 2nd edn, 1902.

PONSONBY, A. *Democracy and the Control of Foreign Affairs,* London, Fifield, 1912.

—— *Democracy and Diplomacy. A Plea for Popular Control of Foreign Policy,* London, Methuen, 1915.

ROLO, P. J. V. *George Canning. Three Biographical Studies,* London, Macmillan, 1965.

ROSEBERY, LORD. *Lord Rosebery's Speeches (1874–1896),* London, Beeman, 1896.

RUSSELL, JOHN, 1ST EARL. *A Letter to the Right Honourable Lord Holland, on Foreign Politics,* 4th edn, London, Ridgway, 1831.

RUSSELL, JOHN, 1ST EARL. *Recollections and Suggestions 1813–1873,* London, Longmans, 1875.

—— *Memoirs of the Affairs of Europe from the Peace of Utrecht,* London, Murray, 1824–29.

—— *Selections from Speeches of Earl Russell 1817 to 1841 and from Despatches 1859 to 1865.* With Introduction by Russell, London, Longmans, 1870.

SALISBURY, MARQUESS OF. *Essays by the Late Marquess of Salisbury: Biographical,* London, Murray, 1905.

—— *Essays by the late Marquess of Salisbury: Foreign Politics,* London, Murray, 1905.

—— *A Speech delivered at Bradford by the Marquis of Salisbury on October 11, 1877,* Publications of the National Union, No. xxxiii, London, 1877.

SETON-WATSON, R. W. *Britain in Europe, 1789–1914. A Survey of Foreign Policy,* Cambridge U.P., 1937.

—— *Disraeli, Gladstone and the Eastern Question. A Study in Diplomacy and Party Politics,* London, Macmillan, 1935.

SHANNON, R. T. *Gladstone and the Bulgarian Agitation 1876,* London, Nelson, 1963.

STRATFORD DE REDCLIFFE, LORD. *The Eastern Question. Being a Selection from his Writings during the Last Five Years of his Life,* London, Murray, 1881.

TAFFS, W. A. *Ambassador to Bismarck: Lord Odo Russell, First Baron Ampthill,* London, Muller, 1938.

TAYLOR, A. J. P. *The Trouble Makers. Dissent over Foreign Policy, 1792–1939,* London, Hamish Hamilton, 1957.

TEMPERLEY, H. *The Foreign Policy of Canning 1822–1827,* London, Bell, 1925.

TEMPERLEY, H. and PENSON, L. M., ed. *Foundations of British Foreign Policy from Pitt (1792) to Salisbury (1902) or Documents, Old and New,* Cambridge U.P., 1938.

THOMPSON, G. C. *Public Opinion and Lord Beaconsfield. 1875–1880,* London, Macmillan, 1886.

TREVELYAN, G. M. *Grey of Fallodon. Being the Life of Sir Edward Grey afterwards Viscount Grey of Fallodon,* London, New York, Toronto, Longmans, 1937.

TWISS, T. *The Law of Nations Considered as Independent Political Communities,* 2 vols, Oxford U.P. and London, Longmans, 1861, 1863.

[VAUGHAN, B.]. *Letters on the Subject of the Concert of Princes and the dismemberment of Poland and France,* by a Calm Observer (1793).

VICTORIA, QUEEN. *The Letters of Queen Victoria. A Selection from Her Majesty's Correspondence between the Years 1837 and 1861,* ed. A. C. Benson and Esher, London, Murray, 1907.

—— *Further Letters of Queen Victoria. From the Archives of the House of Brandenburg-Prussia,* ed. H. Bolitho, trans., London, Thornton Butterworth, 1938.

WALPOLE, S. *The Life of Lord John Russell,* London, Longmans, 1889.

WANDYCZ, P. S. 'Liberal Internationalism. The Contribution of British and French Liberal Thought to the Theory of International Relations', Unpublished Ph.D. thesis, University of London, 1950.

WARD, A. W. *Collected Papers, Historical, Literary, Travel and Miscellaneous,* Cambridge U.P., 1921.

—— *Securities of Peace. A Retrospect (1848–1914),* London, Society for Promoting Christian Knowledge, 1919.

WEBSTER, C. K. *British Diplomacy 1813–1815, Select Documents dealing with the Reconstruction of Europe,* London, Bell, 1921.

—— *The Foreign Policy of Castlereagh 1815–1822, Britain and the European Alliance,* London, Bell, 1925.

—— *The Foreign Policy of Castlereagh 1812–1815, Britain and the Reconstruction of Europe,* London, Bell, 1931.

—— *The Foreign Policy of Palmerston, 1830–1841: Britain, the Liberal Movement and the Eastern Question,* London, Bell, 1951.

WELLINGTON, DUKE OF. *Despatches, Correspondence, and Memoranda of Field Marshal Arthur Duke of Wellington,* ed. his son, London, Murray, 1867–80.

WESTLAKE, J. *International Law,* Cambridge U.P. (1904), 2nd edn, 1910–13.

—— *The Collected Papers of John Westlake on Public International Law,* ed. L. Oppenheim, Cambridge U.P., 1914.

WHEWELL, W. *The Elements of Morality, Including Polity,* London, Parker, 1st edn, 1845; 3rd edn, 1854.

WOOLF, L. S. *International Government: Two Reports . . . prepared for the Fabian Research Department, together with a Project by a Fabian Committee for a Supernational Authority that will prevent War,* London, The Fabian Society and Allen & Unwin, 1916, part i, ch. v.

INDEX

Aberdeen, Earl of, 120, 147
Aix-la-Chapelle, Congress of (1818),
 1, 19, 20, 21, 26, 51
Alexander I, Tsar, 34
Ancillon, Friedrich, 36, 37, 39, 81, 86
Anglo-Turkish Convention, 178
Armed intervention, *see* Intervention
Armenia, 7, 172–4
Ashmead-Bartlett, Sir Ellis, 201

Balfour, A. J., 182
Belgium, revolution in, 120, 132, 139
Béranger, Pierre-Jean, 59
Berlin,
 Conference of (1884–5), 195n
 Congress of (1878), 152, 177n, 181
Bernard, Montague, 158–9
Bernhardi, Friedrich von, 104, 107
Bismarck, Prince von, 5, 13, 41, 44,
 61, 76, 89, 95–100, 106, 109, 112
Bluntschli, Johann Caspar, 66–70,
 78, 85, 187
Bolingbroke, Viscount, 160
Bourbon monarchy, 21
Brailsford, H. N., 175, 184–5
Bright, John, 138, 153, 156–7, 160
Brougham, Lord, 129–30, 154, 164
Bülow, Prince Bernhard von, 5, 100
Bunsen, Christian Carl Josias von,
 35, 54–5
Burke, Edmund, 16
Butler–Johnstone, H. A. M., 200–1
Buxton, Noel, 175, 182

Canning, George, 122, 126, 134, 140
Capo d'Istria, Count, 25
Caprivi, Count von, 76

Castlereagh, Viscount, 3, 4 and n, 54,
 119–20, 122, 124, 134, 136–47,
 181
Chamberlain, Joseph, 174
Chaumont, Treaty of (1814), 136
China, 174n
Clarendon, Earl of, 147
Clausewitz, C. von, 77, 92
Cobden, Richard, 138, 153–6
'Concert of the World', 191, 195n
Constantin, Franz, 5
Crete, 5, 7, 173–4
Crimean War, 110, 140, 152

Delbrück, Hans, 101
Democratic Control, Union of, 184
Denmark, 154
Disraeli, Benjamin, 171, 198–200,
 202
Droysen, Johann Gustav, 55–8, 90,
 95, 106
Dynastic order, preservation of, 15,
 33

Engels, Friedrich, 58–61

Fallati, Johannes Baptista, 107
Ferdinand IV (I), King of Naples
 (and Sicily), 128–9
France,
 dangers to peace from, 1, 15, 16,
 21, 35, 120, 123, 143, 152
 inclusion in European alliance, 2,
 24
Francis Joseph, Emperor, 5, 34
Franz, Constantin, 5, 108–12
Frederick William III, King of
 Prussia, 34

231